INVENTING UNEMPLOYMENT

This book examines the evolution of Australian unemployment law and policy across the past 100 years. It poses the question 'How does unemployment happen?' But it poses it in a particular way. How do we regulate work relationships, gather statistics, and administer a social welfare system so as to produce something we call 'unemployment'? And how has that changed over time?

Attempts to sort workers into discrete categories – the 'employed', the 'unemployed', those 'not in the labour force' – are fraught, and do not always easily correspond with people's working lives. Across the first decades of the twentieth century, trade unionists, statisticians and advocates of social insurance in Australia as well as Britain grappled with the problem of what forms of joblessness should be classified as 'unemployment' and which should not. This book traces those debates. It also chronicles the emergence and consolidation of a specific idea of unemployment in Australia after the Second World War. It then charts the eventual unravelling of that idea, and relates that unravelling to the changing ways of ordering employment relationships.

In doing so, *Inventing Unemployment* challenges the preconception that casual work, self-employment, and the 'gig economy' are recent phenomena. Those forms of work confounded earlier attempts to define 'unemployment' and are again unsettling our contemporary understandings of joblessness.

This thought-provoking book shows that the category of 'unemployment', rather than being a taken-for-granted economic variable, has its own history, and that history is intimately related to our changing understandings of 'employment'.

Inventing Unemployment

Regulating Joblessness
in Twentieth-Century Australia

Anthony O'Donnell

·HART·

OXFORD · LONDON · NEW YORK · NEW DELHI · SYDNEY

HART PUBLISHING

Bloomsbury Publishing Plc

Kemp House, Chawley Park, Cumnor Hill, Oxford, OX2 9PH, UK

1385 Broadway, New York, NY 10018, USA

29 Earlsfort Terrace, Dublin 2, Ireland

HART PUBLISHING, the Hart/Stag logo, BLOOMSBURY and the Diana logo are
trademarks of Bloomsbury Publishing Plc

First published in Great Britain 2019

First published in hardback, 2019
Paperback edition, 2021

A catalogue record for this book is available from the British Library.

Library of Congress Cataloging-in-Publication Data

Names: O'Donnell, Anthony, author.

Title: Inventing unemployment : regulating joblessness in twentieth-century
Australia / Anthony O'Donnell.

Description: Oxford ; New York Hart, 2019. | Includes bibliographical references and index.

Identifiers: LCCN 2019034917 (print) | LCCN 2019034918 (ebook) |
ISBN 9781509928194 (hardback) | ISBN 9781509928217 (Epub)

Subjects: LCSH: Labor laws and legislation—Economic aspects—Australia. |
Labor supply—Australia. | Manpower policy—Australia.

Classification: LCC KU1208 .O36 2019 (print) | LCC KU1208 (ebook) | DDC 344.9401/37—dc23

LC record available at https://lccn.loc.gov/2019034917

LC ebook record available at https://lccn.loc.gov/2019034918

ISBN: HB: 978-1-50992-819-4
PB: 978-1-50995-271-7
ePDF: 978-1-50992-820-0
ePub: 978-1-50992-821-7

Typeset by Compuscript Ltd, Shannon

To find out more about our authors and books visit www.hartpublishing.co.uk. Here you will find
extracts, author information, details of forthcoming events and the option to sign up for our newsletters.

For Belinda and Benjamin,
and to the memory of Dorothy O'Donnell, 1928–2019.

ACKNOWLEDGEMENTS

This book was a long time in the making, the result of two decades of researching and thinking about the evolution of Australian unemployment law and policy. At its genesis I was lucky to work alongside two leading figures in the fields of social policy and labour law: Brian Howe and Richard Mitchell. As well as providing me with unstinting support as a neophyte researcher, each brought a keen historical sensibility to his respective discipline, and there was no better apprenticeship for someone embarking on a project such as this. Christopher Arup was also encouraging, alert to the merits of grounding an examination of unemployment law in labour law, and at an early stage he passed on the manuscript of William Walters' *Unemployment and Government*. That, along with the work of Noel Whiteside and Malcolm Mansfield, provided a crucial spur to the project. The late Alan Jordan, one of the most literate of Australian social policy researchers, also made available an unpublished manuscript on the history of social policy across the last decades of the twentieth century which proved useful. Back then, Joo-Cheong Tham and I discussed the evolution of the work test – or activity test as it had become – and his insights were valuable and welcome. Later, John Grundy generously shared his perceptive and detailed account of the evolution of Canadian manpower policies. I have many other intellectual debts, but that is what footnotes are for.

In Australia, labour law tends to exist as an area of enquiry somewhat separate from social security law, but the community of Australian labour law scholars has provided a really congenial environment for me to test my thoughts on unemployment law and policy. Friendly and collaborative, they can't all be mentioned by name. Several have been involved in an ongoing project to extend the remit of labour law to an examination of labour market regulation more broadly. Instigated by Richard Mitchell and Christopher Arup, that project provided a home for many of the speculations that informed this book. It also made a space for John Howe's valuable work in the cognate field of job creation and employment services and Rosemary Owens' pioneering work on welfare law's role in the reproduction of labour. And Jill Murray has been the staunchest of colleagues – at once curious, probing, and endlessly encouraging – first at the University of Melbourne, and then at La Trobe University.

Parts of the book were completed while I was a visiting scholar at the Centre for Employment and Labour Relations Law at the University of Melbourne Law School in 2013 and again in 2018. I thank the directors of the Centre across those periods – Anna Chapman, Tess Hardy and John Howe – for hosting me. More generally, my students and colleagues at the La Trobe Law School have made it a remarkably convivial place to teach, research and think about law across more than a decade.

Staff at the Melbourne reading room of the National Archives of Australia were always helpful and prompt in retrieving material for me. Final preparation of the manuscript was aided by funds from La Trobe University's Social Research Assistance Platform, with Nicole Shackleton providing meticulous research assistance. Roberta Bassi, Rosamund Jubber, Linda Staniford and Anne Bevan at Hart/Blooomsbury have been enthusiastic, supportive and careful throughout the publishing process.

Some of the arguments in this book have appeared in earlier form. A shorter version of the first chapters emerged as a Master of Laws thesis completed at the University of Melbourne, supervised by Richard Mitchell, and a much abbreviated version of that was published as 'Inventing Unemployment: Labour Market Regulation and the Establishment of the Commonwealth Employment Service' (2003) 31 *Federal Law Review* 342. I developed other parts of the analysis in 'The Public Employment Service in Australia: Regulating Work or Regulating Welfare?' (2000) 13 *Australian Journal of Labour Law* 143; 'Reinventing Unemployment: Welfare Reform as Labour Market Regulation' in C Arup et al (eds), *Labour Law and Labour Market Regulation* (Sydney Federation Press, 2006); 'Unemployment in a Time of Full Employment: Counting and Regulating Worklessness in Mid-Twentieth Century Australia' (2015) 108 *Labour History* 71; and '"Organizing the Labour Market" in a Liberal Welfare State: The Origins of the Public Employment Service in Australia' in S Wadauer, T Buchner and A Mejstrik (eds), *The History of Labour Intermediation: Institutions and Finding Employment in the Nineteenth and Early Twentieth Centuries* (Oxford, Berghahn Books, 2015). Where I have reused words it is with permission.

The true historian in my household is Belinda Robson, whose passion for the discipline continues to inspire and instruct. And she sustains me in so many other ways. Our son, Benjamin O'Donnell, is now old enough to be released from any proscriptions on child labour, and so is free to enter a world of work – and potential joblessness – that promises to be so different from that which I have experienced, which in turn was different from that of my own parents. Across generations, things are in constant flux. This book is for Belinda and Benjamin, both.

As I pulled together the final version of the manuscript, my mother Dorothy O'Donnell became unexpectedly ill and died. Her death was peaceful and mannerly, undertaken with a great sense of purpose, and she was enquiring to the last about this book and its progress. She is sorely missed.

May Day
Northcote, 2019

CONTENTS

Acknowledgements .... *vii*

Introduction 1

1. A Disorganised Labour Market 8
   The British Context 8
   Social Surveys, the Casual Worker and the Problem
       of Unemployment 11
   The Employment Relationship in Australia 14
   Regularising Work in Australia 20

2. Defining Unemployment: Pre-War Endeavours 28
   The Census 28
   Trade Unions 32
   Social Insurance 36

3. The Labour Exchange Solution 45
   The Labour Exchange in British Social Thought 45
   The Labour Exchange in Pre-War Australia 49
   Wartime Labour Administration and the Directorate
       of Manpower 54

4. Social Policy in Wartime 58
   Designing an Unemployment Benefits Scheme 58
   The White Paper on Full Employment 64

5. Unemployment in a Time of Full Employment 72
   The Post-War Labour Market 72
   Statistics: Counting Unemployment 74
   The Work Test: Regulating Unemployment 79
   Unemployment and Industrial Disputes 85

6. Limiting Unemployment 92
   The Married Woman 93
   The Remote-Area Aboriginal Australian 98
   The 'Dole Bludger' 104

7. Reinventing Unemployment 111
    The Demise of the Standard Employment Relationship.............................111
    Towards an 'Active Society' 119
    From Work Test to Activity Test 123
    Making Agreements 126
    Enforcing Compliance...131
    Unemployment Benefit or Basic Income? Manipulating
       the Means Test..133

8. Marketing Unemployment 141
    The CES in the Post-War Labour Market 142
    The End of the Public Employment Service in Australia:
       The First Phase...151
    The End of the Public Employment Service in Australia:
       The Second Phase 153
    The Evolution of the Job Network 156
    Contracts All the Way Down?...161

Bibliography...*167*
Index *179*

Introduction

How does unemployment happen? I mean that question in quite a specific way. Not, how does someone lose their job or fail to find to work. But rather, how does the way we regulate work relationships, gather statistics, and administer a social welfare system produce something we call 'unemployment', and how has that changed over time?

Let's take a stylised example. A 20 per cent drop in the demand for labour within an enterprise or industry could conceivably be managed in different ways. Where there is an extensive system of labour contracting with self-employed workers hired for the duration of specific jobs, a drop in available work simply means no new contracts will be made. The self-employed worker, with a portfolio of contracts, is expected to be responsible for regulating their own amount of work and managing any reductions in work. Where an enterprise relies on an extensive casual labour market, then where once 100 workers at the factory gate each morning might have been hired for the day, only 80 will now be chosen. If those 80 are chosen randomly from a pool of 100, over time each worker will average four days of work a week, but he or she will be uncertain from day to day whether there will be work available on that day. Where an enterprise relies on a permanent workforce of, say, 100 employees, the drop in labour demand could be managed in one of two ways: either all workers are put onto a four-day week or the contracts of 20 workers are terminated – and those workers, permanently severed from their former employer, become available for work at alternative enterprises. Of these examples, it is only the last that we would recognise as giving rise to unemployment as we understand it as a contemporary administrative and legal concept.

That particular understanding of unemployment was consolidated in Australia in the period immediately following the Second World War. There emerged a notion of the unemployed person as someone experiencing more or less absolute lack of work while also signalling their availability and willingness to work. That idea was quite distinct from notions of unemployment that prevailed prior to the war. Unemployment according to this new understanding was a condition clearly distinct from employment on the one hand but also from other forms of joblessness such as disability, sickness and strike action on the other. The idea was embodied in the national unemployment benefit scheme which commenced operation in 1945 and which was administered, in part, by a new labour market institution, the Commonwealth Employment Service (CES). It is an understanding of unemployment that in some respects – as regards our national statistics, for example – has proved remarkably resilient, even into the twenty-first century. In other respects – our administration of a system of out-of-work social security benefits, for example – it dominated much of the post-war period but in more recent decades this idea of unemployment has been dismantled and radically 'reinvented'.

So my approach treats unemployment not as a simple economic variable that waxes and wanes according to prevailing economic conditions, but as institutionally constructed, derived from conventions about how to count it, and administrative rules about eligibility for social security benefits[1] – and importantly, from prevailing labour management practices. This is not an entirely novel approach, and I'm indebted to historians who have traced this line of argument with respect to other countries.[2] But my approach does depart from that of economic historians in Australia, who, rather than exploring how the category of unemployment is constructed over time, have generally been more concerned with examining different historical data sources to find out which give an 'accurate' measure of unemployment.[3]

The way I deal with the category of unemployment differs, too, from the approach taken in much historical sociology of the welfare state. That approach tends to focus on how different social groups mobilise to produce particular policy outcomes.[4] It presumes a pre-established catalogue of social rights or entitlements, waiting to be claimed depending on the degree of influence that any set of actors can have on government.[5] Instead, this book attempts to historicise the process of categorisation itself, arguing that the category of 'unemployment' has its own genealogy.

In this regard my approach is a species of 'social constructionism'. Following Ian Hacking's characterisation of this sort of endeavour, when I talk about the social construction of unemployment, I'm talking about 'the idea, the individuals falling under the idea, the interaction between the idea and the people, and the manifold of social practices and institutions that these interactions involve'.[6]

---

[1] P Baxandall, 'Explaining Differences in the Political Meaning of Unemployment' (2002) 31 *Journal of Socio-Economics* 469.

[2] See N Whiteside, *Bad Times: Unemployment in British Social and Political History* (London, Faber, 1991); M Mansfield, 'Labour Exchanges and the Labour Reserve in Turn of the Century Social Reform' (1992) 21 *Journal of Social Policy* 435; W Walters, *Unemployment and Government: Genealogies of the Social* (Cambridge, Cambridge University Press, 2000); R Salais, N Baverez and B Reynaud, *L'Invention du Chômage: Histoire et Transformations d'une Catégorie en France des années 1890 aux annés 1980* (Paris, Presses Universitaires de France, 1986); P Baxandall, *Constructing Unemployment: The Politics of Joblessness in East and West* (Aldershot, Ashgate, 2004).

[3] See, eg, C Forster, 'Australian Unemployment, 1900–1940' (1965) 41 *Economic Record* 426. For informative exceptions, see T Endres, 'Designing Unemployment Statistics in New Zealand: A History Study in Political Arithmetic c1860–1960' (1982) 22 *Australian Economic History Review* 151; T Endres and M Cook, 'Concepts in Australian Unemployment Statistics to 1940' (1983) 22 *Australian Economic Papers* 68.

[4] See, eg, M Cohen and M Hanagan 'Politics, Industrialization and Citizenship: Unemployment Policy in England, France and the United States, 1890–1950' (1995) 40(S3) *International Review of Social History* 91.

[5] M Gomez Garrido, 'From the Industrial Reserve Army to the Invention of Unemployment: Between Social History and Historical Ontology' (2004) European University Institute Working Paper SPS No 2004/18, available at: cadmus.eui.eu/bitstream/handle/1814/2635/sps2004-18.pdf?sequence=1&isAllowed=y15.

[6] I Hacking, *The Social Construction of What?* (Cambridge, MA, Harvard University Press, 1999) 34.

Hacking in fact identifies six degrees of commitment to constructionism, ranging from the purely historical, through the 'ironic', to the 'rebellious' and even the 'revolutionary'. My approach probably approximates what he calls the 'least demanding':[7] the aim is primarily to argue that the category of unemployment has been constructed through various social processes and, rather than the category being an inevitable result of how the world is, it 'is the contingent upshot of historical events'.[8] There is little of what Hacking calls a reformist or rebellious motive here; I remain pretty non-committal about whether the idea of unemployment that emerged around the middle of the twentieth century was a good or bad thing.

But I would stress that the history of classifications and categories is not solely the examination of language and discourse. Hacking points out that words such as 'construction' and 'invention' signify both a product and a process, both the result and the way one gets there.[9] And the process of inventing unemployment – the emergence, consolidation and reinventing of particular understandings of joblessness – is underpinned by particular *practices*: taking a census, for example, or administering an unemployment benefits scheme, or managing labour in a workplace. Classifications always occur in some sort of matrix: in this instance, legislation, the 'material infrastructure' of labour bureaux, census forms and so on.[10] This focus on how social problems become social problems – how a certain professional expertise allows us to think of 'unemployment' as a discrete social problem – along with an alertness to the role that mundane administrative practices play in this process also means my approach overlaps with, and draws upon, those scholars who take what's known as a 'governmentality' approach to the regulation of the jobless.[11] The shift to privatised or outsourced employment services in particular has also led scholars to more closely examine the role that front-line service provision and discretion play in the administration of the unemployed.[12] However, I'd suggest that an alertness to administrative practice should inform our discussion of earlier regimes of unemployment regulation as well as more recent ones, so the book makes use of departmental office manuals and departmental correspondence from those earlier periods.[13]

---

[7] This should come as no surprise to those who know my work habits.

[8] Hacking, *The Social Construction of What?*, above n 6, 19.

[9] ibid 36.

[10] ibid 10.

[11] A really good overview of what a 'governmentality' approach can offer by way of analysis of unemployment policy can be found in J Grundy, *Bureaucratic Manoeuvres: The Contested Administration of the Unemployed* (Toronto, University of Toronto Press, 2019) 9–10. See also Walters, above n 2, for a pioneering historical study in this vein.

[12] See, eg, E Brodkin and G Marston (eds), *Work and the Welfare State: Street-Level Organizations and Workfare Politics* (Washington DC, Georgetown University Press, 2013); M Considine et al, *Getting Welfare to Work: Street-Level Governance in Australia, the UK, and the Netherlands* (Oxford, Oxford University Press, 2015); G Marston and C McDonald, 'The Psychology, Ethics and Social Relations of Unemployment' (2003) 6 *Australian Journal of Labour Economics* 293.

[13] For one standout study that has paid attention to this aspect of the post-war unemployment benefits system, see A Law, 'Idlers, Loafers and Layabouts: An Historical Sociological Study of Welfare Discipline and Unemployment in Australia' (PhD thesis, University of Alberta, 1993).

I would emphasise, too, that although the focus of this book is the refinement and dissemination of ideas about unemployment proceeding from bureaucrats, statisticians, social scientists (both amateur and academic), legislative draftsmen and so on, it is clear from other historical studies that the unemployed person was not simply invented 'from above' by a community of experts. The autonomous behaviour of jobless people pressing 'from below' created a reality that experts had to find a language for. The two processes, notes Hacking, tend to occur in conjunction: 'our classification and our classes conspire to emerge hand in hand, each egging the other on'.[14]

One of the major contributions of those historians who have pursued this type of enquiry in other countries is to point out that the administrative and legal production of the category of 'unemployment' comes about partly through ordering the labour market in a particular way. Taking regulation in its broadest sense – encompassing a range of more or less formalised norms, conventions and customary practices – it is clear from the example I gave at the opening of this chapter that different types of labour market regulation produce different types of shortage of work. My point is that labour market regulation aimed at producing a homogenous, standardised understanding of the employment relationship, based around full-time 'permanent' contracts of employment, will give rise also to a standardised legal and administrative notion of joblessness that we call *un*employment. The general argument here is that the notion of 'involuntary unemployment' and the eligibility conditions attaching to unemployment benefit are necessarily defined against institutionalised norms about what kinds of work are exemplary while granting other forms of work lesser recognition.[15] So a good part of this book will concentrate on the evolution of the employment relationship in Australia. The consolidation of a relatively homogenous, uniform conception and experience of work is, broadly speaking, the story of labour market regulation in Australia across the first half of the twentieth century; the unravelling of that uniform experience has in turn been the story of the past few decades.

To elaborate on this, the phenomenon of post-war unemployment as an administrative and legal category depended on two conditions. First, that workers were allotted positions within an enterprise through an open-ended or 'permanent' contract of full-time employment. Secondly, that employers adjusted to downturns and depressions through severance of that contract for a given number of positions rather than either absorbing such downturns within the enterprise (through, for example, short-time work) or varying or terminating arm's length market transactions in a volatile and dynamic external labour market (characterised by casual labourers gathered at the factory gate each morning, or the use of labour subcontracting and other forms of 'self-employment').

---

[14] I Hacking, 'Making Up People' in TC Heller, M Sosna and DE Wellbery (eds), *Reconstructing Individualism: Autonomy, Individualism and the Self in Western Thought* (Stanford, CA, Stanford University Press, 1986) 228.

[15] Baxandall, 'Explaining Differences in the Political Meaning of Unemployment', above n 1.

This means I'll be examining a development that is both juridical and socio-economic. The juridical development consisted of bringing different forms of labour hire within a uniform legal conception of the contract of employment, a process that proceeded slowly from the end of the nineteenth century through the early decades of the twentieth.[16] In Australia, this development had a particular impact, not so much because of the emerging common law understanding of the rights and obligations attaching to an employment contract, but because it gradually allowed increasing numbers of wage-dependent workers to be subject to the jurisdiction and determinations of the Commonwealth Court of Conciliation and Arbitration established in 1904. From the 1920s, the Arbitration Court then adopted a policy of stabilising and standardising many of the conditions of the employment relationship, favouring full-time, weekly hiring over casual hire, with accrued entitlements to recreation and sick leave and limitations on employers' right to temporarily stand down workers.

The second aspect is how the temporal and spatial dimensions of work were standardised in practice. Although the decisions of the arbitral tribunals played a vital role in regularising employment, other socio-economic conditions also assured that forms of intermediate labour subcontracting, casual labour and so on, were displaced in favour of bureaucratically controlled, long-term employment relations. With the rise of large, vertically integrated enterprises concerned with the manufacture of standardised, generic products for mass markets, many transactions – including labour allocation – that had been carried out in external markets based on the price mechanism were brought within the firm and subjected to centralised co-ordination and administration. This internalisation of market transactions reduced costs and uncertainties for the firm, particularly in periods of labour shortage. In fact, such 'internal labour markets' ceased to function much like markets at all: unlike subcontracting transactions, they granted the employer an ongoing discretion to direct and control labour within the hierarchy of the firm. The open-ended employment contract proved such a useful legal instrument precisely because it created the space for ongoing co-operation between workers and employers.[17] In Australia, it appears that the type of management practices associated with internalisation – centralised personnel departments, formalised work rules and pay scales, the emergence of a class of professional, salaried

---

[16] See A Merritt, 'The Historical Role of Law in the Regulation of Employment – Abstentionist or Interventionist?' (1982) 1 *Australian Journal of Law & Society* 56; J Howe and R Mitchell: 'The Evolution of the Contract of Employment in Australia: A Discussion' (1999) 12 *Australian Journal of Labour Law* 113; M Quinlan, 'Australia, 1788–1902: A Workingman's Paradise?' in D Hay and P Craven (eds), *Masters, Servants and Magistrates in Britain and the Empire, 1562–1955* (Chapel Hill, NC, University of North Carolina Press, 2004).

[17] See D Marsden, *A Theory of Employment Systems: Micro-Foundations of Societal Diversity* (Oxford, Oxford University Press, 1999). On the efficiency advantages of internal labour markets and the employment contract, see also RH Coase, 'The Nature of the Firm' (1937) 4 *Economica* 386. Coase and his successors tended to underplay the role of conflict within the authority relation created by employment contracts, but their work offers a useful stylised account of why the employment contract came to dominate working life in the mid-twentieth century.

managers – did not become generalised until the 1940s, spurred on first by the need to rationalise production and limit absenteeism during the Second World War, then by acute post-war labour shortages.[18] Interestingly for my enquiry, the dominance of this mode of labour management coincided with the establishment of Australia's system of social security payments for the unemployed.

So in effect, what I'm calling the invention of unemployment is really the invention of a binary opposition: the creation of both employment *and* unemployment as distinct and relatively homogenous labour market statuses, one the obverse of the other. As William Walters puts it:

> A condition of employment could only be delineated from one of unemployment once work came to be concentrated in the socio-spatial form of the factory or office, compressed into a normal working week, and set within a modern bureaucratic system of employment relations.[19]

There is, then, a complex and interactive relationship between the formation of ideas about *employment* and those concerning *unemployment*. Administrators, social investigators and regulators in one field tended to pursue their own lines of enquiry with their own set of concerns, but often were working in a context provided, at least in part, by developments in the other. So, if in the past the regulation of employment and unemployment have been treated as relatively distinct fields of enquiry, I want to approach them as ineluctably intertwined and better understood as carrying on a regulatory conversation with each other.

And then there's the sub-plot. In developing my argument I devote particular attention to the role of the labour exchange, a state-run bureau for matching jobseekers with potential employers. The labour exchange or labour bureau represented one clear instance where the discourses of employment and unemployment came together in a very real way. The labour exchange was conceived as an administrative technology both for the governance and relief of unemployment on the one hand and for the organisation of employment and the labour market on the other. The labour exchange wasn't something that merely became possible after the unemployment was 'invented' as a distinct labour market status. On the contrary, from the early twentieth century exchanges were seen as a useful technology for ordering the labour market in the first instance, and hence for generating 'real' unemployment. The labour exchange could be used to create a 'diagram' of the labour market as a whole.[20] A national labour exchange helped us to conceive a single, national pool of labour where the worker displaced from one enterprise could look for and find a new job in another. It allowed bureaucrats and administrators to think in terms of the formal severance of one contract and availability for rehiring at another enterprise, rather than there being pools of

---

[18] C Wright, *The Management of Labour: A History of Australian Employers* (Melbourne, Oxford University Press, 1995).

[19] Walters, above n 2, 19. A similar point is made in S Deakin and F Wilkinson, *The Law of the Labour Market: Industrialization, Employment, and Legal Evolution* (Oxford, Oxford University Press, 2005) 149.

[20] Walters, above n 2, 47.

casual labour within specific trades or localities or workers maintaining connection with an enterprise during downturns through short-time working and underemployment. Where local and industry practices did not actually correspond to this model, the labour exchange was seen as a useful tool for imposing such a reality and hence organising the labour market around the norm of regular, full-time employment.[21] Labour exchanges rendered unemployment visible in other ways, too. Most importantly in the context of unemployment assistance, exchanges administered the 'work test' that tested claimants' job search by providing constantly updated information on vacancies and bringing this to bear on the case of each individual jobseeker. In this way, the genuinely 'unemployed', temporarily and involuntarily out of work, could be distinguished from the 'malingerer'. So the emergence of the CES in Australia offers a valuable insight into the construction of unemployment. Similarly, the dismantling of the CES over the past few decades is emblematic of changes to the regulation of joblessness.

Despite its subtitle, this book actually ranges from the late nineteenth century to the present and, while the focus is on Australia, it also deals with developments in Britain. Fashions in social policy have become increasingly international, but even as a colonial outpost Australia could not help but be influenced by British ideas while also charting its own distinct course. Particularly influential was the work of what one commentator has called a 'group of intellectual hybrids ... concerned partly with general economic hypotheses, partly with sociological investigation, and partly with administrative reform'.[22] It was this group, including Charles Booth and William Beveridge, along with Sidney and Beatrice Webb, that first began to define unemployment as a social and administrative problem related to labour market organisation and separate from the prevailing cultural or moral interpretations associated with poverty or pauperism. So the first four chapters tic-tac between Britain and Australia, examining ideas of unemployment that prevailed prior to the Second World War, the range of labour management practices and evolving understandings of the employment relationship across that period, and the development of labour exchanges in both Britain and Australia as one particular response to the question of both labour market organisation and the governance of the unemployed.

From chapter five onwards, the book is more directly focused on Australian developments, in particular the administration of a national unemployment benefit scheme, and the role the CES played in this, but also having regard to shifts in how we defined and measured unemployment, and how all this interacted with changing labour market regulation and practice. The global still inevitably intrudes: Australia fell into line as regards international statistical practice regarding the measurement of the unemployed; later, the need to 'activate' them; and more recently we enthusiastically adopted the new international orthodoxy regarding services for the unemployed.

[21] See Mansfield, above n 2, 435.
[22] J Harris, *Unemployment and Politics: A Study in English Social Policy, 1886-1914* (Cambridge, Cambridge University Press, 1972) 11.

1

A Disorganised Labour Market

When, in 1928, Australia's newly established National Development and Migration Commission turned its enquiries to the issue of unemployment, it named the problem as one of labour market 'disorganisation'. Large sections of the Report were spent discussing casual and irregular labour and the need to reform hiring practices.[1] A Royal Commission on National Insurance had similarly concluded, a year earlier, that casual labour constituted 'the greatest problem in connexion with unemployment'.[2] This might strike us as perplexing. Although the perils of *under*employment and precarious work are receiving renewed attention today, for most of the post-war period they were perceived as incidents of a status distinct from that of *un*employment. Yet the conflation in the 1920s of the problem of casual or intermittent employment with that of unemployment was a common one, and perfectly consistent with a body of social and economic enquiry emerging from Britain in the first decade of the twentieth century. William Walters has argued that 'the casual labour problem marks the point at which the problems of poverty and pauperism begin to be linked to forms of employment'. Concerns about irregular work created a space of enquiry where the links between labour markets, forms of employment and forms of social and moral life became established.[3] This preoccupation with casual labour was significant for two reasons: on the one hand it reflected the reality of emergent industrial labour markets; on the other, it pointed to a social and administrative programme in which the labour exchange would play a crucial role.

The British Context

Until the twentieth century, unemployment in British social thought remained an ill-defined concept. The old poor law, originating in Tudor times,[4] covered all

---

[1] Commonwealth of Australia, Development and Migration Commission, *Report on Unemployment and Business Instability in Australia*, Parl Paper No 252 (1926–28).

[2] Commonwealth of Australia, Royal Commission on National Insurance, *Second Progress Report: Unemployment*, Parl Paper No 79 (1926–28) 21.

[3] W Walters, *Unemployment and Government: Genealogies of the Social* (Cambridge, Cambridge University Press, 2000) 26.

[4] An Act for the Punishing of Vagabonds, and for the Relief of Poor and Impotent Persons, 1 Edw 6, c 3 (1547).

forms of poverty, whether caused by sickness, old age, desertion, low wages or lack of work. The main distinction made was that between the 'able-bodied' poor and the sick, old or infirm. For example, the law in the sixteenth century distinguished between the impotent poor who were allowed to beg and the able-bodied vagrant who was to be whipped. As one commentator has observed, the law 'made no provision whatsoever for the man who desperately desired to be employed but had no job to go to'.[5]

The nature of the labour market from the seventeenth through to the eighteenth century meant work was subject to seasonal and cyclical fluctuations and regulated by task rather than time. This made for irregular working days, weeks and years, with periods of intensity and idleness alternating.[6] These fluctuations and irregularities in an occupation could often be offset by a labourer's ability to pick up alternative occupations, often according to seasonal variation, and his or her ability to rely on subsistence forms of provision, or, in the face of regional variations in the availability of work, the practice of 'tramping' in search of work.[7] Overall, the general problem of poverty or pauperism was not easily correlated with labour market status, and lack of work in a given occupation 'cannot have been the threat to livelihood it later came to pose'.[8]

Lack of work would become a greater threat once wages became the 'sole precarious base' of living, rather than one component among many.[9] Over the course of the late eighteenth and early nineteenth century, workers were increasingly incorporated into a monetised, market economy. Their ability to raise their standard of living through non-waged activities decreased, as customary use-rights – such as gleaning or collecting wood – were eroded.[10] The new large cities both concentrated workers and offered only minimal alternatives to waged labour.

Some skilled workers could enjoy more-or-less regular work, for the same employer, for many years. But the small-scale, undercapitalised artisan workshops that predominated in this period were particularly vulnerable to trade depressions, shifts in industrial technique, and business failure due either to bad debts or simply to the 'personal failings of the proprietor which ranged from simple … incompetence to drunkenness and crime' – and any one of these events would likely result in loss of employment.[11] In any case, a lot of the work was organised

---

[5] K Kumar, 'From Work to Employment and Unemployment: The English Experience' in RE Pahl (ed), *On Work: Historical, Comparative and Theoretical Approaches* (Oxford, Blackwell, 1988) 142.

[6] ibid 146–47; EP Thompson, 'Time, Work Discipline and Industrial Capitalism' (1967) 38 *Past & Present* 56.

[7] See EJ Hobsbawm, 'The Tramping Artisan' in EJ Hobsbawm (ed), *Labouring Men: Studies in the History of Labour* (London, Weidenfeld and Nicolson, 1964).

[8] Kumar, above n 5, 149.

[9] ibid 151.

[10] MJ Daunton, *Poverty and Progress: An Economic and Social History of Britain 1700–1850* (Oxford, Oxford University Press, 1995) 179.

[11] J Burnett, *Idle Hands: The Experience of Unemployment, 1790–1990* (London, Routledge, 1994) 92–109.

around discontinuous, irregular employment. Seasonal fluctuations and the multiplicity of small-scale employers produced a highly irregular demand for goods and services, one commentator observing that 'as most trades are "brisk" and "slack" at various periods of the year, a large number of workmen [were] employed only in the busy season and discharged in dull times'.[12] Certain sectors displayed particular variations on this theme: clothing and textile producers tended to enter subcontracting arrangements with outworkers, making it easier for enterprises to utilise workers only as the needs of their business required; port transport and construction industries also relied on short-term engagements, and tended to attract many workers who preferred this lifestyle.[13] For workers in these situations, periods of joblessness were a common occurrence.

Casual labour of this sort dominated London, partly because of its role as a transport and distribution hub, and partly because the city retained its 'pre-industrial' character, dominated not by a factory proletariat but by manifold small commercial enterprises. It was perhaps not typical of the industrialisation that was transforming cities such as Leeds and Manchester. Despite – or because of – this, London became the focus both of a certain political anxiety around joblessness and of various investigations that would attempt to define the unemployed according to some uniform criteria.

Across the middle years of the nineteenth century, the lack of adequate work had become a mobilising force in certain quarters of working class politics and by the 1880s was manifesting itself in street-level demonstrations and rioting in London.[14] For the middle class, the term 'the unemployed' was a dramatic way to refer to a threatening mass of out-of-work men; for speakers at street meetings, the term evoked a clear and proud identity for the assembled jobless.[15] As Noel Whiteside observes:

> It is unlikely that the temporarily unemployed labourer was really much worse off than his father or grandfather had been. Rural underemployment had been much less visible than its urban counterpart ... The new visibility of labour market disorganisation at

---

[12] Henry Mayhew, cited in N Whiteside, *Bad Times: Unemployment in British Social and Political History* (London, Faber, 1991).

[13] Whiteside, above n 12, 31–33.

[14] R Flanagan, '*Parish Fed Bastards*': *A History of the Politics of the Unemployed in Britain, 1884–1939* (New York, Greenwood Press, 1991); Burnett, above n 11, 146. Similar demonstrations of jobless workers had disturbed several North American cities in the 1870s, and between 1890 and 1920 the unemployed in Boston staged some of the 'most powerful, gripping and colourful political protests': A Keyssar, *Out of Work: The First Century of Unemployment in Massachusetts* (Cambridge, MA, Cambridge University Press, 1986) 224.

[15] C Topalov, 'The Invention of Unemployment: Language, Classification and Social Reform 1880–1910' in B Palier (ed), *Comparing Social Welfare Systems in Europe: Volume 1* (Paris, MIRE, 1994) 498. Similarly, in the United States across this period 'involuntary idleness' had, according to Keyssar, become sufficiently widespread and visible so as 'to need its own name and to be measured': Keyssar, above n 14, 4.

home, ... the extension of the franchise to most working men in 1884, the growth of trade and labour organisation and the inability of traditional institutions to cope with the situation all combined to promote the unemployment question as a key issue in national politics in the early twentieth century.[16]

So by the 1890s, the jobless poor in Britain had succeeded in creating a public awareness of their condition, but the government response had been merely to tinker with the poor law, which treated the jobless worker only indirectly, continuing to focus on categories such as the able-bodied poor, the sick or the insane.[17] That is, unemployment had no clear existence in the administrative or legal imagination as a separate and discrete labour market category.

This would change, principally due to the work of a number of social surveyors and investigators. Such surveyors were anxious to discredit many of the claims of socialists and others regarding the extent of poverty and destitution caused by joblessness and to furnish the debate with accurate statistics. Systems of classification like that developed by Charles Booth led to conclusions which were more socially reassuring than the prevailing popular rhetoric of 'starving millions' and the imagery of barbarians of the slums ready to overthrow civilisation.[18] And the work of surveyors such as Booth helped 'unemployment' emerge as a much more potent administrative category. This would be a fairly drawn out process, but by the end of the nineteenth century, it already 'seemed agreed ... that the pool of casual workers lay at the heart of the problem'.[19]

Social Surveys, the Casual Worker and the Problem of Unemployment

Booth was a shipowner and merchant from a wealthy Liverpool family. His interest in social problems led him to fund and organise surveys of the London working class, published in 1903 as the 17-volume *Life and Labour of the People of London*. Booth's preoccupation with disaggregating and classifying the constituent

---

[16] Whiteside, above n 12, 48.

[17] Flanagan, above n 14, 46.

[18] EP Hennock, 'Poverty and Social Theory in England: The Experience of the 1880s' (1976) 1 *Social History* 67, 75. Flanagan asserts that Booth's survey was 'directly inspired' by a survey conducted by the Social Democratic Foundation (SDF) which claimed 25 per cent of Londoners were living in poverty and that Booth was ultimately forced to concede the SDF figure was an underestimate: above n 14, 47. Hennock's close reading of Booth's manuscripts suggests Flanagan is wrong on both counts. Nevertheless, although the link between SDF agitation and Booth's survey might not be as direct as Flanagan wishes it to be, it is clear the preoccupation with statistical surveys was in part driven by the increased prominence and organisation of groups of the jobless poor.

[19] Burnett, above n 11, 156.

elements of the working class was not conceptually that original nor unfamiliar to those who had followed discussions of the 'labouring poor' since the late 1860s. Instead, his contribution lay in an analysis of causes of poverty and strategies for its cure.[20]

Booth distinguished eight classes of labourer in terms of both income and regularity of work. He labelled the classes A to H. Class A was a small group of semi-criminals, 'battered figures who slouch through the streets and play the beggar or the bully', and who could, for purposes of labour market reform, be largely ignored. The real problem of poverty was concentrated on classes B, C and D. Class B represented a casual residuum, men who worked irregularly largely because they were incapable, for 'mental, moral and physical reasons' of steady work. Classes C and D, however, were poor through a mixture of low wages and irregular work, but they were 'decent steady men' whose labour market position was partly the result of competition for jobs from Class B. That is, overall there was a surplus of labour leading to generalised underemployment.[21]

Booth's surveys began to draw greater attention to employment status as an explanation of poverty. In particular, he highlighted the lack of *regular* work as a cause of poverty. Some saw this as a moral problem. The overwhelming concern of the charity organisations of the time was to make the poor self-reliant and to inculcate in them the virtues of thrift, sobriety and familial responsibility. Casual earnings were not conducive to thrift; nor were the habits of casual work conducive to the building of 'character'. As men flitted from job to job, their success in securing work was governed by chance rather than an established employment record.[22]

Booth's approach challenged certain prevailing conceptions of poverty, but still relied upon a distinction between the deserving and undeserving unemployed. A punitive poor law was seen as quite appropriate for those whose poverty could still be attributed to their own failings: drunkenness, profligacy, criminal disposition and so on. By contrast, there was presumed to be a group of deserving unemployed, labourers clearly capable and willing to undertake regular work but who were unable to find it due to trade depressions or unseasonable weather. For this group the poor law was clearly inappropriate.[23]

Constructing such a distinction was well and good; the problem for Booth and others was that the state of the London labour market prevented the easy

---

[20] Hennock, above n 18 76–77, 83–84.

[21] M Mansfield, 'Labour Exchanges and the Labour Reserve in Turn of the Century Social Reform' (1992) 21 *Journal of Social Policy* 435, 442.

[22] See Walters, above n 3, 27–28, discussing evidence from the Charity Organisation Society to the Royal Commission on the Poor Laws. Sidney and Beatrice Webb's minority report for the Commission picked up on this point: chronic underemployment would ultimately render the casual worker unemployable – that is, precipitate the decline of Booth's Class C and D worker into the 'wastage' of Class B. See S Deakin and F Wilkinson, *The Law of the Labour Market: Industrialization, Employment, and Legal Evolution* (Oxford, Oxford University Press, 2005) 155.

[23] Whiteside, above n 12, 51; Walters, above n 3, 23.

identification of two such groups.[24] The growth in major industrial and commercial cities had displaced the household economy with the wage economy, but also produced a labour market where the prevalence of casual labour made it 'quite impossible to make clear distinctions between the employed, the unemployed, the self-employed and the economically inactive'.[25] The almost random distribution of too few jobs among too many men meant the quantity of surplus labour in a given trade was concealed. In such a situation, Booth argued,

> we have to deal not with individuals out of work but with a body of men some of whom are superfluous; though each individual may be doing a job of work the total number of the superfluous is the true measure of the unemployed.[26]

The answer was the decasualisation of the labour market and the transfer of necessary workmen to regular, permanent employment, which would allow the superfluous population to be identified. This superfluous group could then be more easily policed according to the categories of deserving and undeserving: on the one hand, those capable of regular work and able to be absorbed into other industries; on the other, those who, 'if the worst comes to the worst ... pass through the workhouse and finally die'.[27] It is clear that the distinction between regular workers, a legitimate labour reserve and a superfluous population was not an empirical one that reflected the labour market as it then existed. Rather, it was a distinction that could only be made *after* a way was found to regularise the labour market.[28]

Whereas Booth saw the problem of casual labour as endemic to particular trades – most notably the docks – William Beveridge saw it as a general problem of the labour market, with every trade tending to be chronically overstocked. Furthermore, Beveridge depersonalised the problem of unemployment to a greater degree than Booth: the focus was as much the disorganised labour market itself, rather than merely problematic classes of labourer or ways of life.[29] Accordingly, the line between Booth's classes B and C was more permeable for Beveridge. The poverty of Class B was explained for Beveridge 'not by their character alone, but by that and their environment together':

> The casual workman of every grade is the resultant of demand and supply – of the need of employers for casual labour and of the readiness of men to meet that need ... [M]en have not learnt to fight against irregularity of earning as they have learnt to fight against low rates of pay ... These are two sides of the problem of normal poverty which is being forced on public attention in the shape of a problem of unemployment.[30]

[24] Whiteside, above n 12, 127.

[25] ibid 30.

[26] Charles Booth, *Life and Labour of the People in London*, cited in J Harris, *Unemployment and Politics: A Study in English Social Policy 1886–1914* (Oxford, Oxford University Press, 1972) 16.

[27] Harris, ibid, 20.

[28] Mansfield, above n 21, 443, 447.

[29] Walters, above n 3, 30.

[30] WH Beveridge, *Unemployment: A Problem of Industry* (London, Longmans, Green and Co, 1931 [1909]) 144.

This normal 'balance' between casual demand and underemployed supply was disturbed by periodic trade depression, but even then it resulted 'not in the dismissal of regular men, but in the lengthening of the average loss of time by the irregular man'.[31] So the problem was less the existence of Class B exerting competition and dragging down Classes C and D, but the overall organisation of the labour market around short-term engagements and poor recruitment practices in geographically segmented casual labour markets.[32] To some extent, the first step towards a resolution would need to be similar to Booth's: to concentrate available employment on regular, full-time workers rather than spreading a limited amount of employment over a maximum number of individual workers. Added to this, however, was a new concern with the provision of labour market information, labour mobility and the reform of hiring practices. As Beveridge was to go on to occupy a key position at the British Board of Trade, it was his gloss on the problem of casual labour that was to have the enduring effect.

But what's important is the general emergence of unemployment as a matter of labour market reform and policy rather than one of poor relief or social policy. As Christian Topalov notes, 'the notion or language of unemployment emerged ... as a tool to change the reality it was supposed to talk about, and not merely as a concept describing it'.[33]

The Employment Relationship in Australia

The fact that Australian enquiries into unemployment in the 1920s focused on casual labour and the problem of irregular work suggests a similar set of preoccupations on the part of policymakers in both Britain and Australia – and also a similar set of labour market characteristics.

Nineteenth-century Australian labour markets did tend to mirror those of London. Late-nineteenth-century Sydney, for example, had no extensive manufacturing or industrial sector; its commercial functions were tied to the rural sector. Much of this rural work was seasonal, and this had clear repercussions for key sectors of the urban labour market, such as woolwashers, tanners, meat preservers and the arrival and dispatch of sea cargo.[34] Fruit canning and lamb slaughtering were concentrated in the months from November to January; agricultural implement making had two seasonal peaks in late summer (for tillage and planting machines) and late winter (for harvesting machines); and artificial manure production peaked in autumn – provided rain came, otherwise orders

---

[31] ibid 145.
[32] Mansfield, above n 21, 451.
[33] Topalov, above n 15, 494.
[34] SH Fisher, 'An Accumulation of Misery' (1981) 40 *Labour History* 16, 27.

fizzled and workers were laid off.[35] Other industries not so closely linked to the rural seasons – such as construction – fluctuated according to an unpredictable business cycle.[36]

Irregular volumes of short-term orders meant manufacturers could provide few stable jobs. Whereas some clerical and supervisory staff enjoyed ongoing employment, workers on the shop floor tended to bear the brunt of the rise and fall in work, with women and juveniles in particular providing a large pool of short-term, casual labour.[37] Shirley Fisher notes that:

> Many of Sydney's factories were little more than backyard sheds, especially in the food processing and clothing industries, and many of the employees were little more than day labourers. On the other hand, Sydney's handful of large factories tended to be engaged in manufacturing for just those sectors most liable to fluctuating demand – most notably in shipbuilding and repair … [J]ob flexibility has been tied to notions of mobility. The worker turning his hand to anything is seen as an indication of social fluidity and upward occupational mobility. He may just as well be used as an indication of underemployment.[38]

Much early factory production in Australia did little more than bring under one roof artisans who continued to labour in a self-contained way, along with their helpers, as part of a team. Firms often farmed out tasks to a labour boss who contracted to complete them at a specified price and by a certain date, rather than selling his labour by the hour or day. This person would then hire and manage the labour carrying out the task.[39] For example, although mechanised brick works began to displace itinerant brick makers at the beginning of the 1870s, within the factories brick makers were paid on a piecework basis and each paid a helper who carried clay and sand and for whom the brick company itself took no responsibility. Similarly, 'twisters' in some tobacco factories hired and paid assistants who were not included on the firm's books.[40] In the clothing trades, workers would sometimes work on a firm's premises, but often would also take work home, suggesting the distinction between the 'inside worker' and the outworker was not clearly fixed.[41]

These forms of labour management that made for irregularity of employment and underemployment persisted well into twentieth-century Australia. Subcontracting arrangements such as the butty gang system continued into the 1920s.[42]

---

[35] C Fahey, 'Unskilled Labour and the Beginnings of Labour Market Regulation, Victoria 1901–1914' (2002) 33 *Australian Historical Studies* 143, 149; C Fahey and J Lack, 'The Great Strike of 1917 in Victoria: Looking Fore and Aft, and From Below' (2014) 106 *Labour History* 69, 79.

[36] Fahey, ibid, 149.

[37] J Lee and C Fahey, 'A Boom for Whom? Some Developments in the Australian Labour Market, 1870–1891' (1986) 50 *Labour History* 1.

[38] Fisher, above n 34, 27.

[39] C Wright, *The Management of Labour: A History of Australian Employers* (Melbourne, Oxford University Press, 1995) 18–19.

[40] GJR Linge, *Industrial Awakening: A Geography of Australian Manufacturing 1788–1890* (Canberra, Australian National University Press, 1979) 482.

[41] ibid 203, 298.

[42] eg, the butty gang system was actually extended at the Victorian Railways Newport workshops in the mid- to late 1920s: J Spierings, 'Magic and Science, Aspects of Australian Business Management,

In 1927 the Commonwealth government established a Royal Commission to examine proposals for a national insurance scheme. In the course of looking at the question of unemployment insurance, the Commission identified rural employment, the meat and flour industries and building work in the construction industry as characterised by seasonal fluctuations; many collieries in the coal industry as averaging less than four days' work per week; the boot trade and textile industries as relying extensively on short-time work and rostering; and continuous work in the steel industry being supplemented by casual employment of men seeking work gathered at the smelter gates.[43]

It's true that certain large, highly capitalised Australian enterprises of the pre-war period, often enjoying monopolies, were able to offer stable employment, such as State and local government instrumentalities, along with various banks and insurance firms.[44] There is evidence of long-term employment relationships and internal labour markets in the Union Bank of Australia and the Victorian Railways in the first decades of the twentieth century.[45] Even unskilled workers could find secure employment in government instrumentalities: in 1911, around 14 per cent of unskilled manual workers in Victoria found secure employment in the Victorian Railways, the post and telegraph service, the Metropolitan Board of Works, municipal electric plants, and tramways and gas companies.[46] The period of the First World War and the 1920s saw the establishment of some heavy industry, particularly in iron and steel, but also in glass, paper and chemicals. Also, strengthened tariff protection encouraged foreign firms to set up enterprises, resulting in the mass production of complex consumer durables in the automotive and electrical appliance industries.[47] Some of these manufacturers offered employment tenure that endured beyond that of the 'spot' markets associated with many workplaces, but falling short of the secure career employment found at banks, insurance companies and parts of the State railway departments.[48] But in any case, large mass production firms remained the exception, as a small domestic market limited economies of scale, resulting in a large number of small to middling producers.

The introduction of limited liability provided an opportunity for larger, integrated corporations and combines to emerge by way of stock market float,

Advertising and Retailing, 1918–1940' (PhD Thesis, University of Melbourne 1990) 93. This suggests a bifurcated approach to employment relations within the railways.

[43] Commonwealth of Australia, *Second Progress Report: Unemployment*, above n 2, 7–8.

[44] See G Patmore, 'Systematic Management and Bureaucracy: The New South Wales Railways Prior to 1932' (1988) 1 *Labour & Industry* 306; D Merrett and A Seltzer, 'Personnel Practices at the Union Bank of Australia: Panel Evidence from the 1887–1900 Entry Cohorts' (2000) 18 *Journal of Labor Economics* 573.

[45] A Seltzer and A Sammartino, 'Internal Labour Markets: Evidence From Two Large Australian Employers' (2009) 49 *Australian Economic History Review* 107.

[46] Fahey, above n 35, 147–48.

[47] Wright, above n 39, 16.

[48] C Fahey and A Sammartino, 'Work and Wages at a Melbourne Factory, the Guest Biscuit Works 1870–1921' (2013) 53 *Australian Economic History Review* 22; A Seltzer, 'Labour, Skills and Migration' in S Ville and G Withers (eds), *The Cambridge Economic History of Australia* (Melbourne, Cambridge University Press, 2015) 190–93.

takeover or merger.[49] But the introduction of colonial company law acts which mirrored British legislation as early as the 1860s and 1890s seemed to have little immediate repercussion for the growth of colonial enterprise other than in the major industries of mining and banking. Only a minority of companies sought a stock exchange listing,[50] and Australia's domestic capital market across much of this period was underdeveloped compared with those in Britain or the United States. The capital market's prime activity before the 1890s was trading in speculative mining stock. New issues for industrial stocks remained extremely modest until the 1920s and 1930s.[51] By the 1920s, family-owned and managed firms still dominated the economy, with the average number of wage earners per establishment in Australia in 1929 only 15.6.[52] The economy as a whole remained oriented predominantly toward primary production, with the rural sector providing 60 per cent of the national product even in the 1930s, which meant seasonal fluctuations in both the distribution and processing of a wide range of products persisted.

The prevalence of small, technologically unsophisticated workplaces, operating on batch production, with seasonal instability in many industries, produced a volatile labour market. Foremen or labour bosses would hire and fire according to product market fluctuations. The threat of dismissal ensured labour discipline, and subcontracting devolved the responsibility for labour supervision to contractors. From the perspective of management, these modes of hiring and firing suited, on the one hand, product markets subject to uncertainty and, on the other, labour markets characterised by an abundant supply of unskilled labour.[53] But seasonal and casual hiring, along with subcontracting, shifted the risk of unstable product markets to workers, resulting in short-term work with frequent interruptions to earnings.

The Commonwealth Arbitration Court, having identified the existence of intermittent employment in certain industries, attempted to ameliorate its effects through loading a higher hourly rate in the relevant awards. By the second half of the 1920s, this higher rate was written into awards covering wharf workers, builders' labourers, shearers, flour mill workers and those working in the meat export and sugar industries.[54] Wage policy in this way sought to alleviate the possible distress caused by certain forms of irregular work as well as attempting to

---

[49] Deakin and Wilkinson, above n 22, 97.

[50] Rob McQueen's research indicates that in NSW in 1903 there were over 9,000 registrations of partnerships as compared with only 157 company registrations: R McQueen, 'Company Law as Imperialism' (1995) 5 *Australian Journal of Corporate Law* 187.

[51] S Ville and D Merrett, 'The Development of Large Scale Enterprise in Australia, 1910–64' (2000) 42 *Business History* 13.

[52] Wright, above n 39, 16. Comparable figures for Canada were 25.3; for the United States, 41.9.

[53] HF Gospel, *Markets, Firms and the Management of Labour in Modern Britain* (Cambridge, Cambridge University Press, 1992) 77. On the oversupply of unskilled labour in early-twentieth-century Australia, see Fahey, above n 35, 147–48.

[54] G Anderson, *Fixation of Wages in Australia* (Melbourne, Macmillan, 1929) 490.

transfer at least part of the cost of maintaining a reserve army of underemployed workers to employers themselves.[55]

The extent to which the casual 'loading' discouraged such employment is unclear. Income data from the 1933 Commonwealth Census indicate a significant number of 'working' households with an annual income less than that provided by the basic wage, suggesting the continued presence of intermittent or short-time working.[56] In the early 1940s, social commentators were still blaming household poverty on the prevalence of casual labour.[57]

Some commentators have suggested that by the time of the Depression short-time working had effectively disappeared as a response to market fluctuations. Drawing largely on macroeconomic data, Bob Gregory and others have argued that the drop in labour demand in the early 1930s was managed largely through redundancy rather than labour hoarding, short-time work or work rationing. The available figures on durations of individuals' episodes of unemployment support the notion that large pools of jobless labourers accumulated, with little turnover or 'churning'.[58] However, there is what Forster refers to as 'widespread but fragmented' evidence of work rationing and short-time work as a response to the Depression.[59] Writing in 1936, E Ronald Walker recognised work rationing as 'quite a common expedient in Australia in the worst period of the depression'.[60] Histories of the Depression in both South Australia and Victoria make mention of the practice being 'substantial' and 'widespread', affecting both public and private sectors.[61] Gregory et al admit the existence of work rationing in the New South Wales railways[62] and among miners.[63] Broomhill suggests that the practice of short-time work found widespread favour among employers as workers could be put under pressure to complete the equivalent of a full week's work in reduced time, while employees accepted it as a necessary evil.

Gregory et al also support their argument by suggesting that the existence of award coverage prevented any decrease in hours for those workers who

[55] *Waterside Workers Case* (1919) 13 CAR 599, 617–18.

[56] I McLean and S Richardson, 'More or Less Equal? Australian Income Distribution Since 1933' (1986) 62 *Economic Record* 67.

[57] See F Oswald Barnett, *The Poverty of the People in Australia* (Melbourne, Good Companions Christian Social Order Group, 1944) 8.

[58] RG Gregory et al, 'The Australian and US Labour Markets in the 1930s' in B Eichengreen and TJ Hatton (eds), *Interwar Unemployment in International Perspective* (Dordrecht, Springer, 1988).

[59] C Forster, 'Unemployment and the Australian Economic Recovery of the 1930s' (1985) Department of Economic History, Australian National University Working Paper No 45, 11.

[60] E Ronald Walker, *Unemployment Policy: With Special Reference to Australia* (Sydney, Angus and Robertson, 1936) 85.

[61] R Broomhill, 'Underemployment in Adelaide During the Depression' (1974) 27 *Labour History* 31; LJ Louis, *Trade Unions and the Depression: A Study of Victoria, 1930–1932* (Canberra, Australian National University Press, 1968).

[62] See J Pincus, 'Aspects of Australian Public Finances and Public Enterprises, 1920 to 1939' (1985) Department of Economic History, Australian National University Working Paper No 53.

[63] *Official Year Book of New South Wales 1934–35* (Sydney, Government Printer, 1937) 752.

remained employed. This reasoning, however, is based on the supposition that all awards mandated a standard working week. As we'll see, although weekly hiring was the preferred mode of engagement pursued by the Arbitration Court, even in the late 1920s awards in many sectors made allowance for short-time work. For example, the vagaries of the clothing trade saw the Court insert two days' notice of termination provisions and 'turns' for employees in slack times which spread available work over the entire workforce.[64] More awards were modified to accommodate the extreme economic troughs of the Depression, amending weekly hiring and allowing for short-time work, 'turns' and rationing to spread available work as widely as possible employees.[65] There is evidence that even in those trades covered by strong craft unions with established out-of-work benefit schemes, rationing was used as a response to the Depression[66] – perhaps because, with the seriousness of the economic downturn, trade union benefit funds had become so depleted that unions had to find other ways to respond to the crisis.[67]

What we can probably say is that short-time work was a fairly common response to the Depression, as it had been to previous, more minor, cyclical trade depressions within industries, and that the extensive use of casual employment continued into the 1930s, even in larger enterprises.[68] But at the same time the chronic underemployment represented by this mode of labour management was joined in the Depression years by a new phenomenon, highlighted by the data provided by Gregory et al: the redundancy of permanent or core workforces, brought about by a severance of the contract of employment and resulting in joblessness of extended duration. Underemployment was seen as a normal and hence unremarkable feature of the labour market, something that would persist even after the crisis of the Depression had passed.[69] For many commentators in the 1930s, the casual labourer who had been the centre of attention during the 1920s was displaced by the long-term claimant of emergency unemployment relief as the focus of concern. But as Noel Whiteside and James Gillespie point out regarding the British case, this change in official preoccupation should not be taken as evidence for the disappearance of earlier employment practices.[70]

---

[64] See, eg, *Federated Clothing and Allied Trades Union v Andrews* (1923) 18 CAR 1032; see also Anderson, above n 54, 492–95.

[65] *Health Inspectors Association v City of Greater Brisbane* (1931) 30 CAR 322; (1932) 31 CAR 141. See C Arup, 'Job Security or Income Support?' (1976) 7 *Federal Law Review* 145.

[66] J Hagan, *Printers and Politics: A History of the Australian Printing Unions 1850–1950* (Canberra, Australian National University Press, 1966) 242; T Sheridan, *Mindful Militants: The Amalgamated Engineering Union in Australia 1920–1972* (Cambridge, Cambridge University Press, 1975) 113; J Merritt, 'The Federated Ironworkers' Association in the Depression' (1971) 21 *Labour History* 48.

[67] Louis reports that by the early 1930s only six Victorian unions were able to pay unemployment benefit: above n 61, 156.

[68] See, eg, P Cochrane, 'Anatomy of a Steel Works: The Australian Iron and Steel Company Port Kembla, 1935–1939' (1989) 57 *Labour History* 61.

[69] See, eg, E Ronald Walker, 'The Unemployment Problem in Australia' (1932) 40 *Journal of Political Economy* 210; AG Colley, 'New South Wales Unemployment Statistics' (1939) 11 *Australian Quarterly* 96.

[70] N Whiteside and J Gillespie: 'Deconstructing Unemployment: Developments in Britain in the Interwar Years' (1991) 44 *Economic History Review* 665, 680.

Regularising Work in Australia

Walters has made the point in the British context that in the second half of the nineteenth century the notion of *employment* 'acquires a fullness ... as an object and target of governmental interventions'. He pinpoints the rise of factory legislation as one factor 'shaping modern employment relations ... [and which] actively normalised and socialised employment'.[71] The usefulness of this observation for the Australian case is, I think, limited by two factors. First, in nineteenth-century Australia, vast numbers of the workforce were not engaged in factory production. Regulatory interventions targeting factory workers, while important, could only normalise employment for a minority of workers rather than go towards creating a relatively homogenous experience of waged employment. Furthermore, even where people did labour in factories, working alongside each other, undertaking similar types of work, subject to similar levels of subordination, there was no guarantee that they enjoyed the same, generic legal status. This was true in both Britain and the United States, where factory workers in the late nineteenth century were, in certain circumstances, still conceived as independent contractors merely 'renting' bench or machine space.[72] I have already pointed out that subcontracting was also used within factories in the Australian colonies. So in this context, it was first necessary to conceive of all or most forms of work – not just factory labour – as comprising a single, generic legal relationship before the incidents of such a relationship could be regularised. Australia's system of award regulation would provide the crucial spur here, allowing for the emergence of a formalised, 'standard' employment relationship that could be counter-posed to unemployment.

Up to the close of the nineteenth century, much wage-dependent labour in the English-speaking world was covered by master and servant legislation. Although entering service was based on a supposedly consensual transaction between the two parties involved, the transaction was more akin to the passing of property or a lease than what we understand today by a contract of employment.[73] The relationship between master and servant was strongly hierarchical, with extensive implied powers of direction and discipline granted to the master, with sanctions against the employee – including imprisonment – administered by the local magistracy. Master and servant legislation was imported into the Australian colonies in the nineteenth century, but the colonial Acts tended to be cast wider in their coverage than the British acts, to be more coercive, and to specify harsher penalties. For example, sections of the labour force that fell outside the British statutes were

---

[71] Walters, above n 3, 15.

[72] On Great Britain, see R Biernacki, *The Fabrication of Labour: Germany and Britain 1640–1914*, (Berkeley, CA, University of California Press, 1995); on the United States, see E Englander, 'The Inside Contract System of Production and Organization: A Neglected Aspect of the History of the Firm' (1987) 28 *Labor History* 429.

[73] RJ Steinfeld, *The Invention of Free Labor: The Employment Relation in English and American Law and Culture, 1350–1870* (Chapel Hill, NC, University of North Carolina Press, 1991) 55–93.

included in the colonial laws, including dressmakers, laundresses and skilled rural labourers such as shepherds.[74]

The 'service' model underpinning this form of regulation was not seen as applicable to all groups of workers. In Britain, the emphasis on exclusive service meant the task contract tended to be excluded from the scope of the legislation.[75] However, some colonial legislation didn't bother with this distinction, preferring instead to explicitly encompass 'labourer[s] who shall contract with any person whomsoever for the performance of a certain work at a certain price'.[76] At the same time, master and servant legislation did not apply to higher status workers such as managers, agents and clerks. For this group, the employment relationship was understood in more genuinely contractual terms, with an emergent common law that encompassed limits on the employer's right to give orders, and the right of the employee to sue for damages for termination in breach of a notice clause or for the failure of the employer to provide work as agreed.[77]

Furthermore, skilled workers with collective economic power and – through trade unions – control over the labour supply were able to more or less unilaterally regulate their employment conditions. That is, union work rules were simply presented to the employer for acceptance; if the employer failed to comply with the union standards, then union employees were withdrawn. In nineteenth-century Australia, this form of regulation was common in the pastoral and maritime industries, and management attempts to reassert the power to both hire non-union labour and fix individual rather than standard wage rates was at the heart of the industrial conflicts of the 1890s. Finally, collective bargaining could give rise to a form of joint regulation, with bargained agreements playing an important role in metal and coalmining and certain urban craft industries, such as printing, building and engineering.[78]

Skilled and independent workers resisted efforts by employers to bring them within the purview of the broad colonial masters and servants Acts. Otherwise, they used the Acts to litigate what they saw as their 'contractual' rights within

---

[74] M Quinlan, 'Pre-Arbitral Labour Legislation in Australia and Its Implications for the Introduction of Compulsory Arbitration' in S Macintyre and R Mitchell (eds), *Foundations of Arbitration: The Origins and Effects of State Compulsory Arbitration, 1890–1914* (Melbourne, Oxford University Press, 1989) 31–32; see more generally M Quinlan, 'Australia, 1788–1902: A Workingman's Paradise?' in D Hay and P Craven (eds), *Masters, Servants and Magistrates in Britain and the Empire, 1562–1955* (Chapel Hill, NC, University of North Carolina Press, 2004).

[75] S Deakin, 'The Contract of Employment: A Study in Legal Evolution' (2001) ESRC Centre for Business Research, University of Cambridge Working Paper No 203, 17.

[76] Masters and Servants Act 1845 (NSW) s 3.

[77] Deakin, 'The Contract of Employment', above n 75, 24, citing *Emmens v Elderton* (1853) 13 CB 495, a case involving a company solicitor.

[78] M Bray and M Rimmer, 'Voluntarism or Compulsion? Public Inquiries Into Industrial Relations in New South Wales and Great Britain, 1890–4' in S Macintyre and R Mitchell (eds), *Foundations of Arbitration: The Origins and Effects of State Compulsory Arbitration, 1890–1914* (Melbourne, Oxford University Press, 1989).

the employment relationship.[79] While the legislation focused on the enforcement of fixed-term contracts, with strong sanctions against workers absconding prior to the expiration of their term, the length of contracts could vary markedly. In the second half of the nineteenth century, urban employment was probably dominated by weekly to monthly hirings, whereas three- to six-month contracts were the norm in rural areas. So in the cities workers were less likely to run foul of the legislation for absconding, and most actions under the legislation in the cities were employee-initiated actions to recover wages, whereas in rural areas employer-initiated actions for absconding were more common.[80] But generally, at the end of the nineteenth century, the contract of employment remained under-developed as an instrument for regulating the mutual rights and obligations of industrial workers and their employers.

It was in this context that Australian governments began enacting forms of protective legislation around compulsory arbitration and workers' compensation. Courts were increasingly called upon to define the boundaries of legislation of quite a novel type.[81] Up until this time, labour regulation had been directed at certain classes of fairly clearly defined workers, either in specific occupations (shearers, coalminers, workers in factories and workrooms and so on), or in categories that were recognised as clearly not inclusive of all wage-dependent labour (workmen, labourers, servants and so on). By contrast, there was an inchoate understanding that the workers' compensation and arbitral statutes might apply to a larger, more inclusive group of wage-dependent labour across industries – yet without, as despaired one early commentator, there being in 'industrial legislation a sound definition of the industrial class'.[82]

The seemingly protective cast of labour legislation such as workers' compensation law suggested a paternalistic interpretation whereby the workers targeted by the statute were those assumed to be in 'dependent' relationships and incapable of bargaining for themselves.[83] Such an interpretation would exclude higher-status salaried workers and others who could be seen as operating or contracting in an independent manner. So the courts read the legislative terms 'employer' and

---

[79] See A Merritt, 'The Historical Role of Law in the Regulation of Employment – Abstentionist or Interventionist?' (1982) 1 *Australian Journal of Law & Society* 56.

[80] R McQueen, 'Master and Servant Legislation in the 19th Century Australian Colonies' in D Kirkby (ed), *Law and History*, vol 4 (Bundoora, School of Legal Studies, La Trobe University, 1987).

[81] Deakin, 'The Contract of Employment, above n 75, 27; J Howe and R Mitchell: 'The Evolution of the Contract of Employment in Australia: A Discussion' (1999) 12 *Australian Journal of Labour Law* 113, 118.

[82] FAA Russell, *Australian Industrial Problems: Some of the Problems and Results of the Law of Industrial Arbitration Under Statutes of New South Wales and the Commonwealth of Australia Before and During the War, 1914–1918* (Sydney, Butterworths & Co, 1918) 86. Note that Russell still confines discussion of the problem to 'industry', a category that would be interpreted to exclude certain categories of professional and service workers until the 1980s: WB Creighton, WJ Ford and RJ Mitchell, *Labour Law: Text and Materials* (Sydney, Law Book Company, 1993) 442–49.

[83] This was the view expressed in the English decision *Simpson v Ebbw Vale Steel, Iron and Coal Co* [1905] 1 KB 453, 458, and adopted by the Western Australian Supreme Court in *Corcoran v Great Fingall GM Co Ltd* (1907) 9 WALR 192.

'employee' as designating a master and servant relation. Accordingly, the distinction between those workers engaged under a contract of service (ie, a master and servant relation) and those operating as 'independent' contractors emerged as a key legal question in the first decades of the twentieth century as regards workers' compensation law.[84]

Similarly, although most State and federal arbitration legislation applied to the relationship between 'employee' and 'employer', the presumption still tended to be that only restricted classes of 'dependent' labour were entitled to the minimum terms and conditions specified by the arbitral tribunals. The High Court again quickly equated the employer/employee relationship with that of master and servant.[85] It was clear that this relationship could not encompass all 'independent contracts for the supply of labour'.[86] Given the nature of labour contracting arrangements in early-twentieth-century Australia, this approach substantially limited the scope of arbitral legislation. This was a point recognised by Heydon J of the NSW Arbitration Court who in 1907 complained that 'the immense mass of workers who are not, in the technical sense, employees, are shut out [and] the worst sweating is carried on in connection with piecework'.[87] A contemporary commentator noted that the federal Arbitration Court could not regulate 'contracts for the performance of a specific piece of work', including those where a number of labourers agreed to do certain work as co-contractors. Nor could the Court regulate contracts of purchase and sale, whereby a manufacturer sold materials to a worker who then sold the finished product back to the manufacturer, even where such transactions were undertaken between parties on a system of weekly or monthly credits with 'the difference between the relation thus established and ordinary industrial service [being] merely nominal'.[88]

The major doctrinal innovation following the introduction of conciliation and arbitration acts, then, was to conflate the expressions 'master and servant' and 'employer/employee'. The courts adopted the 'control test' to define the limits of the employment relationship. This was ironic given that the 'control test' had been formulated half a century earlier precisely to distinguish 'employees' from 'servants'.[89] Nevertheless, the conflation of the two relationships would prove far reaching in its effects. The subordination associated with 'servants' was married to a framework of contractual rights and obligations associated with 'employee', creating what one commentator has called a 'tension-ridden hybrid'.[90] On the one hand, the notion of subordination institutionalised managerial prerogative and control. On the other, the effect of contractualisation was to place limits on the

---

[84] Howe and Mitchell, above n 81, 119–120.

[85] See, eg, *Amalgamated Society of Carpenters and Joiners v The Haberfield Pty Ltd* (1907) 5 CLR 33.

[86] *Ex parte Haberfield Pty Ltd* [1907] AR(NSW) 12, 13.

[87] *Amalgamated Miners' Association, Wrightville v Great Cobar Ltd* [1907] AR(NSW) 53, 57–58.

[88] VS Clarke, *The Labour Movement in Australasia: A Study in Social Democracy* (New York, Burt Franklin, 1970) 197–98.

[89] *Yewens v Noakes* (1880) 6 QBD 530.

[90] A Merritt, above n 79, 58.

employer's legal powers of command, by way of either express or implied terms. Over time, this hybrid form would come to encompass most forms of wage-dependent labour. However, Simon Deakin in the English context and John Howe and Richard Mitchell in Australia make it clear that initially the 'control test' and the conflation of the master/servant and employer/employee relationships were useful to courts seeking to *limit* rather than to extend the scope and coverage of new, protective social legislation.

For employers wanting to escape the reach of the tribunals, the courts' early restrictive readings provided an incentive to argue either that certain forms of work – such as piecework – indicated an independent contracting relationship rather than an employment or service relationship,[91] or to construct sham arrangements whereby work relationships were disguised as, say, leasing arrangements,[92] or partnerships.[93] However, at the Commonwealth level an activist Arbitration Court, interpreting its mandate as one to regulate relations between capital and labour more widely, moved to more inclusive definitions of the employer/employee relationship. The New South Wales Court also struck down those arrangements where the main purpose was to avoid minimum award rates.[94] And courts managed to some extent to intervene with respect to the wages and conditions of work relationships that remained outside the employment contract. By the end of the 1920s it appeared settled that, whereas persons outside the employer/employee relationship could not be regulated directly – at least by the federal Arbitration Court – they could be regulated as a means of settling disputes between employers and employees. Such a dispute would typically arise where a union had a real and substantial interest in restricting an employer's resort to hiring independent contractors or outworkers in competition with its members' employment.[95] On this basis, the regulation of subcontracting in clothing and textiles was addressed with an award in 1937.[96] Similarly, award clauses could regulate the terms of certain subcontracts themselves with the object of controlling the conditions of the employees of the subcontractor – again so as to protect union members from unfair competition.[97]

---

[91] As in the case of the mineworkers engaged on piecework contracts in *Amalgamated Miners' Association, Wrightville v Great Cobar Ltd* [1907] AR(NSW) 53.

[92] eg, *Re Kahn* [1904] AR(NSW) 387, where hairdressing proprietors entered agreements with journeymen hairdressers whereby the former leased chairs to the latter, took the entire takings and retained a proportion as 'rental' while paying the 'balance' to the journeymen. The court concluded the relationship was thereby one of lessor and lessee rather than employer and employee.

[93] *Henwood v Holmes* [1910] AR(NSW) 451.

[94] E Stern, '"Industrial Disputes" and the Jurisdiction of the Federal Industrial Tribunal' (LLM Thesis, University of Melbourne 1993) 106, citing the NSW tribunal in *Wright v Townsend* [1909] AR(NSW) 377 and *Spriggs v Woodbridge* [1917] AR(NSW) 44.

[95] Stern, ibid, 115–16; *Federated Clothing Trades of the Commonwealth of Australia v Archer* (1919) 27 CLR 207; *Amalgamated Clothing and Allied Trades Union of Australia v Chas F Hawkins Pty Ltd* (1930) 29 CAR 182; *Amalgamated Engineering Union v Metal Trades Employers Association* (1931) 30 CAR 734.

[96] R Frances, *The Politics of Work: Gender and Labour in Victoria, 1880–1939* (Melbourne, Cambridge University Press, 1993) 143.

[97] *Hutcherson Brothers v Australian Builders Labourers Federation* (1948) 62 CAR 355.

Seasonal and casual workers directly employed by an employer presented a different issue. They were clearly employees who came within the scope of the federal Court, but in practice they were hired and fired according to short-term or seasonal fluctuations in demand, resulting in highly irregular or intermittent work. The Commonwealth Arbitration Court largely accepted a certain distribution of casual employment. In those industries where the interruptions to work or the alternation of brisk and slack seasons were fairly predictable, or where idle workers were expected to hold themselves ready for work, the Court granted a higher hourly rate in awards. The Court would consider the 'normal conditions of an industry and the earnings of men of average competency engaged in that industry'. If work averaged out over a year meant they would earn less than the annual equivalent of the basic wage, the Court calculated the appropriate hourly loading.[98] In effect, higher payment in employment for these workers was an offset against periods of intermittent joblessness. By the second half of the 1920s, this higher rate was written into awards covering wharf workers, builders' labourers, shearers, flour mill workers and those working in the meat export and sugar industries.

In other industries, where the Court judged the 'normal conditions' of work to be regular and continuous rather than seasonal or subject to fluctuation, it promoted weekly hiring of employees.[99] So whereas some awards gave recognition to casual hiring, it was increasingly cast as the exception. Weekly hiring clauses meant employees were engaged full-time from week to week, with employment terminable by a week's notice on either side. Weekly hiring came to signify a kind of 'permanent' or open-ended employment with continuity of income, attracting payment for public holidays in the year, for absence from work on account of ill health for up to six days per year, and for time lost where the employee was ready and willing to work but there was a loss of work due to a cause for which the employer could reasonably be held responsible. By the late 1920s, weekly hiring applied to core workforces comprising blacksmiths, engineers, carpenters and joiners in shops, coopers, wool workers, manufacturing grocers' employees, timber workers, furniture trades employees, liquor and allied trades employees, storemen and packers, and workers in the printing industry, clothing industry, meat industry and food preserving industry.[100]

The requirement of a week's notice put a brake on the most abrupt forms of hiring and firing in response to short-term exigencies. In addition to the week's pay, termination of employment would bring on payment of any accrued benefits such as recreation and long service leave as these became standard entitlements across the following decades. Where circumstances beyond the employer's control – in particular strikes, but also physical mishaps – meant interruptions to production, employers were given the benefit of 'stand down clauses'. These clauses were generally inserted in awards from the early 1920s as a quid pro quo for weekly hiring, an attempt to strike a balance between wage security for the employee and

---

[98] Anderson, above n 54, 490.

[99] See *Australian Timber Workers' Union v John Sharp and Sons Ltd* (1920) 14 CAR 811, 887, 836.

[100] Anderson, above n 54, 491.

flexibility for the employer.[101] However, the Commonwealth tribunal tended to interpret stand down clauses strictly, so as to not undermine the security provided by weekly hiring, and stand down clauses could not be used simply to create short-time work during slack periods.[102]

Ultimately, any trade depression – rather than the fairly predictable patterns of intermittency that characterised many industries – meant workers would have to be dismissed until trade revived. The Court in these circumstances refused to adjust awards with loadings simply as a form of unemployment compensation. Loss of earnings in such cases, the Court thought, was a 'social injustice which [could] only be remedied by some form of unemployment insurance'.[103]

The Court's determinations about the 'normal conditions' of an industry – that is, whether work was intermittent or regular – were an attempt to buttress the concept of the 'living wage' rather than see it undermined by casual hiring. However, mirroring British discussions, the Court also harboured a combination of wider moral and economic concerns concerning casual labour. For Higgins J, weekly wages were not only better in guaranteeing workers' subsistence, but also tended to 'greater steadiness in the prosecution of the work required by the community'.[104] Casual work meant 'great bouts of idleness' that led not only to 'bad habits' but a 'tremendous waste of potential human energy'.[105] The ongoing employment relationship was seen as beneficial to employer and employee alike:

> Under weekly wages the employee tends to identify himself with the particular undertaking, to feel interested in the concern, and it takes much more to induce him to throw up a job if it is constant. It is in the interests of the employers as well as in the interests of the employees that the employment should not be casual, that a man should not feel himself to be a piece of flotsam or jetsam in the industry – that he should have a sense of homeship in the concern.[106]

Beeby J more directly echoed the concerns of Beveridge, identifying the problem as one of labour market organisation and refusing to blame the incidence of casual work on workers themselves:

> The status of the citizen with no semblance of security in social life, hawking his labour for sale by the hour, is one of the greatest dangers of the present economic system. It is easy to sit back and criticise the actions of men who gain their livelihood under such conditions. Their actions, to ordinary individuals not concerned with economic

---

[101] C Arup, 'The Power of the Employer to Stand Down: Latitude and Constraints' (1978) 20 *Journal of Industrial Relations* 463, 466. Weekly hiring had been inserted into the federal Metal Trades Award in 1921: *Amalgamated Society of Engineers v Adelaide Steamship Co* (1921) 15 CAR 297, 319, 338. The following year some employers complained of lack of orders and so requested insertion of a stand down clause: *Amalgamated Society of Engineers v Adelaide Steamship Co* (1922) 16 CAR 231, 247, 285.

[102] *Pickard* (1924) 35 CLR 1, 8; *Federated Engine Drivers v Albany Bell* (1922) 16 CAR 1248, 1249.

[103] *Motor Body and Coach Building Employees Federation v General Motors Holden Ltd* (1935) 35 CAR 599, 602. See also *Australian Glass Workers' Union v Australian Glass Manufacturers Coy Ltd* (1927) 25 CAR 289, 291.

[104] *Federated Gas Employees Industrial Union v Geelong Gas Company* (1919) 13 CAR 437, 463.

[105] *Waterside Workers Federation v Commonwealth Steamship Owners Association* (1914) 8 CAR 52, 72.

[106] *Amalgamated Society of Engineers v Adelaide Steamship Company* (1921) 15 CAR 297, 319.

problems, may appear to be arrogant, selfish, and unreasoned, when in reality they are the natural result of the indifference and neglect of society.[107]

Orwell Foenander, writing in 1947, also identified the presence of casualness in industry as 'one of the chief defects of the economic system. Heavy labour wastage to the community is involved, management difficulties are increased, and hardship and impoverishment are inflicted upon many workers'.[108]

The push for decasualisation clearly involved elements of liberal paternalism. It was not necessarily supported by those workers who had negotiated casual working arrangements which they perceived as operating to their benefit as long as they retained control over the labour supply. For example, wharf labourers maintained a closed shop with strict quotas and resisted attempts at decasualisation well into the post-war period.[109] Furthermore, as we've seen, the Arbitration Court's preference for decasualisation and weekly hiring was modified under the extreme economic conditions of the Depression.

All in all, Australia appears to have achieved a 'unitary' model of employment relationships earlier than did the United Kingdom. In that country, as Deakin points out, it required the advent of social insurance legislation in the 1940s to consolidate the binary division between employment on the one hand and independent contracting on the other.[110] In Australia, it was the introduction of arbitral legislation that was to prove crucial. And the advent of compulsory arbitration played two roles in encouraging particular forms of the employment relationship.

First, it gave impetus to a doctrinal innovation that allowed the development of a common law of the contract of employment, based around 'control' as the principal index, and which would apply to the greater mass of dependent wage labour. In many ways, the substantive terms of the contract became less significant under a system of standardised awards; nevertheless the concept of the employment contract was vital as the trigger for the Arbitration Court's jurisdiction. This points to the second role, whereby the emergence of a comprehensive arbitral jurisdiction allowed for the regularisation of the actual conditions of employment across industries. In particular, there was a move towards weekly hiring and limiting the use of stand downs for mere lack of work. The combined effects proceeded slowly across the first three or four decades of the twentieth century, but it was this process that allowed an increasingly formalised and homogenous notion of employment to emerge.

---

[107] *Commonwealth Steamship Owners Association v Waterside Workers Federation* (1928) 26 CAR 867, 875–76.

[108] O Foenander, *Industrial Regulation in Australia: A Study of Awards, Method of Remuneration Fixation, and the Status of Trade Unions Under the Australian Regulative System* (Melbourne, Melbourne University Press, 1947) 134.

[109] T Sheridan, 'Australian Wharfies 1943–1967: Casual Attitudes, Militant Leadership and Workplace Change' (1994) 36 *Journal of Industrial Relations* 258.

[110] See Deakin, 'The Evolution of the Contract of Employment', above n 75. Deakin goes on to note, at 226, the implications for debates within labour law about the role of the contract of employment: 'The contract of employment is often seen as having survived into the modern period *in spite of* the growth of collective bargaining and regulatory legislation ... [I have] suggested that the opposite is the case, that the contract of employment as we know it today is largely the *product* of the welfare state' (emphasis in original).

2

Defining Unemployment:
Pre-War Endeavours

Prior to the Second World War, at least three groups in Australia had an interest in defining unemployment: national statisticians; trade unionists; and those who advocated insurance schemes for the relief of jobless workers. Statistics enumerating the 'unemployed' have been published in Australia since 1891, but the statistical definition has changed, reflecting different understandings of 'normal' employment and labour markets. Trade unions, where possible, tried to offer support to out-of-work members, but 'out of work' carried particular connotations in the context of union industrial campaigns. And there was, in the early decades of the century, the emerging idea of unemployment insurance: but how to define the risk that required insuring?

The Census

In the late nineteenth century there was an upsurge of interest in official statistics. They began to be published in popular form and government statisticians occupied influential positions as both advisers to governments and expert commentators in public forums.[1] Regular conferences of colonial statisticians – often with New Zealand also represented – ensured a uniform approach to the collection of data. After Federation, a Commonwealth Bureau of Census and Statistics was established in 1906, with George Handley Knibbs the first Commonwealth Statistician.[2]

In the late nineteenth century, Australian colonial censuses broke from British census convention by dividing the entire population into 'breadwinners' and 'dependants'. The innovation owed itself to the efforts of Timothy Coghlan and RM Johnston, the government statisticians of New South Wales and Tasmania

---

[1] D Deacon, 'Political Arithmetic: The Nineteenth-Century Australian Census and the Construction of the Dependent Woman' (1985) 11 *Signs: Journal of Women in Culture and Society* 27, 41.

[2] Australian Bureau of Statistics, 'ABS Cat No 1382.0 – Informing A Nation: The Evolution of the Australian Bureau of Statistics' (Australian Bureau of Statistics, 31 December 2005), available at: www. abs.gov.au/ausstats/abs@.nsf/Latestproducts/1382.0Main%20Features12005?opendocument&tabname= Summary&prodno=1382.0&issue=2005&num=&view=.

respectively. This distinction between market and non-market or household activity, first used in the New South Wales census of 1891, was pioneering, and would later become the basis for national accounts worldwide (and it was national income estimates, rather than censuses, that were Coghlan's main preoccupation).[3] Coghlan did not necessarily think of household work as unproductive. Rather, his division hinged on whether work was remunerated or not. But having isolated unpaid household labour he didn't quite know what to do with it.[4] Bracketed off from market activity in this way, the ultimate effect was to efface women's productive activity in the home and to buttress the case for the male family wage. The understanding seemed to be that if women weren't actually 'dependants', they should be. 'The large employment of women in gainful pursuits' wrote Coghlan in his report on the 1891 census, 'is not a matter for gratulation'. Coghlan was happy to explicitly link his preferred classification to a defence of male collective action for labour market control, believing prosperity was to be found where men had to support families and were able to strike in support of better conditions with no competition to drive down wages from illegitimate competitors such as women. Recognising that, in fact, large amounts of 'gainful' work was carried out by most women in family enterprises, Coghlan was eager to classify any 'doubtful' cases as primarily domestic and hence outside the official definition of economic activity.[5]

Once this basic classification was adopted, breadwinners were divided into occupational groups according to their usual 'gainful occupation'. The recording of a person's occupation had no temporal or strictly behavioural dimension: people recorded their *usual* occupation and may not have been working at their occupation on the day or week that the census count was taken. Thus the temporarily or long-term sick along with others who had become incapacitated for work were all included as 'breadwinners' with an 'occupation' as long as they had, at one stage of their life, engaged in gainful activity. The category of breadwinner in all pre-war censuses ended up including retirees, pensioners and people of independent means, all classified according to their previous occupation.[6]

The assumption was that a person played a more or less stable occupational role, irrespective of their physical or mental health.[7] So, first-time jobseekers were omitted from the count of 'breadwinners' as they were yet to establish an occupational role. And a person intermittently engaged in a certain sort of activity at the time of the census would not record that occupation if they had an alternative social definition. For example, a wife who periodically helped in her husband's

---

[3] GD Snooks, *Portrait of the Family Within the Total Economy: A Study in Longrun Dynamics, Australia 1788–1990* (Cambridge, Cambridge University Press, 1994) 154–55.

[4] ibid, 286.

[5] Deacon, above n 1, 35–39.

[6] Australian Bureau of Statistics, 'Census of the Commonwealth of Australia 1947: Statistician's Report' (Canberra, Commonwealth Government Printer, 1952) 179.

[7] T Endres and M Cook, 'Concepts in Australian Unemployment Statistics to 1940' (1983) 22 *Australian Economic Papers* 68, 70. Note however that the unemployed did not include those in institutions such as asylums or gaols.

business would likely be recorded as a 'dependant' undertaking domestic duties.[8] The category of those falling into residual or 'unspecified' categories, and those enumerated as drawing on public support, may have included persons willing to work but unable to find work, but they were not separately identified. Joblessness was merely treated as ancillary to some sorts of poverty or destitution, rather than being a robust category in itself.[9] The primary concern of the census classifications was potential labour supply and the stock of human resources; actual employment status was immaterial, as was the excess of supply over current demand, a focus which served employer interests well.[10]

For those recording a usual occupation, the 1891 census did go on to ask a supplementary question as to their occupational *status*. The status categories were 'employer', 'engaged on own account', 'wage-earner' or 'unemployed'. Just as 'employed' developed a specialised meaning of paid work, by the second half of the nineteenth century 'unemployed' had ceased to mean merely idle, unoccupied, taking no part in working life, and had begun to refer more specifically to working people out of paid employment.[11] We can track the evolution of the term in the US State of Massachusetts census. The old meaning of 'unemployed' is evident in the 1875 census, which went so far as to classify children under 10 and living at home as 'unemployed'. A survey a couple of years later limited the category of 'unemployed' to those able-bodied jobless workers 'who really want employment'. The 1885 Massachusetts census then confined its enquiry to those 'unemployed at that work which constituted the principal trade or calling of each person'.[12] The census report also referred to the extent of 'unemployment', although that abstract noun didn't gain widespread acceptance in either the United States or Britain until the early twentieth century.[13]

The limited definition of 'unemployed' adopted in the 1885 Massachusetts census may have initially been motivated by a desire to obtain 'modest and reassuring figures' as to the extent of joblessness.[14] But the underlying gainful worker approach proved a significant conceptual turnaround: to be 'unemployed' shifted from having no occupation to having an occupation but no job.[15]

---

[8] Deacon, above n 1, 29.

[9] Endres and Cook, above n 7, 70.

[10] S Moses, 'Labour Supply Concepts: The Political Economy of Conceptual Change' (1975) 418 *Annals of the American Academy of Political and Social Sciences* 26. In 1909 Beveridge had also observed that whereas an oversupply of labour appeared to favour employer interests, it remained difficult to get actual 'statistical evidence of excess': WH Beveridge, *Unemployment: A Problem of Industry* (London, Longmans, Green and Co, 1931 [1909]) 70.

[11] R Williams, *Keywords: A Vocabulary of Culture and Society* (London, Fontana, 1988) 325–26; A Keyssar, *Out of Work: The First Century of Unemployment in Massachusetts* (Cambridge, MA, Cambridge University Press, 1986) 2.

[12] Keyssar, ibid, 346.

[13] ibid 5. The US federal Census Bureau persisted with the terms 'nonemployment' and 'idleness' until 1900; 'unemployment' only found its way into the *Encyclopaedia Britannica* in 1911: C Topalov, 'The Invention of Unemployment: Language, Classification and Social Reform 1880–1910' in B Palier (ed), *Comparing Social Welfare Systems in Europe: Volume 1* (Paris, MIRE, 1994) 498.

[14] Keyssar, above n 11, 2.

[15] ibid 3.

The question in the New South Wales census seemed to rely on this new understanding of 'unemployed', without offering any hard and fast definition. But clearly only those who could state a usual occupation could then proceed to be counted as 'unemployed'. As mentioned, this approach meant first-time jobseekers were necessarily omitted from the category of the 'unemployed'. Nevertheless, no age limits were set, and the category ended up covering a wide range of workless persons, and included those more or less permanently incapacitated from following their ordinary occupation. Coghlan estimated that one-third of those recording as unemployed could be classed as 'compulsorily unemployed' in that they were prevented by sickness from following their ordinary vocations.[16] The term 'compulsorily unemployed' hints at the later idea of 'involuntarily unemployed', but refers to quite a different phenomenon: rather than covering those willing and capable of work but prevented from doing so for impersonal economic factors, it referred to incapacity for work.

The 1901 federal census was undertaken prior to the establishment of a Commonwealth bureau of statistics, and was essentially the aggregation of data gathered by each State statistician. It used a time reference that also served to give some indication as to possible 'causes' of joblessness. To be returned as 'unemployed' a person must have not been at work for more than a week immediately prior to the census. This was presumed to exclude those temporarily out of work due to lay-off, industrial dispute or short-term illness. In the 1911 census, the first undertaken directly under the aegis of the new Commonwealth bureau, those returning as unemployed were asked to state the period of unemployment. Again, those out of work for less than a week were excluded from the count, as were those for more than a year, on the assumption that the latter were aged and had permanently retired from the workforce.

The 1921 Commonwealth census enquired more explicitly into the causes of unemployment, asking respondents whether, if out of work at the time of the census, their unemployment was due to scarcity of employment, illness, accident, strike, lockout, old age or 'other' causes. This suggests that 'unemployment' still carried a wide meaning, even though the published data could potentially be used to explore more rigorous or particular understandings of the term. But the taxonomy was heavily weighted towards individualist understandings of unemployment (sickness, age, strike action) rather than labour market causes. The catch-all category 'scarcity of employment' offered little by way of explanation or understanding. For example, it did not distinguish scarcity due to a worker's 'voluntary' refusal to accept work at a particular or current wage rate in the hope of work at a higher wage later, from sheer lack of work at that rate.[17]

While the 1921 census enquired after the number of days 'out of work', the 1933 census asked unemployed respondents to state the time 'since last regularly employed'.

---

[16] Australian Bureau of Statistics, 'Census of New South Wales 1891: Statistician's Report' (Sydney, 1891) 306.

[17] Endres and Cook, above n 7, 72.

This was supplemented for the first time with questions regarding part-time employment, although no distinction was made between part-time work due to normally intermittent or seasonal occupations or that due to 'other factors making for intermittency'. Similarly, no benchmark of what counted as 'full-time' work was provided, so the definition of 'part-time' depended on the view of the person concerned. A special census was carried out in 1939, counting only males of British origin or naturalised Australians, as a way of measuring manpower potential for the War. Given the focus on manpower planning for war, no concern was given for enumerating the causes of joblessness or its alleviation.

So consecutive Australian censuses in the pre-war period enquired with increasing specificity into unemployment. This signified increasing government concern with joblessness – and public consciousness of it – but the category 'unemployed' appeared as a work in progress. It was still a quite different notion from that which prevailed in post-war censuses and labour force surveys. Indeed, the post-war notion of the 'labour force' was yet to be properly articulated. Throughout this earlier period the census starting point remained the distinction between breadwinners and dependants and a focus on those people who had a 'gainful occupation'. As we'll see in chapter five, the gainful occupation approach began to be displaced in the United States in the 1930s, as policymakers became increasingly concerned not with potential labour supply but with creating labour demand through public works programmes.[18] Any movement in this direction in Australia was stymied by the onset of the Second World War, which again oriented concerns towards the estimation and registration of all potential labour.

In any case, the roughly decennial censuses undertaken in Australia from the late nineteenth century up to the Second World War were of little use to policymakers in examining short-term developments and trends in the labour market, especially in moments of seeming economic crisis. For this reason, alternative sources of statistics were sought. In the first decades of the twentieth century, the most promising source appeared to be trade union returns as to members out of work.

Trade Unions

Trade union unemployment statistics were first officially collected and published by the Commonwealth Bureau of Census and Statistics in 1913. Union officials furnished quarterly returns, stating the number of members unemployed on a specific date for more than three days during the last week of the middle month of each quarter. Those out of work due to lack of work, sickness, accident or 'other' causes were included, but those out of work due to strike or lockout were excluded. The returns covered about half the members of Australian trade unions, excluding

---

[18] See Moses, above n 10.

highly seasonal or casualised industries, such a wharf labourers and pastoral and agricultural workers, and those characterised by very stable or 'permanent' employment, such as the State railways. The groups for which they provided a meaningful sample tended to be manufacturing, building and mining. All in all, the returns covered 20–25 per cent of the workforce, substantially biased towards male workers.[19]

Few unions managed to pay their members unemployment benefit, but secretaries tended to keep unemployment registers because provision was often made for out-of-work members to pay reduced subscriptions.[20] Also, many unions operated as de facto labour exchanges, so a register of unemployed members was often kept in order to satisfy employer requests for labour.[21] However in its 1926 report, the Royal Commission examining proposals for a national insurance scheme claimed that returns in 'most cases [are] only based on the secretary's general knowledge of the position' and in New South Wales tended to include both part-time and casual workers 'in addition to the wholly unemployed'. In those cases where unemployment registers were maintained, it was claimed that many unemployed members would either not sign onto the register or, having signed on, would not then advise the secretary when they obtained employment.[22]

By focusing on union members, the trade union returns to some extent replicated the 'gainful worker' approach and excluded many first-time jobseekers. However, whereas early census statistics were concerned with estimating potential labour supply – information that would be useful to employers – trade union records and approaches to joblessness had traditionally operated out of a different set of concerns.

Craft trade unions had operated some of the earliest unemployment benefit systems for their members. British schemes at the beginning of the twentieth century were widespread and diverse.[23] The first friendly societies in Australia, dating from the 1830s, were trade based, serving manual workers and artisans, offering mainly coverage for loss of tools or the costs of a respectable burial, and many offered sickness benefits. A few friendly societies offered benefits for members looking for work, or assisted members who needed to travel in search of employment, and

---

[19] C Forster, 'Australian Unemployment, 1900–1940' (1965) 41 *Economic Record* 426, 429–31, 441. Although the Commonwealth Bureau of Census and Statistics began collecting returns in 1913, an inquiry into trade union unemployment in 1912 came up with figures for the years between 1891 and 1912. A survey had asked secretaries to state the number of unemployed members at the end of each year and, in the absence of direct counts, estimates were accepted: Endres and Cook, above n 7, 73.

[20] Commonwealth Bureau of Census and Statistics, *Labour Report 1925, No 16* (Melbourne, Government Printer, 1926) 111.

[21] Commonwealth Bureau of Census and Statistics, *Labour Report 1936, No 27* (Melbourne, Government Printer, 1937) 108; see also R Mitchell, 'Union Security and the "Hiring Hall": A Note on the Sanctioning of Union Labour Supply Arrangements in Australian Labour Law' (2003) 16 *Australian Journal of Labour Law* 343.

[22] Commonwealth of Australia, Royal Commission on National Insurance, *Second Progress Report: Unemployment*, Parl Paper No 79 (1926–28) 1413–14.

[23] See Beveridge, above n 10, 223–26.

rules relating to sick pay were often interpreted liberally to provide support during trade depressions and strikes.[24] The early trade societies tended to be overtaken by larger friendly societies offering similar benefits, often based around particular interests – for total abstainers, Roman Catholics, Protestants, or white native-born Australians – and membership of these 'affiliated orders' had an over-representation of manual workers and artisans. However, skilled trade unions established in the second half of the nineteenth century, with a relatively small membership of high wage earners, also tended to set up their own 'out-of-work' benefits schemes.

These schemes were intimately tied up with the protection of trade practices and negotiated rates of pay. In Britain, union members were expected to quit when their employer was in breach of a collective agreement and in turn would receive monetary support from the branch for being out of work. Members looking for jobs were expected to refuse work at wage rates below the union scale and would be supported by the branch as well.[25] Support for these 'out-of-work' members thereby exerted union discipline over members who might otherwise have been prepared to work for less than union rates.

Several Australian craft unions established 'out-of-work' funds in the late nineteenth century, where loss of work due to industrial disputation was fully supported. This was the case with the Australasian Society of Engineers,[26] and in the plumbing, bootmaking, carpentry[27] and printing trades.[28] The Operative Plumbers Trade Society rules provided for the payment of members 'unemployed through the maintaining of the Rules and Orders of the Society'.[29] The Victorian Operative Bootmakers' Trade Union also rendered assistance to members 'thrown out of employment in consequence of endeavouring to uphold the … principles' of the Union.[30]

In these instances the notion of unemployment was almost inseparable from the protection of union rates of pay and work rules. It was often possible that a jobless worker could find work if prepared to accept lower than standard or union wages. By setting a reserve wage, benefit schemes enabled union members to not work rather than work for less than standard rates and conditions.[31]

---

[24] DG Green and L Cromwell, *Mutual Aid or Welfare State: Australia's Friendly Societies* (Sydney, Allen & Unwin, 1984) 4–5, 46–47, 60–61.

[25] N Whiteside, *Bad Times: Unemployment in British Social and Political History* (London, Faber, 1991) 52–53.

[26] T Sheridan, *Mindful Militants: The Amalgamated Engineering Union in Australia 1920–1972* (Cambridge, Cambridge University Press, 1975) 13; N Butlin, 'An Index of Engineering Unemployment, 1852–1943' (1946) 22 *Economic Record* 241.

[27] N Ebbels (ed), *The Australian Labour Movement, 1850–1907: Extracts From Contemporary Documents*, 2nd edn (Sydney, Australasian Book Society, 1976) 76–82.

[28] J Hagan, *Printers and Politics: A History of the Australian Printing Unions 1850–1950* (Canberra, Australian National University Press, 1966) 66–67; RT Fitzgerald, *The Printers of Melbourne: The History of a Union* (Melbourne, Pitman, 1967).

[29] Ebbels, above n 27, 76.

[30] ibid 77.

[31] Fitzgerald, above n 28, 141.

Equally, the clear division between sick pay, retirement benefits and unemployment benefits in many trade union schemes was somewhat illusory. Vulnerability to unemployment was linked to health, as was old age – and old age, in turn, was linked to unemployment. Testimony from the Launceston branch of the Amalgamated Society of Carpenters and Joiners to the 1927 Royal Commission on National Insurance indicated that its 'out of work' fund tended to support 'very old members who have been in the society for a considerable number of years' and that 'those on the sick and accident fund are very old members'.[32] As the Amalgamated Engineering Union entered the 1930s depression its payments to 'out-of-work' members soared largely because of the difficulty of older members in finding jobs.[33] Writing in the British context, Southall sums up: '[I]nstead of three quite distinct states we have a blending of unemployment, sickness and old age; the larger share of benefit payments, however labelled, went to older men who had more intermittent incomes due to declining health'.[34] And given that the schemes also handed out unemployment benefits as a form of 'strike pay' to those refusing work at below union wage rates, we have the possibility of an elderly, infirm member claiming 'unemployment' benefit because his wages have been cut.[35]

Although the trade union returns as to 'unemployed' members collated by the Commonwealth Bureau of Census and Statistics excluded striking workers, they included those merely suffering a 'lack of work'. But again, that concept remained ambiguous. Given the support trade unions offered members refusing work below union rates, did it mean 'lack of work' at a certain going rate? Although social reformers saw the mutualism of union schemes and friendly societies as providing a model for social insurance, union schemes were less about thrift and saving than about a broader strategy of controlling craft labour markets and maintaining union discipline.[36]

The difficulty in interpreting trade union returns of unemployment is further complicated in those sectors where short-time work was a common method of managing fluctuating demand. This may lie behind the inclusion of 'part-time' and casual workers in the New South Wales returns. Similarly, an 'unemployed' union member on the books might not necessarily be totally without work, instead taking the odd casual job but on the understanding that it was not work 'in the trade', the search for which would still be supported.[37]

---

[32] Commonwealth of Australia, Royal Commission on National Insurance, *Minutes of Evidence: Unemployment, Destitution Allowances*, Parl Paper No 79 (1926–28) 994; H Southall, 'Neither State nor Market: Early Welfare Benefits in Britain' in B Palier (ed), *Comparing Social Welfare Systems in Europe: Volume 1* (Paris, MIRE, 1994) 74. Southall points out that friendly society and trade union benefit schemes rarely involved a set retirement age: retirement or superannuation allowances were 'essentially an extended sickness benefit to which long-standing members were entitled': 73.

[33] Sheridan, above n 26, 116.

[34] Southall, above n 32, 75.

[35] ibid.

[36] Topalov, above n 13, 500.

[37] Whiteside, above n 25, 53.

Overall, the most we can say is that the 'unemployed' as measured by trade union returns were hardly a uniform group, but varied according to industrial sector and trade practices within that sector. The connection between trade union 'unemployment' and the protection of trade practices was possibly one of the factors that gave rise to scepticism as to the worth of union unemployment returns. Some commentators also suspected that unions might manipulate returns to minimise unemployment if they were pursuing a wage rise in the Arbitration Court, or exaggerate unemployment were they seeking restrictions on entry to the trade.[38]

So despite the fact that the Commonwealth initially encouraged the collection of information as to out-of-work unionists, by the late 1920s the reputation of union returns had fallen.[39] Echoing the concerns of the Royal Commission on National Insurance,[40] local economists such as John Gifford and E Ward expressed reservations as to the worth of the trade union figures.[41] Ward dismissed them as mainly based on 'guesswork' and 'general observation' and hence 'very dubious'.[42] Later, two North American economists would give a more upbeat assessment of the returns – as 'one of the better series, when compared with the character of the data available for other countries'.[43] The Commonwealth Statistician continued to publish the union returns well into the 1940s, while admitting their limitations, glossing them with what one commentator described as a 'delightful truism': the value of the returns lay simply in the fact that they provided an 'indication … of the trend of unemployment amongst trade unionists as reported by the secretaries of trade unions'.[44]

Social Insurance

More sophisticated and focused conceptions of unemployment began to emerge in the context of attempts to design unemployment insurance schemes. To say unemployment is an insurable event is to construct unemployment in a particular way: as a risk, an unwanted contingency brought about by impersonal economic forces.

---

[38] JLK Gifford, *Economic Statistics for Australian Arbitration Courts: Explanation of the Uses Criticism of Existing Statistics and Suggestions for their Improvement* (Melbourne, Macmillan, 1928) 9.

[39] Forster, above n 19.

[40] Commonwealth of Australia, *Second Progress Report: Unemployment*, above n 22.

[41] Gifford, above n 38; E Ward, 'A Sample of Unemployment in Victoria' (1938) 14 *Economic Record* 23.

[42] Ward, ibid, 23.

[43] W Galenson and A Zellner, 'International Comparison of Unemployment Rates' in National Bureau-Universities (ed), *The Measurement and Behavior of Unemployment* (Princeton, NJ, National Bureau of Economic Research, 1957) 482.

[44] Commonwealth Bureau of Census and Statistics, *Labour Report 1946, No 36* (Melbourne, Government Printer, 1946) 102; B Murray, 'Full Employment and the Employment Service: with Special Reference to Australia and the Commonwealth Employment Service' (PhD Thesis, University of Melbourne, 1952) 72.

Unemployment, in this sense, is something that happens *to* people. This insurance-based logic of unemployment as a somehow involuntary status was to prove influential in the design even of non-insurance-based schemes such as Australia's system of non-contributory unemployment benefit inaugurated in the mid-1940s. Further, it meant unemployment was increasingly seen as one insurable event among many: that is, it was a status that could be distinguished from other contingencies such as accident, illness or old age.

This was reflected in British legislation, enacted in 1911. The notion of involuntary unemployment was that of someone who was unable to find work *while capable of being employed*.[45] The key architects of the British insurance scheme were William Beveridge and Hubert Llewellyn Smith at the Board of Trade, the Whitehall ministry charged with overseeing trade and commerce. The Board had established a labour department in 1893, initially responsible largely for the gathering of statistical information. Llewellyn Smith, who had assisted Charles Booth in his social survey of east London, was appointed the department's head, and oversaw its transformation into a centre for policy innovation.[46] The Board's responsible minister, Winston Churchill, brought a draft unemployment insurance bill to Cabinet as early as December 1908. The key features of the bill – that the scheme be funded by tripartite contributions from workers, employers and government, and that benefits be flat-rate, but kept low so as to make for a 'suitable and even severe difference between being in work and out of work'[47] – were to survive the subsequent political and bureaucratic back-and-forth leading up to the introduction of legislation some two-and-a-half years later.[48] As enacted, the scheme would also exclude workers whose joblessness was caused by strikes, voluntary quits, dismissal for misconduct, or 'drunkenness and dishonesty'. Unemployed workers were, however, entitled to receive benefit while refusing offers of work at wages below the prevailing district rate or below that paid in their previous job.[49]

In 1909, Australia's Liberal prime minister, Alfred Deakin, commissioned Knibbs, the inaugural Commonwealth Statistician, to examine social insurance schemes for unemployment, accident, sickness and old age operating in several European countries. Following an exploratory trip to Europe, Knibbs reported to the government in 1910. Unemployment represented the hardest case, he wrote, proving 'hopelessly difficult'. An entire chapter in his report was devoted to the

---

[45] National Insurance Act 1911 (UK) s 86(3) (emphasis added).

[46] L Schweber, 'Progressive Reformers, Unemployment, and the Transformation of Social Inquiry in Britain and the United States, 1880s–1920s' in D Rueschemeyer and T Skocpol (eds), *States, Social Knowledge, and the Origins of Modern Social Policies* (Princeton, NJ, Princeton University Press, 1996) 169.

[47] J Harris, *William Beveridge: A Biography* (Oxford, Clarendon Press, 1977) 171.

[48] For a detailed account of the development of the legislation and its eventual passage, see Harris, ibid, 169–85.

[49] ibid 176. See also L Smith, 'Economic Security and Unemployment Insurance' (1910) 20 *Economic Journal* 513.

distinct problem it posed.[50] He wondered whether it was possible to apply actuarial principles to insurance against unemployment. To do so, the nature of the
risk would have to be specified and then its frequency calculated.

As to the first issue, Knibbs defined unemployment as 'involuntary idleness
not due to physical disability nor to degeneracy of the will'.[51] As in any insurance scheme, it was necessary to limit coverage to unforeseen events and to guard
against the hazard of insuring people against events they could themselves wilfully
cause – hence the emphasis on 'involuntary' idleness. The problem, as Knibbs had
to concede, was that in many cases it 'was well nigh impossible to ascertain whether
the unemployment is attributable to default on the part of the insured or not'. Such
a question necessarily involved normative judgements, as workmen could 'justly
discard' employment if a situation arose whereby they had a 'moral right' to free
themselves. Knibbs thereby preferred the term 'justifiable unemployment' rather
than 'involuntary unemployment'.[52] Clearly, though, what trade unions, in defence
of trade standards, thought was 'justifiable' unemployment could differ from what
economists, actuaries or administrators thought. As noted above, Britain's National
Insurance Act, enacted the year after Knibbs delivered his report, excluded lack of
work due to industrial dispute and voluntary quits from the list of insurable risks.
But as we have also seen, trade union benefit schemes were designed precisely to
support out-of-work members in such circumstances.

Knibbs didn't consider trade union benefit schemes to be true insurance
schemes, as workers' contributions were not actuarially adjusted and members
had no legal claim to the benefit. In fact, there is some indication that craft unions
with benefit schemes did try to exclude 'bad risks', although not on a strictly actuarial basis. That is, they tended to screen applicants for sobriety and regular habits
and their likelihood of making regular contributions, with the result, for example, that only around half the ironworkers in nineteenth-century Australia were
members of the Australian Society of Engineers and eligible for its benefits. But as
to Knibb's second point, entitlement in union schemes, unlike conventional insurance schemes, was based on present membership rather than past contributions,
so expulsion from a union meant the loss of all future benefits regardless of how
much had been paid in.[53]

By contrast, in Britain Beveridge and Llewellyn Smith, familiar with trade
union schemes, believed that unions were exceptionally well placed to implement
insurance for unemployment: union officials had both detailed knowledge of the
local labour markets in which insured individuals were seeking work, and the

---

[50] GH Knibbs, *Social Insurance: Report of the Commonwealth Statistician*, Vol 2, Parl Paper No 72
(1910) 15.

[51] ibid 69.

[52] ibid 70–71.

[53] As to the first point, see I Turner and L Sandercock, *In Union is Strength: A History of Trade
Unions in Australia 1788–1983*, 3rd edn (Melbourne, Nelson, 1983); on the second, see Southall,
above n 32, 79.

ability to monitor such individuals' behaviour.[54] The state, assisted by a network of labour exchanges, was one of the few actors that could take over such a role. Yet the idea of 'involuntary' unemployment that emerged from Britain's national insurance legislation fundamentally subverted that of the trade unions.[55]

The actuarial calculation of the frequency of risk depended on collecting information and producing aggregate data about workforces in a way that had not been done before. The nature of the 'unemployment' risk and its frequency inevitably varied between industry sectors, and depended on management practices, unionisation, product markets and so on. If 'unemployment' meant more or less absolute inactivity in response to a cyclical downturn, then an insurance scheme would only gain purchase in those trades where lay-off and redundancy were the normal response to slack demand, rather than reduced hours or variations in the use of casual and intermittent workers. Indeed, the British legislation did initially limit itself to workers in construction, shipbuilding, engineering and the metal trades: that is, those trades where 'the line between being in or out of work was fairly clear cut'.[56] But the problem, as Noel Whiteside and James Gillespie observe, was not simply a question of insufficient data and missing information. Rather, there was 'a mismatch between actual working practices and official appraisal of them; the superimposition of uniform categories and classification systems on a situation where no single mode of labour management was dominant'.[57]

Knibbs ultimately recommended further research and enquiry before any legislative proposals be introduced in Australia. His report was delivered the year before the British scheme came into effect. Had he had the chance to study that scheme in operation, his conclusion might not have been so circumspect. The subsequent success of unemployment insurance in Britain kept the matter on the Australian policy agenda at least until the 1915 Premiers' Conference.[58] At the Commonwealth level, there was then a hiatus until the conservative United Australia Party (UAP) government appointed a Royal Commission to re-examine the possibility of an unemployment insurance scheme in the mid-1920s.

That Commission again ran up against the problem as to which groups of worker were to be included in the scheme. It suggested a distinction be made between seasonal unemployment which was the normal characteristic of many trades, and which was partially compensated for with loadings in award wages, and unemployment 'over and above this'. The latter was a matter for insurance, but not the former.[59] The alternative would be to revise awards to remove loadings for

[54] Southall, ibid, 80–81.

[55] M Mansfield, 'Labour Exchanges and the Labour Reserve in Turn of the Century Social Reform' (1992) 21 *Journal of Social Policy* 435, 458.

[56] N Whiteside and J Gillespie: 'Deconstructing Unemployment: Developments in Britain in the Interwar Years' (1991) 44 *Economic History Review* 665, 675.

[57] ibid 674.

[58] TH Kewley, *Social Security in Australia, 1900–72* (Sydney, Sydney University Press, 1973) 150.

[59] This echoed the Arbitration Court's own understanding of what it saw as two different types of unemployment requiring distinctive responses: see above, ch 1.

intermittent work and to include the entire workforce in such a scheme, with the exception of those intermittent and casual workers who were habitually excluded from such schemes operating overseas.[60] While it was recognised that 'employers who give, and employees who receive, constant employment could not equitably be included in the scheme', the issue of short-time or work rationing, common in such trades as clothing and textiles as a response to trade fluctuations, was left unaddressed: would these workers be forced to pay contributions while rarely being in a position to claim benefit because management practices meant they were rarely 'unemployed' according to most insurance definitions? Nevertheless, the Commission perfunctorily recommended, and roughly costed, a scheme to insure against those risks of unemployment 'found to be unavoidable'.

However, when the UAP government introduced a National Insurance Bill in 1928 following on from the Commission's reports, it contained no provision for unemployment insurance, concentrating instead on sickness, disability, old age and widowhood. José Harris observes in the British context that while the problems surrounding unemployment insurance were largely technical, those around sickness and disability insurance were overtly political.[61] The latter tended to draw the ire of vested interest groups, in particular doctors and friendly societies. Within 12 months, in the face of opposition primarily from employer groups, the UAP bill was shelved.[62] John Murphy links employer opposition to the bill with the existence of the arbitration system: employers were worried that workers' contributions to the scheme would end up being taken into account in the cost of living adjustments to wages, so in effect the scheme would simply end up being financed largely by industry.[63] Ten years later, the Commonwealth government again introduced similar legislation for a social insurance scheme, and again it excluded any form of unemployment insurance. This time resistance to the bill came from the Labor opposition as well as the medical profession, women's groups and the UAP's coalition partner, the Country Party. The legislation was again abandoned.[64]

In the meantime, Queensland went it alone. At the 1915 Premiers' Conference it had been the Queensland attorney-general, Thomas O'Sullivan, who was most vocal in pressing for national legislation along the lines of Britain's National Insurance Act 1911. O'Sullivan's party lost office very soon after, replaced by a Labor government that eventually enacted an unemployment insurance scheme in 1922, based on equal contributions by workers, employers and government. That a Labor

---

[60] Commonwealth of Australia, *Second Progress Report: Unemployment*, above n 22, 22–23.

[61] Harris, *William Beveridge: A Biography*, above n 47, 169.

[62] For a detailed account, see J Murphy, *A Decent Provision: Australian Welfare Policy, 1870 to 1949* (London, Routledge, 2011); R Watts, *The Foundations of the National Welfare State* (Sydney, Allen & Unwin, 1987); Kewley, above n 58, 143–49.

[63] J Murphy, 'Path Dependence and the Stagnation of Australian Social Policy Between the Wars' (2010) 22 *The Journal of Policy History* 450, 458.

[64] ibid 462–66. This time, in an attempt to defuse employer opposition, a special provision in the Bill prohibited the Arbitration Court from including workers' insurance contributions when calculating the cost of living increases that would determine the basic wage.

government established Australia's one and only contributory unemployment insurance scheme was, as Carmel Black observes, somewhat 'incongruous'. As early as 1912 the national Australian Labor Party conference had clearly signalled the Party's opposition to any form of contributory scheme.[65] The 1922 legislation is best seen as a compromise after a more radical 1919 bill failed to get through the Queensland upper house. That earlier proposal enabled workers registered at the recently established State labour exchange to claim unemployment benefits if they failed to find work after 14 days – but those benefits were to be funded solely by a levy on employers. Rather than fund benefits directly, the government undertook to fund job creation schemes by way of public works, and to establish 'labour farms' for 'unemployables', and in any case its own employees would rarely have recourse to benefits. The reliance solely on employer contributions to fund an insurance scheme would have resulted in a genuinely radical and redistributive outcome, consistent with Labor policy,[66] but it also sounded the legislation's political death knell.

The 1922 legislation was similarly based around registration at the labour exchange. It excluded striking workers along with professional and high-income workers, but was designed to specifically include seasonal workers in the sugar and pastoral industries as well as dock workers.[67] Receipt of benefit could be suspended where a jobseeker refused to accept an offer of work, refused to join a union as a condition of accepting work, or became unemployed through their own fault. Benefits were flat-rate rather than earnings related, varied according to region, made allowance for dependants, and were capped at half the minimum award wage or the prevailing rate in the trade. The legislation also included provisions relating to the funding of public works and labour farms. In short, it more or less replicated the 1919 bill except for two crucial concessions to ensure its passage: benefits were now to be funded by way of equal tripartite contributions from employers, employees and the government; and receipt of benefits was capped at 15 weeks in any one year.

* * *

It's tempting to think of social science as a tool for discovering things that already exist, and then to see social policy as 'providing practical answers to social issues which supposedly pre-exist any action taken to face them'.[68] This chapter has explored a potentially more intriguing question: to what extent did attempts to count and classify the unemployed *impose* a binary categorisation of 'employment' and 'unemployment' in a situation where diverse modes of labour management

---

[65] C Black, 'The Origins of Unemployment Insurance in Queensland 1919–1922' (1991) 60 *Labour History* 34, 49.
[66] ibid.
[67] Kewley, above n 58, 151.
[68] Topalov, above n 13, 493.

and forms of work organisation confounded any such classification?[69] Definitions and understandings of unemployment across the early decades of the twentieth century changed over time, and varied between groups such as trade unionists, economists and statisticians. What we are observing is less the measurement of a simple economic variable, and more the social and political construction of an administrative category.[70]

At the time of the Royal Commission in 1925, unemployment insurance was seen as merely one among a number of policies for the prevention and relief of poverty. Given the passage of unemployment insurance legislation in Britain as early as 1911, it is odd that the development of an Australian scheme seemed to present such an intractable political challenge. Yet despite the failure of an Australian scheme to materialise, discussion around the practical application of insurance here and overseas was important in refining the idea of unemployment. More clearly than census or trade union statistics, proposed insurance schemes attempted to identify unemployment as a particular risk understood as distinct from old age, industrial disputation, accident and sickness. In particular, though, unemployment insurance presumed unemployment was a condition distinct from employment. And as Simon Deakin and Frank Wilkinson observe, by defining what was *not* employment, the category implicitly defined what *was* employment: continuous, regular work at a breadwinner wage.[71] It assumed a bipolar labour market, split between the 'employed' and the 'unemployed' with workers moving unambiguously between those categories according to the prevailing level of economic activity.[72]

But as the discussion of the Australian labour market prior to the Second World War in chapter one has shown, this crude division captured only some of the diverse ways that fluctuations in the demand for labour were managed by employers or negotiated by workers. Instead, shifts in economic activity were often managed through the use of irregular, intermittent and casual employment arrangements, short-time work, or through 'disguised' employment such as labour-only subcontracting. This diversity is reflected in policymakers' uncertainty and prevarication as to which groups of workers to include in any unemployment insurance scheme. Ultimately, if the insurance definition of unemployment was to find purchase, the labour market would have to be 'organised' – a realisation that turned most policymakers' eyes towards the institution of the labour exchange, which we'll examine in the next chapter.

Unemployment insurance also tried to extend the principles that governed the insurance of other risks to the new risk of unemployment. This affirmed a view

---

[69] Whiteside and Gillespie, above n 56, 674.

[70] See Whiteside, above n 25, 50–51.

[71] S Deakin and F Wilkinson, *The Law of the Labour Market: Industrialization, Employment, and Legal Evolution* (Oxford, Oxford University Press, 2005) 149.

[72] Whiteside and Gillespie, above n 56, 674.

of unemployment as distinct but normal, an inevitable and necessary feature of industrial life.[73] While this stood partly at odds with what William Walters calls 'a moralising, fault-finding perspective', the insurance principle did focus attention on fault and 'involuntariness' in a new way that drew further and finer distinctions not only between unemployment and other risks, but between different types of unemployment. These distinctions were necessary to define unemployment as an insurable risk according to general principles[74] – and, again, the labour exchange became a key institution in policing and adjudicating these distinctions.

The distinction made in the 1921 census between unemployment due to 'scarcity of work' and absences from work due to causes such as illness, strike and lockout also indicated a more complex understanding of unemployment. It showed a concern not only with an individual being without work but also his or her willingness and ability to work if work were available or not 'scarce'. Tony Endres and Malcolm Cook have suggested that economists were running ahead of the statisticians in this instance.[75] Arthur Pigou, Professor of Economics at Cambridge University, had published a popular book on unemployment in 1913 as part of the Home University Library series, and again considered the matter in a 1933 book. In the latter he wrote: 'A man is only unemployed when he is *both* not employed and *also* desires to be employed'.[76] This also implied a question of capacity: for Pigou, the definition of unemployment excluded 'those who are definitely incapacitated from wage-earning work by extreme old age, infirmity or temporary sickness'.[77] Then there was the question of the wage rates at which people desired employment. Can a worker who refuses work at a current rate but who would be willing to work at a higher rate be said to desire work? Pigou is clear that 'involuntary' unemployment relates to the frustration of the desire and willingness to work 'at the current rate of wages under current conditions of employment', in both the district and trade in which he was last employed.

Yet Pigou's definition of 'involuntary' unemployment was itself largely inspired by Britain's National Insurance Act 1911.[78] So it appears the economists themselves had been outflanked by those social investigators, statisticians and bureaucrats who had already recognised that the administrative category of unemployment was a

---

[73] W Walters, *Unemployment and Government: Genealogies of the Social* (Cambridge, Cambridge University Press, 2000) 58.

[74] ibid 61.

[75] Endres and Cook, above n 7, 72.

[76] AC Pigou, *The Theory of Unemployment* (London, Macmillan, 1933) 3.

[77] AC Pigou, *Unemployment* (London, Williams and Norgate, 1924) 15.

[78] Note, however, that whereas Pigou refers to the 'current rate of wages', the National Insurance Act 1911 referred to wages negotiated by collective agreement. Pigou's phrasing is compatible with his ideal of a largely unregulated, competitive labour market that will tend towards market-clearing wage rates. 'Involuntary' unemployment thereby only occurs where rigidities and uncompetitive practices stop wage rates from adjusting. Also, Pigou's calculation of the amount of unemployment considered the number of hours work by which the employment of persons occupied in or attached to an industry falls short of the number they would be willing to provide at the current wage rate. It thus embraced people who were underemployed, whereas such people lay outside the scope of the 1911 legislation. See Mansfield, above n 55, 458–59.

cultural artefact, both reflecting regulatory norms regarding paid labour and in turn reinforcing those norms.[79] Harris notes that the burgeoning British literature on unemployment from the mid-1890s was dominated by amateurs – 'journalists, practical reformers, heretics and cranks' – with academic economists playing only a very muted role.[80] The careers of Beveridge and Llewellyn Smith illustrate the informal culture of 'clubs, associations and public activity linking Oxford liberals with London's political elite'.[81] And ultimately, it was the practical, administrative insurance-based understandings of unemployment that would displace both trade union out-of-work schemes and the blunter census classifications of joblessness.

---

[79] JL Williams and K Williams (eds), *A Beveridge Reader* (London, Allen & Unwin, 1987) 102.

[80] J Harris, 'From Sunspots to Social Welfare: The Unemployment Problem 1870–1914' in B Corry (ed), *Unemployment and the Economists* (Cheltenham, Edward Elgar, 1996) 52, 65.

[81] Schweber, above n 46, 166.

3

The Labour Exchange Solution

In the first half of the twentieth century, one institution was seen as central to tackling the problem of joblessness. The labour exchange or labour bureau was a government-run agency that aimed to match jobseekers with job vacancies. Reformers in both Britain and Australia saw the exchange as undertaking two tasks. The first, more comprehensive task was to organise the labour market and minimise the incidence of casual labour by redistributing available work to regular workers in full-time employment. This would in turn produce a clearly identifiable group of workers suffering unambiguous unemployment – that is, a more or less absolute lack of work. The second, supplementary task of the labour exchange in matching supply and demand in an organised labour market was to 'test' these jobless workers' willingness to work and hence the genuineness of their unemployment, which could then be compensated by way of an insurance scheme. In short, reformers planned a two-pronged attack on unemployment: unemployment insurance coupled with a national labour exchange.

The Labour Exchange in British Social Thought

The idea of the labour exchange was probably not as novel as that of unemployment insurance. Exchanges had a respectable history in Britain. William Beveridge traced the concept back to the sixteenth century. In the nineteenth century various philanthropic and commercial agencies existed to help the jobless look for work, although these tended to be confined to particular trades or classes of client. The most notable example that caught the eye of reformers was the Egham Free Registry, established in Egham, Surrey, in 1885. The Egham Registry was not concerned with charity but efficiency, with priority given to a registrant's suitability for work rather than the level of their distress, putting local employers in contact with workmen of 'authenticated good character', and aiming to diminish the 'waste of time and energy involved in the search for work'.[1] By 1892, there were 17 private agencies modelled on the Egham Registry, and over 30 permanent or temporary registries operated by local authorities across England and Wales concerned with

---

[1] J Harris, *Unemployment and Politics: A Study in English Social Policy 1886–1914* (Oxford, Oxford University Press, 1972) 279.

charitable relief rather than being commercial operations.[2] The Labour Bureaux (London) Act 1902 allowed for the establishment of municipal bureaux funded out of local rates.

Outside their connection with emergency relief, labour exchanges as institutions capable of 'organising the labour market' received little attention prior to 1905.[3] But social investigators such as Charles Booth and William Beveridge perceived the problem of unemployment as precisely one of labour market disorganisation. Examining dock and wharf labour – the pre-eminent examples of casual work – Booth favoured a scheme whereby employment could be concentrated on 'regular' workers as a precondition for the exclusion of 'surplus' workers. This would be done through 'call stands' and preference lists. Preference would be given to workers in order of regularity of attendance, and telephones connecting the call stands would mobilise waiting workers in accordance with variations in the location of activity over the whole dock area. Thus a unified waterside labour market would be created and a job with variable manpower requirements could be reconciled with the provision of work for regular workers.[4]

Booth's plan for the docks was picked up and further developed by other reformers. Beveridge's thinking on the issue evolved across the first decade of the twentieth century. Like Booth, he initially saw exchanges primarily as an instrument of decasualisation, but later saw their value as a response to seasonal and cyclical trade fluctuations, then as offering a service to the general labour market and, finally, as a prerequisite for any system of unemployment insurance.[5] By 1907 he was calling for the 'universal application of the principle of the labour exchange' as a prerequisite for decasualisation, forestalling depressions and maintaining a 'maximum mobility' throughout the economy.[6]

Beveridge was encouraged by Sidney and Beatrice Webb to present evidence on effective existing labour exchanges to the Royal Commission on the Poor Laws. Beveridge visited Germany in September 1907 to inspect their labour exchange system, comprising over 4,000 bureaux, financed at municipal level, and filling one-and-a-quarter million vacancies each year.[7] He submitted a proposal for a national scheme of British exchanges, centrally controlled and managed on a business rather than a charitable basis, to the Royal Commission in October 1907.

The aims of his proposal were ambitious: to reduce unemployment caused by lack of labour fluidity; collect the relevant statistics to help predict and stabilise depressions; arrange schemes to regularise employment and dovetail seasonal and casual occupations; and to verify 'authentic' unemployment as a necessary

---

[2] ibid 280.

[3] ibid 199.

[4] M Mansfield, 'Labour Exchanges and the Labour Reserve in Turn of the Century Social Reform' (1992) 21 *Journal of Social Policy* 435, 447.

[5] J Harris, *William Beveridge: A Biography* (Oxford, Clarendon Press, 1977) 126–40.

[6] WH Beveridge, 'Labour Exchanges and the Unemployed' (1907) 17 *Economic Journal* 66, 76.

[7] WH Beveridge, 'Public Labour Exchanges in Germany' (1908) 18 *Economic Journal* (March) 1.

precondition for the payment of unemployment insurance.[8] The exchange would rationalise hiring procedures by favouring full-time, regular employment. 'For the man who wants to get a casual job now and again' explained Beveridge, 'the exchange will make that wish impossible ... The result of the exchange is the direct opposite from that of assisting the lazy or incapable; it makes it harder for them and compels them to be regular.'[9] As did Booth, Beveridge saw labour exchanges as performing an implicitly moral function in separating the deserving and undeserving unemployed: they would 'enable the idle vagrant to be discovered unmistakably and sent to an institution for disciplinary detention'.[10]

It's clear in these policy prescriptions that labour exchanges were not seen as responding to the empirical reality of unemployment, but were creating the very subject they sought to act upon. Classical economics assumed a fluid and friction-less labour market, tending towards an equilibrium of supply and demand, making 'involuntary' unemployment an impossibility except in fairly transient form. In Beveridge's honest admission, a national system of exchanges was a 'policy of making reality correspond with the assumptions of economic theory'.[11]

In their Minority Report for the Poor Law Commission, the Webbs echoed Beveridge's recommendation that employment practices be rationalised through the compulsory registration of all job vacancies and all unemployed at state-run labour bureaux. This would enable vacancies and the unemployed to be matched with minimal delay. Those workers deemed immediately surplus to requirements, those disinclined to work regularly, and those deemed physically unfit could all then be dealt with as required.[12]

Beveridge's ideas found a champion in Winston Churchill, who recruited Beveridge to the Board of Trade in 1908 precisely because of his expertise in the area of exchanges. Having the Board of Trade take carriage of labour exchanges accorded with Beveridge's insistence that exchanges were an aspect of employment policy, not merely a response to pauperism or the relief of distress that character-ised the approach of, say, the Local Government Board. Arthur Lowry, assistant inspector to the Local Government Board, conceded as much. Any labour bureau, he argued, 'should occupy itself solely with the normal labour market', and any association with charity would frustrate this aim – a view that was difficult to put

---

[8] Harris, *Unemployment and Politics*, above n 1, 206. Beveridge's championing of unemployment insurance distinguished his approach from that of the Webbs.

[9] Evidence to the Royal Commission on The Poor Laws, cited in N Whiteside, *Bad Times: Unemploy-ment in British Social and Political History* (London, Faber, 1991).

[10] Harris, *Unemployment and Politics*, above n 1, 285.

[11] WH Beveridge, *Unemployment: A Problem of Industry* (London, Longmans, Green and Co, 1931 [1909]) 237. The extent to which the reality of British industrial relations in the first decades of the twentieth century refused to conform to the economic theory embodied in the national labour exchange system is explored in M Mansfield, 'Flying to the Moon: Reconsidering the British Labour Exchange System in the Early Twentieth Century' (2001) 66 *Labour History Review* 24.

[12] National Committee to Promote the Breakup of the Poor Law, Royal Commission on The Poor Laws and Relief of Distress, *The Minority Report of the Poor Law Commission Vol 2* (London, 1909).

into practice, as bureau administrators were often understandably preoccupied with giving priority to clients on the basis of social need rather than suitability or capacity for work.[13]

Later that year, the Liberal government decided to go ahead with a scheme for unemployment insurance. From then on, observes José Harris, the two schemes – exchanges and insurance – were planned in close conjunction, with Hubert Llewellyn Smith, the Board of Trade's Permanent Secretary, working closely with Beveridge on both.[14] Indeed, the draft bill Churchill presented to Cabinet in late 1908 was an omnibus one, proposing both unemployment insurance and a national system of labour exchanges. The two were seen as mutually reinforcing: an exchange could test the authenticity of a claimant's unemployment, while the promise of insurance payments provided the incentive to register at an exchange.[15] The schemes ended up following separate legislative trajectories – the Labour Exchanges Act passed in 1909, the National Insurance Act not until 1911 – primarily because the government wished to hitch unemployment insurance to a wider social insurance scheme covering sickness and disability. Within three years of the passage of the Labour Exchanges Act, over 400 exchanges were opened.[16]

According to the arguments put forward by Beveridge, if exchanges were to allocate work so as to organise the labour market around a new paradigm of regular, full-time work, their coverage of the labour market would have to be extensive and their control over hirings almost total. In other words, notification and registration of vacancies through the labour exchange would need to be compulsory for employers. Churchill stopped short of proposing compulsory registration and, observes Harris, also 'shrank from the social consequences of the evolutionary logic that Booth and Beveridge had prescribed for the labour market during the previous seventeen years'. That logic had entailed the delineation of a superfluous residuum of workers but, as Churchill recognised, without any scheme to deal with that surplus.[17]

The 1909 legislation had two main priorities: to regularise placement and hiring practices, and to exclude the undeserving from unemployment relief. As to the first, by decasualising and concentrating work on a restricted group of full-time workers, the labour exchange in effect constructed unemployment as absolute – and possibly prolonged – inactivity.[18] 'In making work more regular for some', admitted Beveridge, decasualisation 'throws others out altogether. The fact is undeniable. The avowed object of decasualisation is to replace every thousand half-employed men with five hundred fully employed men'.[19] The consequent

---

[13] Harris, *Unemployment and Politics*, above n 1, 202.

[14] Harris, *William Beveridge*, above n 5, 150.

[15] ibid 171.

[16] J Burnett, *Idle Hands: The Experience of Unemployment, 1790–1990* (London, Routledge, 1994) 195.

[17] Harris, *Unemployment and Politics*, above n 1, 288.

[18] Mansfield, 'Labour Exchanges and the Labour Reserve', above n 4, 456.

[19] Beveridge, *Unemployment*, above n 11, 204.

creation of 500 unemployed men in turn points to the need to use the labour exchange for the re-employment of those displaced workers and for the administration of a system of unemployment insurance to sustain them in the meantime.

It was in the administration of unemployment insurance that an equally innovative role for labour exchanges came to the fore: their operation as a system of social surveillance. The principle governing the poor laws was one of deterrence or 'lesser eligibility', whereby the position of the pauper on relief had to be made less comfortable than that of the lowest paid labourer. This was done, for example, through the harsh conditions and dull work typical of the workhouse. The belief was that unless a worker was really unable to obtain work, they would not accept relief under such conditions.[20] Beveridge's concern was that levels of unemployment relief not be so low as to encourage 'degeneracy', but low enough to maintain industrial discipline, particularly the desire among workers to retain secure, regular employment. Any fear that rates and conditions of relief more generous than the workhouse would encourage idleness and malingering was eased by a system of labour exchanges. This is because the labour exchange presented an alternative to the old poor law methods: 'If all the jobs offering in a trade or a district are registered at a single office, then it is clear that any man who cannot get work through that office is unemployed against his will'.[21] The exchange provided a method of measuring willingness and intent, and placed these states of mind at the centre of any understanding of 'unemployment'. As Mansfield concludes:

> The labour exchange is supposed to be capable of so counterposing job-vacancies and the dossiers containing the qualifications of unemployed workers that it can identify individuals 'voluntarily' avoiding work, 'scrounging' or 'malingering' being phenomena created by the imposition of this form of surveillance. Indeed, the 'voluntarily unemployed' did not exist prior to the labour exchange.[22]

The Labour Exchange in Pre-War Australia

The colony of New South Wales had experimented with a government labour bureau as early as 1892. Established just a year after a similar exchange had been set up in New Zealand, it was one of the earliest government bureaux in the world. By 1902 labour bureaux had been set up in Queensland, Victoria, South Australia and Western Australia.[23]

These early bureaux were largely a response to the concentration of jobless men in the major colonial towns or cities. The bureaux typically registered men as artisans and labourers available for employment on government works. Some also

---

[20] ibid 215.

[21] ibid.

[22] M Mansfield, 'The Why Work? Syndrome' (1988) 22 *Social Policy & Administration* 235, 238.

[23] WP Reeves, *State Experiments in Australia and New Zealand Vol 2* (Melbourne, Macmillan, 1969) 217.

sent men out to private employers seeking labour, and would provide the railway fare for men willing to leave urban centres in search of work.[24]

The New Zealand bureau favoured placing men in permanent work where possible and made no attempt to 'share' the available work around.[25] Although the New South Wales bureau was ostensibly modelled on the New Zealand system, it initially operated 'more as a means of social control and as a charitable institution than as a full scale labour exchange',[26] and tended to register men for temporary or casual work.[27] All applicants, irrespective of their usual trade, were placed on equal footing. After 1900, the New South Wales bureau was arranged on a more rational basis, attempting to classify registered jobseekers who were then selected according to the specific skills required by employers. Nevertheless, in the first decade of the twentieth century the bureau still sent the majority of the registered unemployed out to casual and irregular work,[28] and the predominant destination remained government work rather than private employment.[29] It was not until the second decade of the century that the proportion of registered unemployed sent out to government work declined noticeably (dropping to around 30 per cent by 1912) and the bureau began to blend its operations with the demands of the general labour market.[30]

Other colonial labour bureaux were even more explicitly tied to the provisioning of manpower for public works rather than private employment. The South Australian bureau, established in 1898, came under the control of the Commissioner for Public Works, although private employers were able to recruit workers through the bureau.[31] The Victorian system for registering those unemployed in search of work, established in the second half of the 1890s, was situated within the colonial Railway Department and supplied workers only to government departments and only for engagements of three months or less.[32] An exception to this pattern was the government labour bureau of Western Australia, established

---

[24] ibid 219–20; TA Coghlan, *Labour and Industry in Australia: From the First Settlement in 1788 to the Establishment of the Commonwealth in 1901* (Melbourne, Macmillan, 1969) 1457.

[25] Victoria, *New Zealand: Report on the System of Dealing with the Unemployed*, Parl Paper No 32 (1899–1900).

[26] T Endres and M Cook, 'Administering "The Unemployed Difficulty": The NSW Government Labour Bureau 1892–1912' (1986) 26 *Australian Economic History Review* 56, 58.

[27] Reeves, above n 23, 219–20.

[28] Endres and Cook, above n 26, 66.

[29] By the end of the nineteenth century, placement into government employment accounted for seven-eighths of the placements made by the New South Wales bureau. This dominant activity of the bureau was recognised in 1900, when the New South Wales Bureau was brought under the administration of the Ministry of Public Works: Reeves, above n 23, 226. In contrast, in the 1890s, of those who found work through the New Zealand bureau around 40 per cent went to private employers, although skilled tradesmen rarely used the bureau: see Victoria, *New Zealand: Report on the System of Dealing with the Unemployed*, above n 25.

[30] Endres and Cook, above n 26, 69–70.

[31] Victoria, *New Zealand: Report on the System of Dealing with the Unemployed*, above n 25.

[32] ibid.

in 1898, which placed a larger proportion of jobseekers with private employers than other colonial bureaux.[33]

These Australian bureaux were operating at the same time as debates on the decasualisation of labour markets were proceeding in Britain. Indeed, the Australian bureaux were operating in advance of British attempts to establish a national government-run exchange. Yet their operations in the early stages were hardly, if at all, informed by those British debates. In responding to social distress at the turn of the century, the New South Wales bureau tended to distribute available jobs in rotation over a large number of the registered unemployed in order to provide 'relief work'. In effect, rather than stamping out casual labour in the manner advocated by Booth and Beveridge, the bureau became the headquarters of a mobile casual labour reserve – and arguably perfectly suited to the volatile and seasonal conditions and the irregular demand for labour that characterised the colonial labour market.[34] That exchanges could facilitate the increased mobility of labour and so lead to an increased tendency towards casual employment was recognised by some economists of the period.[35]

Nevertheless, British policy in this area was being watched with interest by Australian promoters of social insurance. In his 1910 report on social insurance, Knibbs quoted the reflections of a New South Wales actuary, J Farrell, on contemporary British proposals for exchanges:

> All irregular men for each group of employers should be taken from a common centre or exchange, and this exchange should so far as possible concentrate employment on the smallest number that will suffice for the work of the group as a whole; that successive jobs under different employers should as far as possible be made to go in succession to the same individual, instead of being spread over several men, each idle for more than half his time.

This system, pointed out Knibbs, would thus 'render possible discrimination between the loafer and the honest workman'.[36] This echoed earlier claims that government labour bureaux were essential for distinguishing between the 'unemployed' and the 'unemployable', or the 'worthy' and 'unworthy',[37] those 'capable and fully vouched for' and those 'inefficient for physical or moral reason'.[38]

The idea of a national labour exchange resurfaced in reform proposals in the 1920s. As long as unemployment was viewed as largely a problem of casual labour,[39] the regularisation of employment in those industries only providing

[33] Reeves, above n 23, 242.

[34] Endres and Cook, above n 26.

[35] DH Macgregor, 'Labour Exchanges and Unemployment' (1907) 17 *Economic Journal* 585.

[36] GH Knibbs, *Social Insurance: Report of the Commonwealth Statistician*, Vol 2, Parl Paper No 72 (1910) 78.

[37] Victoria, *New Zealand: Report on the System of Dealing with the Unemployed*, above n 25.

[38] Victoria, *Unemployment: Report of the Board of Inquiry*, Parl Paper No 5 (1900).

[39] Commonwealth of Australia, Royal Commission on National Insurance, *Second Progress Report: Unemployment*, Parl Paper No 79 (1926–28).

intermittent work was central to addressing the problem. Such intermittent work in turn was seen as related to disorganised hiring practices, a lack of labour market information, and the immobility of labour. 'Diverse arrangements for the filling of vacancies' (trade unions, private employment agencies, hiring halls, State exchanges registering men for relief works and so on) were seen as 'confusing, inefficient and wasteful' and contributing 'to the creation of numbers of separate reserves of labour within the respective industrial groups'[40] and in separate geographic localities. Whereas arbitral tribunals and courts, through the imposition of casual loadings, could compensate workers in those industries where intermittent work persisted, they could not address the wider issues identified by those concerned with labour market disorganisation. Therefore, what was required was a mechanism that created one national pool of labour. A national network of labour exchanges would provide a centralised clearing house, connecting areas experiencing labour shortage with those experiencing labour surplus: the 'lay-off in one industry may, as the result of organisation, be absorbed by the busy period of another industry'.[41]

Labour exchanges would also be a vital source of labour market information. By presenting 'all jobs on offer', they in effect offered a whole new representation of the labour market.[42] Previous attempts to measure unemployment, such as those examined in chapter two, were hampered by the difficulty in distinguishing between those in underemployment – caught in a cycle of seasonal or temporary work – and those in unemployment. A network of labour exchanges that regularised employment in the manner envisaged by reformers would address this. And by making unemployment 'visible' in this way, labour exchanges would also allow for new ways of administering the unemployed. Generally, advocates of unemployment insurance in Australia expressed a view similar to those in Britain: labour management practices and prevailing forms of employment would have to change as a *precondition* of any successful insurance scheme, and labour exchanges had a key role to play in this.

In practice, though, State labour exchanges continued to operate as ad hoc responses to problems of social control and charitable relief – a situation that was exacerbated with the onset of the Depression of the 1930s.[43] Except in Queensland, which operated its system of unemployment insurance from the early 1920s, Depression relief or 'sustenance' tended to be financed from consolidated revenue and took the form of a mixture of cash and in-kind benefits. After 1931, New South Wales and Victoria established unemployment relief funds financed by special

[40] Commonwealth of Australia, Development and Migration Commission, *Report on Unemployment and Business Instability in Australia*, Parl Paper No 252 (1926–28).

[41] Commonwealth of Australia, *Second Progress Report: Unemployment*, above n 39.

[42] W Walters, *Unemployment and Government: Genealogies of the Social* (Cambridge, Cambridge University Press, 2000) 49.

[43] For an overview of the functions and scope of State labour exchanges in the 1930s, see Australian Bureau of Census and Statistics, *Labour Report 1939, No 30* (Melbourne, Commonwealth Government Printer, 1941) 134–41.

unemployment relief taxes. In the early 1930s each State also devised methods of distributing relief work among the unemployed. This was usually achieved by dividing the amount of sustenance allowed a man (which depended on family size) by the prevailing hourly award rate, typically resulting in a few hours work per week in return for sustenance, although some States experimented with rotational or intermittent relief work schemes.[44] Generally, registration at the State labour bureau was a precondition for receiving sustenance. A range of conditions as to the 'genuineness' of a claimant's unemployment tended to apply, but these were usually adjudicated at a municipal level. For example, sustenance and relief work in Victoria were refused to claimants who had turned down offers of work without 'reasonable excuse', or who were in short-time work, but it was the relevant Public Assistance Committee, appointed by the municipal council, rather than the labour bureau that had 'absolute discretion' as to who was unemployed for the purposes of obtaining relief.[45]

It seems, then, that although there was continued discussion of the potential role of labour exchanges in Australia, along similar lines to that in Britain, the actual practice of State labour bureaux tended not to reflect these emerging ideas. A retrospective summation of the pre-war experience was provided by Wallace Wurth, the wartime Director-General of Manpower, in 1944. He recognised that all States had established institutions to place unemployed workers and administer unemployment relief and other social benefits. But he pinpointed only Queensland and New South Wales as having a well-developed and decentralised system of exchanges, with considerable experience in both administering relief and in 'handling and placing labour'. In other States, decentralised organisations to administer unemployment relief had sprung up only during the worst of the Depression years, and had gradually reverted to their pre-Depression size. In these States,

> [t]he labour departments existed in embryo; they were attached to other departments and could be enlarged, if necessary, to meet the problems associated with any considerable increase in unemployment. They represented spare parts, as it were, of an administrative machine which could be supplemented and fitted together into a working mechanism, and experience showed that they were in fact, under appropriate guidance, capable of considerable expansion.[46]

JM Garland, looking forward at war's end to an era of full employment overseen by new forms of labour administration, summed up the pre-war experience of labour exchanges more concisely than Wurth, but echoing the gist of his observations: '[L]abour administration in the Australian States has somewhat

---

[44] GD Snooks, 'Robbing Peter to Pay Paul: Australian Unemployment Relief in the Thirties' (1985) Flinders University Working Paper in Economic History No 41.

[45] See Victorian Department of Labour, Sustenance Branch, *The Administration of Social Services (Unemployment Relief)* (Melbourne, Government Printer, 1933).

[46] W Wurth, *Control of Manpower in Australia: A General Review of the Administration of the Manpower Directorate, February 1942–September 1944* (Sydney, Government Printer, 1944) 14, 39–40.

dingy antecedents. It has never been able to shake itself free from the associations of its origins, the misery of unemployment and the apathy of the dole'.[47]

Wartime Labour Administration and the Directorate of Manpower

With the onset of the Second World War, the Australian Commonwealth government was able to secure unprecedented control over matters of labour administration and the direction of manpower. The constitutional 'defence power'[48] enabled the federal Parliament to enact any laws that had a real connection with the defence of the Commonwealth or which were associated with the prosecution of the war, greatly extending the valid scope of the Parliament's legislative power compared with peacetime. The key legislation was the National Security Act 1939 (Cth), under which the government made a series of National Security Regulations.

In the early stages of the war, the government was faced with the challenge of securing and maintaining a proper distribution of manpower between the armed services and essential industries. The Commonwealth was loath to depart from the voluntarism that characterised labour engagement practices in Australia. Initially, the conservative United Australia Party government attempted to induce workers to transfer to key industries through incentive mechanisms. A Reserved Occupations List exempted workers in key industries from call-up and offered higher wage rates and improved conditions. Gradually, though, employees in certain skilled occupational classes and, later, employees in entire industries or enterprises ('protected undertakings') had their mobility effectively frozen, with both the employee's right to move jobs and the employer's right to fire severely circumscribed.[49]

The accession of a Labor government and the onset of the Pacific War at the end of 1941 saw an even stronger movement towards near total control of both hiring and firing under a range of new bureaucratic and administrative arrangements. For example, under the earlier regulations, employers were still permitted to dismiss workers in cases of serious misconduct. In 1942 this was modified so that an employer who had reason to believe an employee was guilty of serious misconduct could suspend the employee from duty but then needed to submit to the Director-General of Manpower a written statement setting out the grounds of the suspension. The Director-General would then decide whether to confirm or remove the suspension, with right of appeal available for both parties.[50]

---

[47] JM Garland, 'Some Aspects of Full Employment, Part II' (1945) 21 *Economic Record* 23, 30.
[48] Australian Constitution s 51(vi).
[49] See Statutory Rules No 128 of 1940; No 128; No 287 of 1940; and No 151 of 1941.
[50] Statutory Rule No 102 of 1942.

The emergence of wider wartime manpower issues – not just around the allocation of labour between industries, but also the expedited training of skilled workers, wage fixing and industrial peace[51] – led the Commonwealth Statistician and Economic Adviser to the Treasury, Roland Wilson, to propose a federal Department of Labour and National Service (LNS) in July 1940. Announcing the establishment of the Department – with Wilson as its permanent head – the new minister, Harold Holt, explained its functions as covering general labour policy, manpower priorities, investigations of labour supply and demand, the effective placement of labour, training, industrial relations and welfare and planning for post-war rehabilitation and development.[52]

The initial organisation of the Department provided for a Secretariat and six divisions, covering industrial relations, technical training, industrial welfare, employment, records and analysis, and post-war reconstruction. The initial wartime labour controls were largely administered not by LNS, but by the Labour Directorate of the Department of Munitions, and were overwhelmingly directed at securing a supply of labour for munitions production at the expense of other industries.[53] But in January 1942 the Employment Division of LNS was subsumed into a new Directorate of Manpower, established by the incoming Labor government, and it was this new Directorate that took responsibility for enforcing the National Security (Manpower) Regulations.

The inaugural Director-General of Manpower was Wallace Wurth, a career public servant from New South Wales with a background in labour administration and seconded to the Commonwealth for the duration of the war. Although based in LNS, Wurth was answerable directly to the Minister, Eddie Ward, rather than to the permanent head of LNS. Wurth's staff grew from 324 in January 1942 to nearly 2,500 by June 1943.[54] His Directorate operated on a decentralised basis. Its creation coincided with the establishment of a nationwide system of National Service Offices, based on local military districts. This occurred, primarily, through the takeover of existing State labour offices and their staff. As noted, New South Wales and Queensland had fully operational State Departments of Labour; in Victoria, the Commonwealth was involved in building a virtually new department 'from its foundations'.[55] The National Service Offices were to compile and maintain a manpower register for each district; issue certificates of exemption from war service under the protected undertakings controls; and place 'disemployed' labour

---

[51] See O Foenander, *Wartime Labour Developments in Australia: With Suggestions for Reform in the Post-War Regulation of Industrial Relations* (Melbourne, Melbourne University Press, 1943); E Ronald Walker, *The Australian Economy in War and Reconstruction: Issued under the Auspices of the Royal Institute of International Affairs* (New York, Oxford University Press, 1947) ch XII.

[52] SJ Butlin, *War Economy 1939–1942* (Canberra, Australian War Memorial, 1955) 249–50.

[53] C Fort, 'Developing a National Employment Policy, Australia 1939–45' (PhD thesis, University of Adelaide, 2000) 68–75.

[54] P Hasluck, *The Government and the People, 1942–1945* (Canberra, Australian War Memorial, 1970) 284.

[55] Wurth, above n 46, 19.

in new employment. 'Disemployed' labour referred to those workers who were out of work due to rationing controls of non-essential industries.

Under the National Security Regulations, Wurth was to obtain increasing powers of labour direction, so much so that the National Service Offices became virtually the sole channel for the engagement of labour by all employers, both government and private. By March 1942 almost the entire civilian population over 16 years of age was required to register. All employers not in protected undertakings required a permit from Manpower before engaging any new male employee – a requirement that was extended in August to include any female employee under 45.[56] A number of exemptions were made, including the engagement of casual labour for periods less than three consecutive days, waterside workers (whose employment was under the control of the Stevedoring Industry Commission) and women aged over 45, but the effect was to sharply curtail the advertising of vacancies through newspapers and the activities of private employment agencies.

The regulations also gave the Director-General power to direct any person registered as unemployed at a National Service Office to accept such employment as the Director-General thought fit, provided that the person was capable of performing the work, the wages and conditions of the work were those set by the appropriate industrial tribunal, and suitable accommodation was available if the employment entailed the person moving from home. Wurth admitted there was always 'some doubt as to the precise meaning to be accorded to the word "unemployed".[57] This perhaps reflected the relatively underdeveloped nature of unemployment insurance or benefit schemes in Australia. Elsewhere, however, in explaining the administration of the regulations, Wurth referred to those who were 'technically unemployed' and distinguished these individuals from 'those who were not gainfully occupied, the latter group comprising relatively large numbers of females who were not actively seeking employment.[58] This suggests an understanding of 'unemployment' as necessarily encompassing job-seeking activity, and anticipates both the eligibility conditions that would attach to the post-war unemployment benefit scheme and the 'labour force' approach that would come to dominate national economic statistics. But in the meantime, any distinction between the 'technically unemployed' and those 'not gainfully occupied' did not seem to overly preoccupy Wurth and his staff. In fact, the priority was to mobilise *all* available labour, including women – that is, to efface any such a distinction.[59] Accordingly, Wurth thought it best to proceed by relying 'largely on the psychological effect of the existence of the Regulation rather than on any strict legal interpretation of its provisions.[60]

[56] Statutory Rules No 34 of 1942; and No 345 of 1942.
[57] Wurth, above n 46, 95.
[58] ibid 95, 132.
[59] ibid 132.
[60] ibid 95.

In any case, the expansion of the armed forces on the one hand and the high wages and attractive conditions offered by the war industries on the other tended to minimise the number of unemployed registered at National Service Offices. As for those remaining people who might be capable of direction to essential employment, they were selected from the civilian register and required to attend an interview at the National Service Office where they were offered a choice of several positions. Only if they did not voluntarily accept the employment offered was a direction issued. Between January 1942 and January 1946, an estimated three million people were placed in employment through the Offices, with directions issued to about 10,000. Appeals against a direction could be made to a magistrate. Appeals were made by around 100 directed persons and upheld in two-thirds of cases.[61]

Due to the war, Australia now had a national system of labour exchanges, under the aegis of the Directorate of Manpower. Could such a system outlive the exigencies of wartime? The Commonwealth government's plans for post-war reconstruction, including both an unemployment benefit scheme and pursuit of a policy of full employment, potentially provided the Manpower Directorate with precisely that opportunity.

---

[61] Walker, above n 51, 318–19. For a case study in the wartime direction of labour, see C Fort, 'Regulating the Labour Market in Australia's Wartime Democracy' (2003) 34 *Australian Historical Studies* 213.

4

Social Policy in Wartime

Administrators, statisticians and legislators of the 1920s and 1930s struggled with the problem of defining unemployment as an insurable risk. But by the late 1930s the Australian Labor Party's opposition to any scheme of contributory insurance had become entrenched. Labor was adamant that workers should not have to pay for a social security system directly out of their own wages.[1] This lack of cross-party support, along with divisions in the conservative Coalition government and resistance from the medical profession and some trade unions, spelled the death of the government's plans for social insurance, even though a proposed scheme had gone as far as being legislated in 1938.[2] Any successful proposal for an unemployment benefits scheme had to break the impasse as to how it should be financed.

Designing an Unemployment Benefits Scheme

Bipartisan support for a scheme of national unemployment benefits was finally secured through the work of the parliamentary Joint Committee on Social Security. The Committee was established by the United Australia Party (UAP) government of Robert Menzies in July 1941, although the impetus appears to have come from Labor opposition leader John Curtin, then a member of the National War Advisory Council. Menzies wanted to make a call for national unity in the war effort. Curtin suggested any increased burdens imposed on the civilian population be balanced by some indication that workers' 'efforts and sacrifices were going to result in making social conditions better' and that a parliamentary standing committee be appointed to report on proposed social reforms.[3] The Joint Committee was to report to the Minister for Social Services with a brief to consider – as part of a 'full programme of social security' – widows' and orphans' pensions, unemployment insurance, contributory pensions, a national housing scheme and a comprehensive health scheme. As reflected in the reference, the UAP government and the

---

[1] R Watts, *The Foundations of the National Welfare State* (Sydney, Allen & Unwin, 1987) 92.

[2] ibid, 18–24; J Murphy, 'Path Dependence and the Stagnation of Australian Social Policy Between the Wars' (2010) 22 *The Journal of Policy History* 450, 464–66.

[3] Watts, above n 1, 62; S Macintyre, *Australia's Boldest Experiment: War and Reconstruction in the 1940s* (Sydney, NewSouth Press, 2015) 204–05.

Minister, Frederick Stewart, remained committed to the idea of a contributory unemployment insurance scheme.

Labor was able to form a government in late 1941, and would go on to credit the Committee for the social services legislation it eventually enacted. This partly reflected the political advantage of pointing to the recommendations of an all-party committee to defuse or weaken any opposition criticism. But in fact, many of Labor's welfare initiatives were being promoted from other quarters, in particular from Treasurer Ben Chifley and members of Treasury staff, and they may well have passed into law regardless of the Committee's recommendation.[4] The Joint Committee's recommendations proved useful in the meantime in offering a post-war sweetener that offset increased wartime taxes – the latter being necessary to dampen more immediate inflationary pressures and to finance the war effort.[5]

But one of the Joint Committee's real achievements was to secure all-party support for a non-contributory system of unemployment benefit.[6] That consensus was hardly a stable one. When the Unemployment and Sickness Benefits Bill came to be debated by Parliament two years later, members tended to retreat to the positions that characterised the 1930s standoff, with UAP parliamentarians continuing to spruik the virtues of contributory schemes. One UAP member of the Joint Committee, Rupert Ryan, used the parliamentary debate to insist that the Committee had not been unanimous on the issue of financing and that he still supported a contributory model.[7] And as late as 1949 the UAP's successor party – the Liberals – went to the federal election espousing a policy to establish a contributory scheme of social insurance.

Perhaps the Committee managed to sidestep the impasse by showing that it was easy to overstate the differences between 'social insurance' models of welfare and any proposed 'social assistance' model. The Committee argued, in effect, that there was little material distinction between contributions on the one hand and progressive income taxes on the other, with claimants in the latter case having 'earned' their benefits through the taxes they paid. This meant, of course, extending income taxes down the income scale so that those likely to receive the new social security benefits were being asked, for the first time, to pay for them, and to pay for them via a tax based largely on participation in the employment relationship. So in the space of a single paragraph, the Committee could refer to 'the obligation of all the potential beneficiaries *to contribute* to the scheme' and then go on to

---

[4] TH Kewley, *Social Security in Australia 1900–72* (Sydney, Sydney University Press, 1973) 179; W De Maria, 'New Society Blueprint or Political Ploy: The Work and Impact of the Joint Committee on Social Security' (1989) 35 *Australian Journal of History & Politics* 164, 167.

[5] Watts, above n 1, 96–98.

[6] S Shaver, 'Design for a Welfare State: The Joint Parliamentary Committee on Social Security' (1987) 22 *Historical Studies* 411.

[7] J Murphy, *A Decent Provision: Australian Welfare Policy, 1870 to 1949* (Farnham, Ashgate, 2011) 218. In fact, Ryan's dissenting 'Minority Report' tabled in 1942 merely took issue with the Committee's proposed *level* of benefit payment, not with the mode of financing: Commonwealth of Australia, Joint Committee on Social Security, *Second Interim Report*, Parl Paper No 71 (1940–43) 5.

propose that 'the simplest and most equitable plan in the present circumstances is to impose a [graduated] *general tax* on every income-earner in the community'.[8]

The Committee's Second and Third reports highlighted the shortcomings of established social insurance schemes. Those reports were mostly written by the Committee's research officer, Ronald Mendelsohn. An economist who had worked for a major bank and an appointee of UAP Minister Stewart, Mendelsohn was initially viewed with suspicion by Labor members of the Committee. But Mendelsohn had definite socialist sympathies and was happy to make the case for a non-contributory scheme of social security.[9] He completed drafts of the reports by 5 March 1942 and they were signed by the Committee and presented to the Minister the next day.

The reports relied on only a handful of submissions from within the public service, most notably from Jim Nimmo, a junior Treasury official.[10] Nimmo argued for the idea of a 'national minimum of real income': that is, a minimum limit below which no citizen need fall in the advent of adverse circumstances. It was to be made up of cash transfers and financed from a progressive income tax. The resulting cash payment would be means-tested and set considerably below prevailing wage rates. In this last aspect, the proposal mirrored the old British poor laws, whereby the recipient of relief was not to be 'made really or apparently so eligible as the situation of the independent labourer of the lowest class'.[11] The Committee ended up recommending a weekly payment of 80 shillings for an unemployed adult male who was supporting a wife and one child. The basic wage at that time, notionally meant to cover the same type of household, was 86 shillings a week, so Nimmo's suggestion regarding the rate of payment seems to have gone unheeded by the Committee. In the end, the government would legislate for a far lower rate of 50 shillings a week for such a household, which amounted to less than 60 per cent of the basic wage. It was 'more than New Zealand provided, a little less than that Beveridge had proposed recently in the United Kingdom'.[12]

The principle of 'lesser eligibility', achieved by keeping payment rates at a parsimonious level, did not do away with the need for a work test. Nimmo pointed out that the 'one important danger' in establishing a Commonwealth minimum, even

---

[8] Joint Committee, *Second Interim Report*, above n 7, para 12, emphasis added. For liberals, contributory schemes weren't simply a means to address a technical problem concerning financing: they embodied a particular societal model based around prudence, the alliance 'of labour with frugality and thrift', with benefits appearing as a legal right linked to contributions, 'an exchange between equals that did not vitiate independence': P O'Malley, *Risk, Uncertainty and Government* (London, Glasshouse Press, 2004) 32, 30.

[9] Macintyre, above n 3, 179, 205.

[10] Watts, above n 1, 76.

[11] Report of the Poor Law Commission (1834), cited in S Deakin and F Wilkinson, *The Law of the Labour Market: Industrialization, Employment, and Legal Evolution* (Oxford, Oxford University Press, 2005) 134.

[12] Macintyre, above n 3, 207.

considerably below prevailing wage rates, was 'that it may weaken or destroy for many persons the incentive to work':

> There is only one effective means to prevent malingering and that is by the application of a work test. Wherever a work test has been applied it has proved a most unpopular measure. Nevertheless it is an essential part of any scheme to guarantee a minimum income to able-bodied workers.[13]

He went on to observe that 'the necessity to apply a work test means that the organisation responsible for the administration of any scheme to guarantee a minimum income to unemployed persons must also act as an employment agency' and that such an agency be most appropriately established within the federal Department of Labour and National Service (LNS). This would render State relief organisations and employment exchanges redundant, although Nimmo thought they could provide a core of experienced personnel for any new, federal agency.[14]

The Committee's Third Report, published on 25 March 1942, affirmed the merits of a non-contributory scheme, financed from a progressive income tax.[15] Apart from that, the Committee's analysis of unemployment reiterated the concerns of the 1926 Royal Commission, suggesting that a system of 'employment exchanges under Commonwealth supervision are without doubt the most important and the most urgent reform required in the Australian system for the organisation of labour'. The Report recognised that the wartime National Service Offices under the Directorate of Manpower provided the nucleus of

> an efficient system of employment exchanges which may be expanded to carry out any function associated with unemployment benefits including the application of a work test, while also recognising that such a system would help in 'the placing of Australian labour to the best advantage.[16]

As already mentioned, the principle of financing unemployment benefits through a progressive income tax tied in nicely with the imperatives to both finance the war and soak up excess consumer demand that could otherwise give rise to an inflationary spiral. A progressive income tax was made possible by the Commonwealth's new position as the sole taxing authority in the field of income tax.[17] The main problem for Labor in instituting such a tax, which would mean extending

---

[13] Parliamentary Committee on Social Security, *Minutes of Evidence* (Canberra, Commonwealth Government Printer, 1943) 234–35.

[14] ibid 235, 237.

[15] Commonwealth of Australia, Joint Committee on Social Security, *Third Interim Report*, Parl Paper No 72 (1940–43) para 25.

[16] ibid para 18.

[17] This was achieved through a suite of legislation which gave priority to Commonwealth taxes over State-levied taxes, authorised the transfer of State public servants to collect the new Commonwealth income taxes, and made Commonwealth grants to States conditional on the States not raising income taxes of their own: Income Tax Act 1942 (Cth); State Grants (Income Tax Reimbursement) Act 1942 (Cth); Income Tax (Wartime Arrangements) Act 1942 (Cth).

tax rates down the income scale, was political. The Australian Labor Party (ALP) had long maintained a public opposition to any increase of the tax burden on low-income earners – indeed, this was one of the grounds for the Party's opposition to contributory social insurance schemes.

Between September 1942 and February 1943, key advisers and officials from the Treasury worked out how to increase taxes while defusing potential political objections. In December 1942, Chifley was able to secure Cabinet's approval to link an increase in tax to the establishment of a 'National Welfare Fund'. The government would pay a proportion of its increased revenue each year into the fund, from which an extended range of social security benefits would be paid. A month later, the details of the new social security benefits were agreed upon: an immediate increase in maternity allowances and the introduction of funeral benefits and pensions to dependants of pensioners, together with a promise that a scheme of unemployment benefits would be introduced in the near future.[18] Curtin reiterated his government's commitment to a scheme of unemployment benefit in a policy speech for the 1943 election. The legislation was nearly another 12 months in the making, with a bill finally introduced into the February 1944 session of Parliament.

The Unemployment and Sickness Benefits Act 1944 received royal assent on 5 April 1944. It provided for unemployment benefit to be paid to people who were out of work, were capable of undertaking and willing to undertake suitable work, and had taken reasonable steps to obtain work.[19] Direct participation in a strike disqualified a person from receiving the benefit[20] and voluntary unemployment, unemployment by reason of misconduct, and refusal of an offer of suitable work could all result in a cancellation or postponement of benefit.[21] Benefit was payable to men 16 years of age and over but not 65 and women 16 years and over but not 60.[22] Applicants were required to have resided continuously in Australia for not less than 12 months immediately prior to the date of application.[23] A married woman was not entitled to benefit unless it was not 'reasonable for her husband to maintain her';[24] any Aboriginal native was not eligible unless the Director-General of Social Services was satisfied that it was 'reasonable' that he or she receive it.[25]

The details of the benefit's administration remained to be worked out, however, and would involve questions of both Federal–State relations and the division of responsibilities between the Commonwealth departments of Social Services and Labour and National Service. Curtin had informed State premiers on

---

[18] Watts, above n 1, 94–99; see National Welfare Fund Act 1943 (Cth).
[19] Unemployment and Sickness Benefits Act 1944 (Cth) s 15(c)(ii) and (iii).
[20] ibid s 15(c)(i).
[21] ibid s 28(a), (b) and (c).
[22] ibid s 15(a).
[23] ibid s 15(b).
[24] ibid s 18.
[25] ibid s 19.

31 October 1944 that it was the Commonwealth's intention to administer the Unemployment and Sickness Benefits Act 1944 and that, further, this could not be divorced from the establishment of a Commonwealth employment service. The Victorian premier replied it was absolutely necessary to retain State employment services and he opposed any attempt to duplicate at the federal level a service 'which has always been carried on successfully by the State'. This last comment was greeted with scepticism by Jack Holloway, the new federal Minister for Labour and National Service, who advised Curtin that 'it is a fair comment that Victoria really had no employment service that could be reasonably so described'.[26]

As to the issue of interdepartmental relations at the Commonwealth level, Nimmo did not consider the Department of Social Services an appropriate body to take sole responsibility for administering a 'national minimum'. The administration of a work test in particular was seen as fundamentally different from the type of administration already being undertaken by the Department in regard to child endowment and widows' pensions. Curtin, anxious to get the unemployment benefit scheme running by early 1945, favoured Nimmo's suggestion to use the resources of the Manpower Directorate situated within LNS.[27]

Manpower was only too happy to claim administration of unemployment benefits, not least because it strengthened the Directorate's prospects for surviving into the post-war period as a peacetime national employment service. At the end of 1944 William Funnell, who had succeeded Wallace Wurth as Director-General of Manpower a few months earlier, informed his Deputy Directors-General in each State that the unemployment and sickness benefit scheme would come into force on 1 March the following year and that it seemed 'not unlikely that the actual administration of this scheme will devolve upon this Department'.[28]

Here, however, Manpower had to tread a fine line. Funnell had reservations about tying the employment service too closely to the administration of the Unemployment and Sickness Benefit Act 1944 for fear of the service being seen as a dole and social security organisation rather than a generalist labour exchange. For political reasons, however, he thought it unwise 'to dissociate the independent need for an Employment Service from the requirement of an organisation to handle administration of the [Unemployment and Sickness Benefit] Act'.[29] By February 1945 the ministers of LNS and Social Service, together with their departmental heads, had reached an agreement that Manpower would administer the work test but play no part in policy formation surrounding unemployment benefits. The latter would be the sole responsibility of Social Service. For the duration

[26] Cabinet Agendum, January 1945, National Archives of Australia, Series B551, Item No 43/101/5246, 'Unemployment and Sickness Benefits Act. Administration of'.

[27] Curtin to Holloway, 18 September 1944, National Archives of Australia, Series B551, Item No 43/101/5246, 'Unemployment and Sickness Benefits Act, Administration of'.

[28] Unemployment and Sickness Benefit Circular No 1, 1 December 1944, National Archives of Australia, Series MP 243/3, Box 2.

[29] ibid, Director General of Manpower Minute, 13 February 1945.

of the war, the existing National Service Offices would be used for local operation of the Act, with officers acting as Registrars of Social Service under the Act.[30]

On 10 March, Funnell was able to report to his State deputies that Cabinet had approved the establishment, within LNS, of a Commonwealth Employment Service (CES). Established under the Re-establishment and Re-Employment Act, the CES would, inter alia, participate in the peacetime administration of the unemployment benefits scheme.

The White Paper on Full Employment

In July 1944 Prime Minister Curtin returned from a visit to Britain, impressed by that country's White Paper on Employment Policy. He announced to Parliament that his government would prepare a similar document and handed the task to the Ministry of Post-War Reconstruction.

A Reconstruction Division had been created within LNS at the end of 1940. The Division served as secretariat to an Inter-Departmental Advisory Committee on Reconstruction that drew in representatives of 15 departments and instrumentalities. Over the next two years, and with a change of government, pressure grew for a separate Ministry of Post-War Reconstruction. Curtin and Chifley saw political advantage in a specialist ministry acting as a focus for post-war aspirations. LNS departmental head Roland Wilson supported the separation of the Reconstruction Division from LNS on the grounds that he had little faith that his minister, Eddie Ward, could oversee such an important task. The Joint Committee on Social Security, in its Fifth Interim Report of October 1942, had also recommended the appointment of a dedicated minister responsible for reconstruction co-ordination. In November 1942, the ALP National Conference added its voice to the call for the establishment of Post-War Reconstruction as a separate department with its own minister. In December 1942 Curtin announced Ben Chifley's appointment as Minister for Post-War Reconstruction and in January 1943 the appointment of HC Coombs as Director-General of the new department.[31]

Australia had already pressed for an international policy on full employment as a precondition for any acceptance of a post-war free trade regime as envisaged by the Mutual Aid Agreement between Britain and the United States. Full employment became the focus of international negotiations conducted by Foreign Minister Bert Evatt in 1943, with Australia pressing for recognition of the issue at the United Nations Food and Agriculture Conference in 1943, at the April 1944

---

[30] ibid, Cabinet Agendum 790, 14 February 1945.

[31] SJ Butlin and CB Schedvin, *War Economy 1942–1945* (Canberra, Australian War Memorial, 1977) 629; T Rowse, 'The People and Their Experts: A War-Inspired Civics for HC Coombs' (1998) 74 *Labour History* 70; Macintyre, above n 3, 128–33.

meeting of the International Labour Organization, and at the United Nations Monetary and Financial Conference at Bretton Woods in May 1944.[32]

However, preparation of the White Paper outlining a domestic policy did not commence until Curtin's announcement in July. By this stage there was an added imperative for the Labor government to declare its commitment to full employment. The government planned to introduce its Re-establishment and Re-employment Bill to Parliament the following autumn. Under the proposed legislation, employers would be obliged to give demobilised servicemen preference in employment for seven years following the cessation of hostilities. This angered the Australian Council of Trade Unions (ACTU). During the war, the Labor government had made sure that the Commonwealth, as a major employer and procurer, adhered to a policy of preference for trade union members, and the ACTU was agitating for legislation that would require all employers to give preference to union members in peacetime. And there was a significant number of unionised workers who were refused enlistment in the armed forces because they were engaged in essential wartime occupations. Despite their contribution to the war effort, these workers would be denied the benefit of preference in employment afforded to returned servicemen. So its policy of preference in employment for returned servicemen, rather than for unionists, put the Labor government on a collision course with the ACTU. For the government, the immediate political utility of a commitment to full employment was to defuse the preference issue altogether: in a full employment economy, there would simply be jobs for all.[33]

But the Re-establishment and Re-employment Bill would also establish Australia's first Commonwealth peacetime labour exchange. This novel institution, its scope and purpose, its role in addressing the problem of joblessness, needed to be sold to the Australian people, and the White Paper would provide the space for this.

Coombs took on the drafting of the White Paper, assisted by Jim Nimmo and Gerald Firth from Post-War Reconstruction. At the end of February 1945, Coombs circulated a version to departments outside Reconstruction. By this stage it was already a third draft, having gone from Firth and Nimmo to Coombs and back again to Firth and Nimmo. It was now titled a government statement on 'Employment, Production and Expenditure in the Transition from War to Peace'.[34] Seventy pages in length, the document was partly intended as a 'political instrument ... designed to rally community support for the war and to stimulate

---

[32] See Butlin and Schedvin, ibid, 630–73; E Ronald Walker, *The Australian Economy in War and Reconstruction: Issued under the Auspices of the Royal Institute of International Affairs* (New York, Oxford University Press, 1947) 369–76.

[33] T Rowse, 'Curtin and Labor's Full Employment Promise', paper presented at 'From Curtin to Coombs: War and Peace in Australia' seminar (Curtin University of Technology, 25 March 2003).

[34] National Archives of Australia, Series B551, Item No 45/78/12162, 'White Paper on Full Employment'.

willingness to bear continuing hardships'[35] and partly a detailed discussion, drawing on Keynes' *General Theory*, of the economics of maintaining full employment through aggregate demand management, complete with detailed statistical forecasts of expenditure, savings and investment patterns, drawn from estimates of national income and expenditure prepared by the Commonwealth Bureau of Census and Statistics.

The draft argued that the 'fundamental human problem' of the transition from war to peace was 'that of helping men and women to find steady civilian jobs'. The war had shown it was possible to redirect economic production when there was general agreement about national objectives and understanding of the nature of the changes required. The post-war period offered a 'unique opportunity to lay down new patterns of employment, production and expenditure directed towards important objectives of national policy'. Full employment was defined as a 'high and stable level of employment', which meant slightly more jobs than the number of people seeking work, with as far as possible the jobs being 'of the right kind and in the right place', and with people who found it necessary to change occupations being helped to do so 'as promptly as possible'. The aim of the government was to keep unemployment below a maximum of 5 per cent, with a rate of perhaps 4 per cent for males and 2 per cent for females.

To achieve these aims, the paper proposed a particular industrial strategy, based on secondary industry, and a 'more adequate machinery for ... job finding' and 'adequate financial provision ... for the maintenance of those moving from job to job'. Achievement of full employment would only be practicable if every effort was made 'to increase the mobility of labour as between districts and between industries and occupations'. To this end, an efficient Australia-wide employment service was proposed:

(a) To bring to the notice of men and women seeking employment the full range of opportunities offering, and in particular to find employment offering scope for their abilities.

(b) To enable employers to draw upon suitable labour throughout the Commonwealth.

(c) To provide assistance where necessary to enable employees to move to where employment is available.

(d) To provide information necessary for planning public expenditure and for economic policy generally.

Promoting the mobility of labour was also seen as important for industrial peace in a full employment economy, stopping local or industrial shortages where 'advantage may be taken' by workers 'to exact concessions out of line with earnings in other comparable occupations'. The draft pointed out that 'it would greatly assist' the work of the employment service and enable better facilities for employers and

---

[35] HC Coombs, *Trial Balance: Issues of My Working Life* (Melbourne, Sun Books, 1981) 49.

employees 'if they will inform the local office of the Service well ahead of prospective changes in their employment'.[36]

A copy of the draft paper was sent to Funnell on 27 February, who in turn sought comments from staff in Manpower. One staff comment was that insufficient detail had been paid to the importance of the Employment Service and

[t]he need for its recognition by the community, ie. by employers and employees. I feel that a much more definite statement of the Government's policy to support the employment service, to force the development of a really effective employment service, one which will not only give service to employers and employees but provide the basis on which plans for full employment could be implemented, is required.

Funnell relayed this principal criticism to Coombs in mid-March, saying that instead of the 'sporadic' references to the Employment Service, its functions 'might be given more prominence'. He suggested 'a few cohesive paragraphs indicating the Government's intention to develop a high calibre Commonwealth-wide service ... and the reasons why both sides of industry should co-operate to the full in achieving the government's object'.[37]

Funnell's comments were not received by Coombs in time to be incorporated into the next draft. Nevertheless, many of Manpower's more general concerns had obviously been echoed by other departments and influenced the final shape of the paper. The revised version that Coombs circulated on 15 March was now entitled 'Full Employment in Australia' and represented its 'transformation from a seminar paper to a policy statement'.[38] The quantitative estimates of spending, production and employment were eliminated (it was proposed that they appear in a separate statistical memorandum to be issued as the work of the public service, not as a ministerial statement). The notion of full employment was not given the percentage estimate that had appeared in the earlier draft, replaced instead by the comment that it merely meant 'more jobs offering than people seeking work'. A clearer distinction was also made between the special problems of transition to peace and more general policy regarding the maintenance of full employment. Perhaps reflecting the fact that Manpower had failed to communicate its comments to Coombs in time to be considered in relation to the revision, the revised version left the references to the proposed employment service virtually unchanged.[39]

On 20 March Cabinet referred the revised draft to a Cabinet sub-committee, comprising the Minister for Post-War Reconstruction, the Treasurer, the Minister for Labour and National Service and the Minister for Information. Again, the

---

[36] 'Employment, Production and Expenditure in the Transition from War to Peace', Draft, 27 February 1945, National Archives of Australia, Series B551, Item No 45/78/12162, 'White Paper on Full Employment'.

[37] Funnell to Coombs, 13 March 1945, National Archives of Australia, Series B551, Item No 45/78/12162, 'White Paper on Full Employment'.

[38] Butlin and Schedvin, above n 31, 676.

[39] 'Full Employment in Australia', Draft, 15 March 1945, National Archives of Australia, Series B551, Item No 45/78/12162, 'White Paper on Full Employment'.

timing seems to be linked to the preference issue: the second reading of the Re-establishment and Re-employment Bill was to commence on 23 March and the need to placate trade union discontent on the matter of servicemen's preference in employment had attained a certain urgency.[40]

Funnell again wrote to Coombs at the beginning of April, having suspected his previous comments in relation to the revised paper had not been considered. Noting that the paper's introduction read 'rather more like a political manifesto than a proposed white paper', he again stressed the problems associated with a full employment economy. These included the filling of uncongenial jobs, which had proven a problem even with the existence of extensive wartime labour controls. More specifically, Funnell suggested that the references to the Employment Service on the one hand gave the impression that the Service would provide the panacea for full employment, yet on the other still gave insufficient attention to the significance of the Service in the post-war scheme of things:

> In one sense I think the paper dismisses too lightly the part the employment service has to play, and in another sense it gives the impression that the employment service is the key to the full employment economy. Actually, the truth lies somewhere between these two extremes. I feel that the Government should categorically state its intention to build up a high calibre service and invite the co-operation of both sides of industry. I don't think we can be too positive about this matter or assume that the community understands the functions which an employment service can perform.[41]

Funnell then referred specifically to the International Labour Organization's Philadelphia resolutions of the previous year that had recognised the role that public employment agencies might play in the promotion of employment.[42] He emphasised the fourth of the Service's proposed functions ((d) above) as missing the important point about the role the Service could play in measuring employment trends and contributing to manpower planning, as well as the Service's role in retraining workers.

Coombs replied that Funnell's suggestions regarding the Service would be 'taken fully into account' in the work of revision, so that the treatment would preserve 'the necessary balance between undue emphasis and cursory mention'.[43] By this stage the paper was already with an 'expert committee' of public servants to further simplify the text. The Cabinet sub-committee made a series of excisions, representing 'not disagreement with the ideas expressed but rather doubts about their political acceptability to the electorate'.[44] All this tended to result in further

---

[40] Rowse, 'Curtin and Labor's Full Employment Promise', above n 33.

[41] Funnell to Coombs, 4 April 1945, National Archives of Australia, Series B551, Item No 45/78/12162, 'White Paper on Full Employment'.

[42] See Employment (Transition from War to Peace) Recommendation (No 71) and the Employment Service Recommendation (No 72).

[43] Coombs to Funnell, 7 April 1945, National Archives of Australia, Series B551, Item No 45/78/12162, 'White Paper on Full Employment'.

[44] Coombs, above n 35, 52.

dilution of the economic analysis, while still leaving the politicians dissatisfied. The final draft approved by Cabinet for publication in May 1945 was 'an amalgam of ministerial statement and specialist report which served neither purpose adequately ... Nevertheless, there can be no question that the White Paper carried an unambiguous message and a policy commitment of the very highest order'.[45]

As it happened, the final version did see many of Funnell's concerns addressed. The proposed Employment Service was given eight paragraphs under the sub-heading 'Mobility of Resources' – although the earlier admission that occupational and residential mobility were necessary to prevent labour 'taking advantage' of a full employment economy was omitted. Explicit reference was made to the 1944 Philadelphia declaration, with the CES proposed to be 'on the general lines' of this recommendation. Functions (a) to (c) of the Service as outlined in the draft were reiterated, but function (d) was replaced by an extended statement on the Service's capacity to 'affect the employment situation' by developing retraining schemes, advising on the location of industry, public works, housing and similar measures, and disseminating information concerning labour supply, employment opportunities, skill requirements, employment trends, seasonal and casual employment and 'other information of value in promoting full employment'. Paragraph 59 made the kind of categorical statement that Funnell was seeking, referring to the government's commitment to building a 'thoroughly efficient service' staffed by 'suitably qualified and experienced personnel' using the 'best modern practice in placement, training and vocational guidance'. The government wished to make it clear 'that no effort will be spared in building a service of the highest quality in both its personnel and procedures, and accordingly invites both employers and employees to collaborate in ensuring its success'.[46]

***

Australia's new Commonwealth Employment Service came about in the context of wartime centralisation of powers, including powers of labour administration. This centralisation was accompanied in peacetime by a new optimism regarding the scope and possibilities of state planning. The post-war 'reconstruction ethos' to some extent represented a continuity with the outlook of administrative reformers such as Beveridge and other champions of 'organising the labour market': theirs was 'a kind of Edwardian idea of reform "above class" introduced by a benevolent state staffed by technocrats'.[47] However, those earlier reformers, in both Britain and Australia, saw unemployment as 'primarily a problem of rationalizing the market for labour by administrative means; [and] were only peripherally concerned with

---

[45] Butlin and Schedvin, above n 31, 679.

[46] Commonwealth of Australia, *Full Employment in Australia*, Parl Paper No 11 (1945).

[47] R Skidelsky, *John Maynard Keynes, Volume Two: The Economist as Saviour 1920–1937* (London, Macmillan, 1992) 687.

the kind of macroeconomic analysis that revolutionised the study of unemployment [in the 1940s] by relating it to public investment and consumer demand'.[48]

Beveridge had succeeded in partially depersonalising unemployment, removing
it from the realm of moral character and relabelling it a 'problem of industry' –
although the genuineness of an individual's claim for benefit remained a preoccupation of reformers. Keynes' approach abstracted the category even more.
The focus was no longer on the *unemployed*, but on *unemployment* as a key macroeconomic indicator responsive to the levers of supply and demand.[49]

But it would be wrong to see this evolution as simply a series of displacements.
Rather, it is better thought of as a species of layering. Writing in the mid-1940s,
Beveridge admitted that his earlier writings on the role of labour exchanges in alle-
viating unemployment had ignored the question of aggregate demand – although
this oversight, he insisted, was 'in accord with all academic economists and most
practical men' of the time.[50] In the wake of the Keynesian revolution, he stressed
that his and Keynes' approaches were complementary rather than in opposition.

It's true that in the early drafts of Australia's White Paper, the role of the
labour exchange was peripheral to the vision of economists and planners such as
Coombs, Firth and Nimmo. For them, the pre-war concern with labour market
inefficiency had been eclipsed by a concern with the macroeconomic management of demand. To the extent that planners like Coombs turned their mind to
the idea of the labour exchange, it was to recognise its more limited role as a mechanism for reducing frictional unemployment, as well as facilitating the mobility
of labour in a way that would discipline workers in a full employment economy.
The kinds of state intervention that the Keynesian planners were pursuing were
more focused on quantitative analysis of spending, consumption and investment.
Whether a lack of effective demand would manifest itself as the total inactivity
of a few or the underemployment and irregular work of the many – the issue of
labour market organisation that had preoccupied Booth and Beveridge – was left
unexamined. But the Directorate of Manpower's contribution to the White Paper,
growing out of its wartime experience in the direction of labour, was to highlight
a more proactive role for the Employment Service, indicated by activities involving training, vocational guidance and more general manpower planning. This
in turn meant greater promotion of the Service, the expertise it could offer, and
its preferred profile within the labour market, resulting in a stronger statement
as to the continued post-war role of the new Service than Coombs and others
had originally envisaged. The evolution of Australia's White Paper supports
William Walters' contention that the new Keynesian approach to securing full

[48] J Harris, *Unemployment and Politics: A Study in English Social Policy, 1886–1914* (Oxford, Oxford
University Press, 1972) 11.

[49] As William Walters points out, there was no entry for 'the unemployed' in the index to Keynes'
General Theory. On the novelty of the Keynesian approach in the British context, see Walters' discussion
in *Unemployment and Government: Genealogies of the Social* (Cambridge, Cambridge University Press,
2000) 100–05.

[50] WH Beveridge, *Full Employment in a Free Society* (London, Allen & Unwin, 1944) 106.

employment did not supplant the role of the labour exchange in organising the labour market, but took shape alongside it.[51]

In particular, the preoccupation of pre-war reformers with clarifying the boundary between employment and unemployment survived into the post-war period because it became a central issue in the administration of a new system of unemployment benefits. The new Commonwealth Employment Service had managed to secure itself a key role in adjudicating what was seen as the perennial problem of unemployment relief schemes: making the crucial distinction between the genuinely unemployed and the malingerer.

[51] Walters, above n 49, 103.

5

Unemployment in a Time
of Full Employment

By the middle of 1945, Australia's Labor government had introduced the first federal unemployment benefit scheme and was publicly committed to establishing the country's first peacetime national labour exchange. The Commonwealth Employment Service (CES) was established under the Re-establishment and Employment Act 1945 (Cth) and commenced operations in May 1946. Guy Anderson, a member of the Australian Council of Trade Unions (ACTU) executive, wrote a piece on 'The Benefits of the CES to the Trade Unionist' which he authorised Labour and National Service to use as it saw fit for the purposes of publicity. In it, he contrasted the 'old scramble for jobs ... and much time tramping from job to job' that existed prior to the war with the wartime arrangement of registering with National Service Offices, an arrangement whereby 'the unsatisfactory pre-war features of the engagement of labour were largely eliminated'. The CES would replicate this efficiency in job search. Anderson concluded:

> My experience is that the happiest person in the community is the man who is employed on congenial work in keeping with his ability, whilst the most dissatisfied person is one who follows the job, hangs around the factory gates, and is unable to gain suitable employment ... Unionists, the CES is a free service – use it in your own interests.[1]

Anderson's touchstone was the pre-war labour market, characterised by small enterprises reliant on pools of seasonal and casual labour. The CES would commence operations in a radically different type of labour market. And the CES's role in administering the new unemployment benefit scheme would help to define the boundaries of 'unemployment' and legitimate job search, reflecting a new, mid-century understanding of employment relationships.

The Post-War Labour Market

As we saw in chapter one, the first decades of the twentieth century saw increasing numbers of wage-dependent workers brought under the jurisdiction and

---

[1] 'The Commonwealth Employment Service and Its Public Relations', 5 March 1946, National Archives of Australia, Series B550/0, Item No 46/27A/112 Pt 1 – 'CES Publicity at inception and in immediate post war years'.

determinations of the Commonwealth Court of Conciliation and Arbitration. From the 1920s, the Court adopted a policy of stabilising and standardising many of the conditions of the employment relationship, favouring full-time, weekly hiring over casual hire, with accrued entitlements to recreation leave and limitations on the employer's right to temporarily stand down workers. This led to a de facto type of 'permanent' employment.

But the generalisation of this employment model depended on developments that were as much economic and social as legal. The Second World War had boosted the size and scale of manufacturing in Australia and helped employers realise the benefits of planned production, product standardisation and economies of scale. The proportion of metal workers, for example, in small establishments of 100 hands or fewer fell from 42 per cent in 1935–36 to 24 per cent in 1942–43.[2] By 1945 the combined effects of depression and wartime rationing also meant many Australian households had endured 15 years of austerity, despite the fact that the war years – in particular, the incorporation of many women into the labour market – had seen household purchasing power increase. The resulting pent-up demand fuelled a post-war boom in car, home and appliance ownership. Trade barriers ensured much of this demand was met by domestic manufacturers, or by foreign-based manufacturers setting up Australian-based enterprises. This ensured the wartime modernisation and expansion of manufacturing continued into the post-war period.

The new mass market for generic, standardised products resulted in changes in the labour process. Vertically integrated enterprises took on long production runs, limited to repetitive and standardised tasks within established rhythms.[3] Mass production for mass markets offered the organisational capacity to manage risk and to maintain minimum revenue in the face of market fluctuations, in turn enabling more enterprises to offer stable employment to a substantial workforce.[4] In fact, in this new environment, stable employment underpinned by the open-ended employment contract offered employers distinct advantages over earlier forms of labour hire. It enabled employers to contract for future availability of labour, often with firm-specific skills, when they knew roughly what kind of work would need to be undertaken but were unable to specify precisely what tasks should be done. Workers in turn were willing to give management the authority to specify future tasks, within certain limits, in return for a stable wage.[5] One indicator of employment being increasingly absorbed within the corporate form, rather than transacted for on a task basis in the market, is the decline in the proportion

---

[2] T Sheridan, *Mindful Militants: The Amalgamated Engineering Union in Australia 1920–1972* (Cambridge, Cambridge University Press, 1975) 146 – although the proportion engaged in small-scale enterprises rose again in the immediate post-war years: ibid, 164.

[3] C Wright, *The Management of Labour: A History of Australian Employers* (Melbourne, Oxford University Press, 1995) 50–65.

[4] R Salais, 'Labour Conventions, Economic Fluctuations and Flexibility' in M Storper and A Scott (eds), *Pathways to Industrialization and Regional Development* (London, Routledge, 1992).

[5] D Marsden, *A Theory of Employment Systems: Micro-Foundations of Societal Diversity* (Oxford, Oxford University Press, 1999) 22.

of 'own account' workers, from 16 per cent of the workforce in 1921 to 8 per cent in 1966.[6]

The usefulness of the open-ended employment contract as a means of ensuring availability of workers was reinforced in post-war Australia by the emergence of an extremely tight labour market.[7] The offer of long-term stable employment, greater job security, rewards for seniority, common enterprise policies with company-wide job descriptions and procedures, and centralised personnel departments that regularised both external hiring and internal promotion were all seen as ways to attract and retain all grades of labour and to reduce industrial unrest resulting from trade unions' increased bargaining power.[8]

Such standard, company-wide rules tended to suit a labour process – both manual and clerical – that was increasingly routinised around rationalised 'work stations', substitutable as between one worker and another. Yet while this form of employment relationship gave employers a certain level of flexibility, it also limited the scope for adjustments. Short-term fluctuations could be managed through the build-up of inventory; in the case of more serious downturns those older forms of labour management, such as work rationing, the hiring and discharge of casual labour, and wage rate adjustments, were harder to implement. So adjustments in response to severe fluctuations tended to take place around the number of 'work stations' occupied, with downturns managed primarily through redundancy. While many personnel management functions were internalised, ultimately more severe fluctuations were externalised through the dismissal of workers and the severance of the employment contract.

Statistics: Counting Unemployment

The post-war period saw a major break in the way unemployment was defined and counted in Australia, a break first proclaimed in the Commonwealth Census of 1947 and consolidated in a more frequent sample-based population survey instituted in 1964. These surveys utilised the idea of the 'labour force' to schematically

---

[6] RW Connell and TH Irving, *Class Structure in Australian History: Documents, Narrative and Argument* (Melbourne, Longman Cheshire, 1980) 294.

[7] The *Bulletin of Industrial Practice and Personnel Management*, issued by the Department of Labour and National Service, carried over a dozen articles focusing on the problems of high labour turnover in the six years from 1945.

[8] See Wright, above n 3, 50–65. For a good case study of a large firm's response to the tight post-war labour market, see C Fahey and J Lack, 'Working at Sunshine: A Case Study of the Recruitment and Management of Labour in a Melbourne Manufacturing Enterprise, 1946–63' (2006) 90 *Labour History* 95. Another response, prevalent in the automotive and steel industries, was to rely on a steady stream of newly-arrived immigrant labour to address the problem of high turnover: C Lever-Tracy and M Quinlan, *A Divided Working Class: Ethnic Segmentation and Industrial Conflict in Australia* (London, Routledge & Kegan Paul, 1988) 103, 196–7; R Tierney, 'The Pursuit of Serviceable Labour in Australian Capitalism: The Economic and Political Contexts of Immigration Policy in the Early Fifties, with Particular Reference to Southern Italians' (1998) 74 *Labour History* 137.

divide the population into three mutually exclusive categories: the employed, the unemployed and those outside the labour force. The unemployed, along with the employed, are counted as 'in the labour force', as opposed to those without work and unavailable for work and who are 'outside the labour force'.

As explained in chapter two, statistical practice prior to the Second World War relied on what has been referred to as the 'gainful worker' approach. The gainful worker approach was based largely on status: that a person played a more or less stable occupational role throughout their life, irrespective of their physical or mental health and capacity to work at any given time.[9] By contrast, the labour force framework focused on behaviour or activity. In doing so, it had a temporal dimension. Rather than describing a person's usual activity, it sought to describe a person's actual labour force activity (working or seeking work) at a certain time (during, say, a period of one week or four weeks); and it embodied a set of priority rules.[10]

The framework operated through a series of sorter questions. These tended to become more detailed and specific over time in an attempt to eliminate elements of subjective self-definition on the part of interviewees.[11] Generally, however, the questions first ascertained whether someone was working during the reference week: these were the 'employed'. Then of those not working it enquired as to whether they were available for work and looking for work. If they were, these were the 'unemployed'. All other persons were considered not to be in the labour force. This resulted in the three mutually exclusive categories mentioned above: 'employed', 'unemployed' and 'not in the labour force'. By aggregating the 'employed' and the 'unemployed', we arrive at a figure for the 'labour force'. As Gertrude Bancroft observes, the 'labour force' itself is merely a 'by product' of this sorting process: 'it has no independent definition ... Persons are not tagged as members of the labour force then queried about their employment status'.[12]

A willingness and ability to work, frustrated by impersonal economic forces beyond an individual's control, was central to this post-war understanding of unemployment. A definition that combined lack of work with the *desire* for work can be traced back to censuses undertaken in the US State of Massachusetts in 1878. The innovation of the post-war period was that such desire had to be expressed

---

[9] T Endres and M Cook, 'Concepts in Australian Unemployment Statistics to 1940' (1983) 22 *Australian Economic Papers* 68.

[10] It's also worth noting that the framework directed its attention to the activity of a certain age group – roughly those aged 15 to 65 years of age. This reflects earlier welfare state interventions in many industrialised nations that defined the acceptable span of working life: compulsory schooling and restrictions on child labour in the last decades of the nineteenth century; age pension provisions in the first decades of the twentieth century.

[11] F Di Giorgio and A Endres, 'The Changing Fortunes of CES Unemployment Statistics' (1983) 55 *The Australian Quarterly* 307, 313; J Innes, *Knowledge and Public Policy: The Search for Meaningful Indicators*, 2nd edn (New Brunswick, Transaction Publishers, 1990) 128–29.

[12] G Bancroft, *The American Labor Force: Its Growth and Changing Composition* (New York, John Wiley and Sons, 1958) 186.

through the activity of looking for work.[13] Without such activity, a person's desire for a job remained purely 'speculative'.[14] Then there remained scope for continued redefinition according to the vigour of a person's job search. For example, the 1966 Census directed that the following activities counted as 'looking for work': registration with the CES; approaching prospective employers; placing or answering advertisements; and writing letters of application. In contrast, registering only with private employment agencies or at trade union offices, reading the 'positions vacant' columns, or asking among friends and family did not count as looking for work. This exclusion of registration at private agencies most likely reflected both a widely held view that such agencies were not legitimate labour market actors, indicated by a long antipathy towards them by bodies such as the International Labour Organization (ILO), and their declining importance in placement of workers in the post-war period.[15] And although trade unions remained important channels of recruitment in many occupations well into the post-war period, they only referred registered workers to work 'in the trade', and so registration with a trade union seriously curtailed the search for 'work' more generally.

Finally, by posing the sorter questions in the order that it does, the labour force framework also prioritises certain activities over others. Rather than recording a respondent's predominant activity at a point in time, labour force activities take priority over non-labour force activities, and having a job takes priority over looking for a job.[16] To take an example used by one post-war commentator, a young woman might do five hours of babysitting during a survey week and spend 25 hours job-hunting: she would be classified as 'employed'.[17] This contrasts with the gainful worker approach where people could choose their own social definition based on their 'usual' or predominant activity.

The 1947 Census Statistician's Report declared that the gainful worker approach was being superseded by the 'labour or workforce approach ... defined primarily on the basis of activities during a stated period'.[18] However, the 1947, 1954 and 1961 censuses only imperfectly mirrored the labour force approach. The 1947 Census made provision for a category 'not at work' but 'usually engaged in work' and within this category distinguished between people 'out of a job ... [and] ... not at present seeking a job' on the one hand, and those 'able and willing to work but unable to secure employment' on the other. It was the latter group which were

---

[13] K Hancock, et al, *Report of the Advisory Committee on Commonwealth Employment Service Statistics* (Melbourne, Australian Government Publishing Service 1973) para 2.2.

[14] Bancroft, above n 12, 187.

[15] A O'Donnell and R Mitchell, 'The Regulation of Public and Private Employment Agencies in Australia: A Historical Perspective' (2001) 23 *Comparative Labor Law & Policy Journal* 7.

[16] Bancroft, above n 12, 192–93.

[17] J Steinke, 'Some Problems in the Measurement of Unemployment' (1969) 11 *Journal of Industrial Relations* 39, 42.

[18] Census of the Commonwealth of Australia 1947, *vol III: Statistician's Report* (Canberra, Commonwealth Government Printer, 1952) 179.

defined as 'unemployed', apparently on the basis of their job-seeking activity. Yet despite this activity-based definition of unemployment, the figure for 'Total in Workforce' was obtained simply by aggregating the 'at work' and 'not at work' groups, even though the second category included not just the unemployed but also those out of a job who were not seeking a job.[19] In the 1954 and 1961 census reports, the category of 'not at work' was replaced with the specific heading of 'unemployment', but still included both those 'able and willing to work' *plus* those 'not at present actively seeking a job'.[20]

So despite a stated determination to define labour force status on the basis of economic 'activity' (either working or looking for work),[21] the total 'workforce' reported in these censuses included inactive persons.[22] The problem appears to be that the form of enquiry in many ways still mirrored that of pre-war censuses. The starting point was a notion of the 'workforce' defined by people's usual activity, rather than allowing a concept of 'labour force' to emerge as the final product from a series of sorter questions about a person's current actual activity.

It was not until the instigation of the Labour Force Survey in 1964 and then the 1966 Census that a notion of a 'labour force' defined according to labour market 'activity' became settled. The distinction between the unemployed being 'in the labour force' and others not at work as being 'out of the labour force' was now clear. The labour force or workforce figure was obtained by aggregating those people with a job or business; those that did any work at all;[23] those without work and who looked for work; and those temporarily laid off. Those who fell into either or both of the last two categories were considered 'unemployed'. This new definition of unemployment excluded those out of work and not looking for work because of accident, illness, strike or lockout. In short, employed people were those with jobs while the unemployed were those who did no work at all but were looking for work, or whose search for work was postponed because they expected to be called back to their job.[24]

So why did the labour force approach, however imperfectly realised, begin to displace the gainful worker approach when it did?

---

[19] ibid 237.

[20] ibid 196; Census of the Commonwealth of Australia 1961, *vol VIII: Statistician's Report* (Canberra, Commonwealth Government Printer, 1967) 244.

[21] Census of the Commonwealth of Australia 1954, *vol VIII: Statistician's Report* (Canberra, Commonwealth Government Printer, 1962) 197.

[22] However, the reports admitted that the category of 'not at work' did not 'represent the number of unemployed available for work and unable to obtain it': *Statistician's Report*, 1954 Census, 221; *Statistician's Report*, 1961 Census, 292.

[23] Even as unpaid helpers in the family farm, or members of religious orders – although members of purely contemplative orders were excluded.

[24] 'The net effect of this new definition ... [was] ... a proportionate increase in the Australian workforce of approximately 2.3 per cent. The major factor in this change was females working part-time (sometimes only a few hours a week) some of whom in 1961, did not consider themselves as "engaged in an industry, business, profession, trade or service"': *Census of Population and Housing, 30 June 1966*, Volume 1, Part 8 (Canberra, Commonwealth Bureau of Census and Statistics, 1969–73) 7.

One explanation is that Australia simply fell into line with what was recognised as 'modern Census practice'.[25] In 1947, the ILO's Conference on Labour Statistics had endorsed the labour force approach to measuring unemployment.[26] In doing so, the conference was endorsing and adopting an approach that had been pioneered in the United States in the 1930s. In the 1937 Enumerative Census Check, all non-workers who in the United States Census had expressed a desire to work were asked if they were able to work and were actively seeking work. This was the first national sample survey that defined unemployment on the basis of activity undertaken in the previous week.[27] This approach was then adopted by the Works Progress Administration in subsequent monthly sample surveys called the Monthly Report of the Labour Force (MRLF). The MRLF questions were then more or less replicated in the US population census of 1940.

The context for all this was a Democrat agenda for a nationally organised policy to fight unemployment through job creation schemes.[28] The advantage of the labour force approach over the gainful worker approach was that it provided a way to measure the 'immediate unmet demand for work under prevailing conditions', rather than trying to measure some potential labour reserve.[29] A notion of 'unemployment' that excluded both those who might have become jobseekers under different economic conditions and those who had done any work whatsoever gave a figure that 'equated with the minimum number of jobs needed'.[30] In effect, the definition of unemployment that arose from the labour force framework and its sorter questions was driven by pragmatic decisions about how unemployment relief should best be targeted. Rather than a settled definition of unemployment being the necessary precursor to any policy response to joblessness, the preferred policy response itself generated a particular definition of unemployment.

A further explanation for the emergence of the labour force approach in Australia in the post-war period is hinted at by the discussion in the preceding section. Not only did the labour force approach have a better fit with the type of policy interventions that emerged in the US New Deal, it was also more appropriate for the type of labour market and type of employment relations that were consolidated in post-war Australia. Arguably, the gainful worker approach,

---

[25] Census of the Commonwealth of Australia 1947, *Statistician's Report* 179.

[26] ILO, *Employment, Unemployment and Labour Force Statistics: A Study of Methods* (Geneva, ILO Studies and Reports, New Series, No 7, Part 1, 1948); ILO, The Sixth International Conference of Labour Statisticians, Montreal, 4–12 August 1947 (Geneva, ILO Studies and Reports, New Series, No 7, Part 4, 1948).

[27] D Card, 'Origins of the Unemployment Rate: The Lasting Legacy of Measurement Without Theory' (paper prepared for the 2011 meetings of the American Economic Association) 6.

[28] A Desrosieres, *The Politics of Large Numbers: A History of Statistical Reasoning* (Cambridge, MA, Harvard University Press, 1998) 202. See also S Moses, 'Labour Supply Concepts: The Political Economy of Conceptual Change' (1975) 418 *Annals of the American Academy of Political and Social Sciences* 26.

[29] P Baxandall, *Constructing Unemployment: The Politics of Joblessness in East and West* (Aldershot, Ashgate, 2004) 181.

[30] Bancroft, above n 12, 185; see also Innes, above n 11, 129, 186.

focusing on a person's usual occupation rather than their activity in any given week, better suited the intermittency of employment that prevailed in many sectors prior to the war. Post-war, this picture had begun to change. Rather than respond to fluctuations in demand by way of the old practices of work rationing or the hiring and discharge of casual workers, large rationalised enterprises increasingly 'externalised' idle labour time.[31] This post-war labour market enabled statisticians and administrators to conceive of unemployment in terms of the formal severance of one contract and a worker's availability for rehiring at another enterprise, rather than there being pools of casual labour within specific trades or localities or workers maintaining connection with an enterprise during downturns through short-time working and underemployment. Unemployment became 'visible' in a way that it hadn't been prior to the war. Conversely, underemployment was minimised and, in any case, remained invisible within the labour force framework and the set of priorities established through its sorter questions.

Finally, the notion that unemployment should involve some sort of labour market activity – that is, seeking work – also aligned with another major development in the regulation of joblessness in the post-war period: the inauguration of a system of unemployment benefits.

The Work Test: Regulating Unemployment

Once the Unemployment and Sickness Benefit Act 1944 was passed into law, it remained to finalise the rules that would guide CES officers in determining eligibility for the new benefit. Section 15(c)(ii) and (iii) of the Act required that the Director-General of Social Services satisfy himself that a claimant for unemployment benefit was unemployed and was 'capable of undertaking and willing to undertake work which, in the opinion of the Director-General, is suitable to be undertaken by that person' and that the claimant had 'taken reasonable steps to obtain such work'. Section 28 of the Act empowered the Director-General to postpone or cancel the payment of benefit if a claimant had become 'voluntarily unemployed without good reason'; had become 'unemployed by reason of misconduct'; or had 'failed or refused without good and sufficient reason to accept an offer of employment which the Director-General considers to be suitable'. The administrative procedures intended to ensure claimants met the requirements of sections 15(c) and 28 – later sections 107(1) and 120(1) of the Social Services Consolidation Act 1947 – were referred to as the 'work test' or sometimes as the 'works test'.[32]

---

[31] M Mansfield, 'Blind Spots and Awkward Corners: "Precarisation" through the Perspective of Unemployment Construction' (paper prepared for the 11th biennial French Sociology of Work Conference, London Metropolitan University, 20–22 June 2007); Salais, above n 4.

[32] The relationship between the eligibility conditions set out in s 15 on the one hand, and the postponement or cancellation penalties for various types of 'voluntary' unemployment in s 28 on the other, is not entirely clear. The sequencing of the provisions suggests that s 28 is meant to come into

Writing about the administration of the work test at the beginning of the 1980s, Alan Jordan concluded that the function or objective of the test was to distinguish the person 'who is a current although unemployed member of the labour force from the person who, although jobless, is not'.[33] Yet this begs the question as to why we define unemployed people as members of the labour force in the first place. As we've seen, the 'labour force' approach to unemployment was not operationalised in Australian statistical measurement until the 1947 Commonwealth Census – that is, *after* the commencement of the 1944 Act.

Rather, the work test had two stronger antecedents. One was Beveridge's concern to weed out the malingerer – not by the principle of 'lesser eligibility', but by a system of administrative surveillance that the labour exchange made possible. As noted in chapter four, a similar concern was expressed by government officials proposing an unemployment benefit system in Australia in the early 1940s. The second antecedent was the idea of 'voluntary unemployment' that arose most clearly in the debates around social insurance. But voluntariness as a qualifying condition was never limited to insurance-based schemes. The original old age and disability pensions legislation in Australia tended to disqualify claimants who were somehow responsible for their current circumstances. Claimants for invalid pension, for example, were disqualified where their incapacity was self-induced 'with a view to obtaining a pension'.[34] Similarly, widows pension supported widowed and deserted wives, but not unwed mothers. The administration of emergency unemployment relief during the 1930's Depression similarly incorporated a set of conditions that disqualified claimants who had refused offers of work 'without reasonable excuse'.[35]

The first thing to note about the work test as enacted in 1944 is that it was expressed in relatively strong terms. A work test had been at the core of Britain's unemployment insurance scheme, but it merely spoke of 'availability' for work. Britain had instituted a test based on 'actively seeking full-time work' in 1921, but it was dropped in 1930. Beveridge saw the 'actively seeking work' formula as undermining his original vision for labour exchanges as it would drive men back into the 'hawking of labour' and 'fruitless journeys' for work outside the ambit of the exchange.[36] The Australian legislation, by insisting, as a condition of

---

effect where the claimant otherwise satisfies the eligibility conditions set out in the earlier section. Nevertheless, refusal of a job offer, for example, could be sanctioned either by refusal of benefit under s 15 (that is an unwillingness to work or a failure to take reasonable steps to find work), or be taken as grounds for the postponement of a new claim or as grounds to cancel an existing benefit under s 28. Similarly, failure to follow up a referral to a vacancy from the CES could be sanctioned under either head (clearly, failure to follow up a referral does not amount to a refusal of an offer of employment, but could be construed as a voluntary act contributing to a person's unemployment). The relationship between the provisions – and departmental practice in the 1980s – is further discussed in ch 7.

[33] A Jordan, *Work-Test Failure: A Sample Survey of Terminations of Unemployment Benefit* (Canberra, Department of Social Security, 1981) 6–7.

[34] Invalid and Old Age Pension Act 1908 (Cth) s 22(d).

[35] See, eg, Unemployment Relief (Administration) Act 1932 (Vic) s 7(1)(b).

[36] WH Beveridge, *Unemployment: A Problem of Industry* (London, Longmans Green and Co, 1931 [1909])) 280. The British government reintroduced an 'actively seeking employment' requirement in 1989: Social Security Act 1989 (UK) s 12.

benefit, on 'reasonable steps' to find work, sought to more actively mobilise the unemployed as a source of labour supply. In effect, by mobilising the unemployed as clear participants 'in the labour market', it provided the juridical and institutional underpinning for the labour force framework that would come to dominate national economic statistics.

A second point is that the legislative articulation of a work test, couched in broad terms of 'suitable' work and 'reasonable' steps, allowed both an inevitable degree of discretion in application at the District Office level, and considerable scope for the government of the day to expand or contract its requirements, according to prevailing labour market conditions or social mores. This could be achieved by altering administrative criteria without changing the legislative provisions themselves.[37] Indeed, there was no major legislative amendment to the test until the late 1980s but, as we'll see, there was considerable alteration to the way the work test was administered both across time and between District Offices.

In March 1945 the Director-General of Manpower, William Funnell, in his communications with HC Coombs concerning the drafting of the White Paper, had already recognised the particular set of demands that would arise regarding peacetime employment policy. Commenting on the draft of the White Paper that Coombs had circulated to all departments, Funnell thought that 'the difficulties of a full employment policy [had] been somewhat understated'. In particular, from the perspective of Manpower, the draft White Paper's principal omission was 'the failure to state the difficult social and administrative problems involved in the achievement of a high employment policy and the provision of unemployment benefits'. These problems included getting workers to accept 'uncongenial employment'; inducing workers to engage in public works in remote locations; and the 'social and industrial difficulties of obtaining a satisfactory balance between male and female employment'.[38] In short, having anticipated the emergence of a full employment economy – whether by circumstance or design – the problem for the government now became one of disciplining labour under such conditions. For this reason, as Funnell noted in a communication to the Director-General of Social Services, FH Rowe, 'specification of the works test has considerable political as well as administrative significance and I quite agree with your proposal that Ministerial approval should be obtained for whatever formula is ultimately decided upon'.[39] As envisaged by the White Paper, the CES provided a country-wide

---

[37] In practice, this took the form of roughly quinquennial updates to the DSS district office procedure manual which incorporated accumulated instructions and circulars emanating from head office: A Law, 'Idlers, Loafers and Layabouts: An Historical Sociological Study of Welfare Discipline and Unemployment in Australia' (PhD thesis, University of Alberta, 1993) 81. The malleable nature of the legislative provisions was identified as problematic by various commentators: see Commonwealth of Australia, *Unemployment Benefit Policy and Administration: Report of Inquiry*, Parl Paper No 243 (1977) para 4.11.11; and later the Federal Court in *Director-General of Social Services v Thomson* (1982) 53 FLR 356, 361.

[38] Funnell to Coombs, 13 March 1945, National Archives of Australia, Series B551, Item No 45/78/12162, 'White Paper on Full Employment'.

[39] Funnell to Rowe, 29 March 1945, National Archives of Australia, Series B551, Item No 43/101/5246, 'Unemployment and Sickness Benefits Act, Administration of'.

register of both jobseekers and vacancies and made possible a fluid, national labour market. Now, by administering the work test, it could compel workers' mobility across that labour market.

In December 1945, federal Cabinet considered the works test formula. Jack Holloway, Minister for Labour and National Service, and Richard Keane, acting Minister for Health and Social Services, had made a joint submission. They recognised that, up to this point, unemployment had been negligible, but cited evidence of:

(a)   An increase in local unemployment in districts where purely wartime activity was responsible for an 'abnormal' high level of employment absorbing nearly all local labour.
(b)   Approaching seasonal slackness in those districts where seasonal industries predominated, such as the north Queensland meat and sugar industries.
(c)   A dimunition of job prospects in certain trades.
(d)   A disinclination by workers to accept available employment less attractive than those to which they had become accustomed during the war.

What was sought was a precise work test formula 'consistent with the government's policy of creating conditions designed to secure a high and stable level of employment' and with 'the government's conception of social justice'; but one that also guarded against 'abuse of a social service and consequent heavy expenditure from the National Welfare Fund' and didn't jeopardise the planned national works programme due to a lack of workers prepared to move geographically. Holloway and Keane warned that any formula that allowed able-bodied persons to receive benefit while vacancies for suitable work waited to be filled would not only be inconsistent with these principles but 'would have a profound effect on the social structure'.[40]

Cabinet resolved that all applicants for benefit would be required to register with the CES and to accept any suitable work available that was offered them. As the legislation made clear, failure to accept such work would render them ineligible for benefit. A lot hinged, then, on the understanding of what counted as 'suitable work', a concept not spelled out in the legislation. Cabinet approved the following approaches, which subsequently were incorporated into the 1949 District Office Manual of the CES.[41] Employment which was not covered by an award or collective agreement was not considered suitable unless it carried remuneration at least equivalent to the recognised rate. Male claimants under 19 years of age, female claimants under 21, claimants residing with dependent children, claimants residing with a pregnant wife or claimants who were themselves pregnant were able to

---

[40] Unemployment and Sickness Benefit Circular No 8, 2 January 1946, National Archives of Australia, Series MP 243/3.

[41] ibid. See also CES, *District Office Manual*, January 1949, section 10,004.

refuse employment which would involve living away from home, unless they were accustomed to undertaking such employment, and all claimants were entitled to refuse work that involved living away from home where the 'conditions and amenities' did not reach the standards usually applying to that type of employment. However, claimants would be disqualified where work was not available of the type for which they possessed particular experience or qualifications, or for which they had indicated a personal preference, and the claimant had refused to accept other employment which the District Employment Office considered suitable, even should such employment require working outside a trade calling or transfer of union membership.[42]

The administration of the work test in this way attempted to delineate an understanding of *involuntary* unemployment: that is, unemployment as an impersonal economic condition, beyond the control of the individual. But, as indicated by Holloway and Keane's Cabinet submission, it did so in a specific labour market and social context. The test attempted to inculcate an industrial discipline consistent with the drive for national development, along with a tight labour market and enhanced worker bargaining power. But the test also took into account certain labour standards – the prevalence of award rates – and certain social mores, particularly the value placed on preservation of 'home' life for the traditional family unit.

The way that the work test pivoted on the notion of 'suitable work' indicates the mutually constitutive relationship between notions of employment and unemployment. Involuntary unemployment can be seen as a social and cultural practice and norm in part constituted by Australia's prevailing system of labour regulation.[43] That is, unemployment did not refer to an inability to find *any* work but an inability to find work under conditions laid down by regulation. The idea of 'involuntary' unemployment therefore clearly still embodied a right to refuse work under certain conditions.

However, whereas trade union out-of-work schemes made it possible for an unemployed person to hold out for a job in their own occupation or trade, under customary conditions, the work test in Australia meant the unemployed could be directed to take up work outside their usual trade, rather than being supported while waiting for 'better' work to show up. As Funnell put it in a letter responding to a query from federal Labor parliamentarian Eddie Ward in December 1946, the result of Cabinet's approval of the work test formula (as subsequently incorporated into the 1949 Manual) was that 'a tradesman may be offered a job as a labourer if better paid employment is not available and he is not allowed Benefit if he declines to accept this position, provided the Registrar considers he is capable of undertaking labouring work'.

---

[42] Unemployment and Sickness Benefit Circular No 8, 2 January 1946, National Archives of Australia, Series MP 243/3.

[43] *cf* W Walters, *Unemployment and Government: Genealogies of the Social* (Cambridge, Cambridge University Press 2000) 64.

In practice, though, there was room for discretion at the branch office level when it came to directing unemployed workers to take up work outside their trade. In February 1952 Labor leader Bert Evatt pointed out in correspondence to the Liberal Minister for Labour and National Service, Harold Holt, that some CES officers would apply this aspect of the work test 'most ruthlessly. Others are more humane and will readily endorse the claim form "No suitable employment available". The latter, I would say are a minority'. Holt replied merely by referring to the District Office Manual as authority for the proposition that the unemployed must, in the last resort, be prepared to accept any job on offer, subject to the qualifications outlined.[44]

All this represents a shift from the notion of stable occupation embodied in the 'gainful employment' approach of pre-war censuses, to a more generic understanding of work, characteristic of both the new, emerging labour practices outlined earlier in this chapter, and an extensive system of labour regulations and standards. The work test essentially reconstructed the job search from one of looking for work 'in the trade' to a more generic search for 'work' per se. By contrast, a claimant under the UK national insurance scheme was able to refuse work outside their usual occupation for a reasonable period. According to Simon Deakin and Frank Wilkinson, this meant the condition of unemployment signified 'a status for workers who had lost regular employment through no fault of their own, and who were expected to return, after a short interval, to a similar type of regular employment'.[45] Of course, a contributory scheme meant eligible claimants necessarily could point to a 'usual' occupation; in contrast, the non-contributory Australian scheme provided for first-time entrants into the labour market who could not point to a usual occupation. Also, the existence of a national system of labour regulation, rather than locally bargained collective agreements, meant that workers could be more easily expected to be mobile across the uniform space of a protected, national labour market in their search for work. At the same time, the scope of the job search was limited in geographic terms for certain classes of workers – suggesting workers were not seen solely as interchangeable units of labour power, but were also conceived of as constrained by social context, particularly the ties of family life.

The crucial thing is to see the category of 'involuntary' unemployment as something that was administratively constructed, generated by the specific web of rights and duties put in place by an unemployment benefits scheme.[46] Rather than starting from a definition of unemployment (and there were several competing,

---

[44] National Archives of Australia, Series MP537/1, Item No 251/57/2, 'Unemployment and Sickness Benefits: Application of the Works Test 1946–1952'.

[45] S Deakin and F Wilkinson, *The Law of the Labour Market: Industrialization, Employment, and Legal Evolution* (Oxford, Oxford University Press, 2005) 167.

[46] B Studer, 'Social Policy as Gender Technology: The Social Construction of "the Unemployed" in Switzerland in the First Half of the Twentieth Century' (paper prepared for the 5th European Social Science History Conference, Berlin, 24–27 March 2004).

plausible but contested definitions),[47] there was initially a series of practical, policy related questions that needed to be addressed in any scheme of unemployment compensation. What type of work should unemployed people be expected to present themselves for? Should the search for work require the unemployed to move from their normal place of residence or did the idea of unemployment retain a reference to a local rather than a genuinely national labour market? When can a worker be taken as having caused his or her own unemployment? In a country with a strong and extensive trade union movement and compulsory arbitration, what role was there for norms around pay and conditions and industrial disputation in an understanding of unemployment? The work test and its administration represented the detailed working out of these questions, and gave birth to a particular, contingent notion of unemployment.

Unemployment and Industrial Disputes

One of the key features of trade union out-of-work benefits was the practice of giving financial support to workers engaged in industrial disputes. This was not reflected in the new unemployment benefit scheme. Section 15(c)(i) of the 1944 Act required the Director-General of Social Services to be satisfied that a claimant's unemployment was not due to direct participation in a strike. How the CES chose to administer this disqualification was an important negotiation of a key aspect of a post-war labour market riven by industrial disputes.

The role trade union benefit schemes played in industrial disputes, examined in chapter two, suggests there were in fact two related issues at stake. First, by financing those members who undertook the industrial action, the trade union schemes effectively functioned as 'strike pay' and helped the union maintain solidarity among striking members. Secondly, the provision of trade union benefits recognised that a member could be 'unemployed' despite there being work available. Whatever the availability of work, an unemployed member would not feel compelled to act as a strike breaker. The new unemployment benefit system administered by the CES had to address each of these questions: would the benefit be available to unionists stood down because of industrial action, in effect financing those workers' industrial action? And would a jobseeker refusing work at an enterprise affected by an industrial dispute be deemed as 'unemployed' and satisfying the work test?

It is not always easy to separate the two issues, or to distinguish between the differing rationales that inform discussion of them. Refusal of a job offer at an enterprise where industrial action is afoot is clearly a subset of the question of what

---

[47] See, eg, the discussion in C Long, 'The Concept of Unemployment' (1942) 57 *Quarterly Journal of Economics* 1, 2–5.

counts as 'voluntary' as opposed to 'involuntary' unemployment. It is tempting to conceive of the trade dispute disqualification outlined in section 15(c)(i) as merely one other aspect of whether a striking worker could be thought of as having 'voluntarily' made themselves unemployed.[48] But the disqualification is better thought of as having its own rationale. That is, it derives from the principle that the authorities administering unemployment benefits should remain neutral in industrial relations. This was particularly the case where benefits were funded out of an insurance fund administered jointly by workers, employers and the state, but the principle remained applicable to the case where the fund was solely funded by the state. The principle could be extended by analogy to bodies such as the public employment service: the service was seen as meeting the needs of both employers and workers and so could not be seen to be taking sides when the interests of those groups were opposed.

The general point was recognised quite early on in the development of government labour bureaux.[49] However, the principle of state neutrality can be interpreted and put into practice in different ways. William Beveridge thought labour exchanges wanting to maintain neutrality in industrial disputes were presented with three options. The first was to ignore strikes and lockouts altogether, filling vacancies and referring jobseekers without drawing any special attention to the fact of the strike or lockout. The second was to suspend the operations of the exchange within the trade and district affected by the dispute. The third was not to refuse to fill vacancies, but to refer jobseekers to vacancies subject to a warning to applicants that the vacancies arose from an industrial dispute.[50]

It was this third course that was followed by the CES in its placement activity. The CES continued to receive and record all requests for labour notified by an employer at whose establishment there was a strike. All jobseekers using the Service were to be informed of all vacancies for which they were qualified and suitable, but were also to be told when those vacancies had arisen due to strikes or black bans. In such a case, the acceptance of the employment was then to be entirely a matter between the applicant and the employer: the applicant was not to be influenced by CES staff either for or against accepting such work. The CES's neutrality here depended on process. If the applicant were to accept the referral to the vacancy, they were to be given no introductory slip from the Service, nor any assistance with transport to the interview. Rather disingenuously, the applicant, despite having just been notified of the vacancy by the Service, was to be 'regarded as having obtained the employment of his own initiative'.[51]

---

[48] See, eg, the justification given by Sir John Simon, one of the architects of the British unemployment insurance scheme, cited in KD Ewing, *The Right to Strike* (Oxford, Clarendon Press, 1991) 64.

[49] See the discussion on the establishment of the British exchange in D King, *Actively Seeking Work? The Politics of Unemployment and Welfare Policy in the United States and Great Britain* (Chicago, IL, University of Chicago Press, 1995) 41 ff.

[50] Beveridge, above n 36, 299.

[51] CES, *District Office Manual*, January 1949, section 4400.

In its attempt to maintain neutrality, the quid pro quo for the CES was to not consider vacancies arising as a result of a dispute to be 'suitable work' for the purposes of determining eligibility for benefit. In practice, then, the doctrine of 'neutrality' in industrial disputes inevitably became entangled with the administration of the work test and the policing of 'involuntary' unemployment.

These issues had to be confronted quite early in the CES's life. In September 1945 the dismissal of an employee at Australian Iron and Steel, Port Kembla, led to one of the biggest industrial upheavals since the First World War.[52] The initial action involved 2,400 steel operatives going on strike. They were subsequently joined by 700 workers from John Lysaght and Company and another 500 from Commonwealth Rolling Mills, in addition to workmen from three coalmines belonging to Australian Iron and Steel. Employers across several industries were forced to stand men down. Senator Keane, the acting Minister for Social Services, advised the Federated Ironworkers' Association (FIA) that unemployment benefit would be paid to workers stood down and to those workers refusing to perform the duties of a position vacated by a striking worker. But the striking workers themselves would not be paid benefit, in accordance with section 15(c)(i).[53]

The question of participation in a strike was complicated where a union called out certain 'key men', a tactic that could result in the paralysis of an enterprise and the stand down of practically all employees. The FIA used this tactic at Lysaghts in March 1946, calling out 41 men, which resulted in the stand down of 1,700 employees. James Fraser, the Minister for Social Services, advised Cabinet that the payment of unemployment benefit to the 1,700 men stood down would mean the government was

> being forced into the position of financing a strike … If the Government concedes the right of the Union to call one or two members out on strike and pay U[nemployment] B[enefit] to all other members of the Union when they cease work, it would appear that the temptation to enforce industrial disputes by a powerful union will be considerably encouraged.[54]

Yet although Fraser couched the issue initially as a question of the state 'financing' a strike, he slipped from this to the language of 'voluntary' versus 'involuntary' unemployment: the question put to Cabinet was one of the collective responsibility of those employees – both members of the union and non-members – stood down as a result of a union's decision to call out 41 members. While only 41 members appeared to be 'directly' participating in a strike, had the stood-down employees become 'voluntarily' unemployed by virtue of the decision of their union sub-branch?

---

[52] T Sheridan, *Division of Labour: Industrial Relations in the Chifley Years, 1945–1949* (Melbourne, Oxford University Press, 1989) 90.

[53] Cabinet Agendum 1127, prepared by JM Fraser, Minister for Social Services, 21 March 1946, discussed at Cabinet 2 April 1946, National Archives of Australia, Series B 550/0, Item No 46/48/195, 'Payment of Unemployment Benefit During Industrial Disputes'.

[54] ibid.

A sub-committee of Cabinet thought the issue of 'key man' strikes be best addressed by amending section 15 of the Act so that a worker would be disqualified from benefit if he or she were 'one of a class or body of employees', any of the members of which were direct participants in a strike at the establishment at which that person is employed and which resulted in the unemployment of that person. At the same time, the proposed amendment would insert a specific clause stating that a person would not be disqualified from receiving benefit 'by reason only of his refusal to undertake work which has become available by reason of a strike' or lockout. In short, Cabinet believed the first proposal would deal with the Lysaght situation, while the second would incorporate the principle 'approved by the Government when the Bill was before Parliament, to ensure that a person would not be deprived of benefit solely because he would not act as a strike breaker'.[55]

Holloway, still Minister for Labour and National Service, opposed the amendment, but ultimately a similar proposal became incorporated into social service practice when a Cabinet sub-committee again considered the issue in April 1947. The following year a ministerial direction to the Department of Social Services noted that trade unions had been represented at a conference with the Minister and all had 'accepted the principle that the Commonwealth could not permit unemployment benefit to be used for financing strikes'. Apart from this, the union deputation was informed by the Minister that 'no hard and fast rule should be laid down to cover cases where a strike of key worker unionists in one industry threw out of work members of the same union in another industry but that all the circumstances would have to be taken into account', including the conduct of the union and its executive.[56]

A principle of 'collective responsibility' is sometimes invoked as justification for extending the disqualification beyond direct participants in a strike to members of the same union or people with a direct interest in a dispute. That was not the paramount issue here.[57] Rather, it was the government's desire to thwart unions using 'key worker' strikes to leverage de facto strike pay from the unemployment benefit system. Furthermore, any principle of collective responsibility was difficult to reconcile with the preoccupation as to whether an individual's unemployment was voluntary or involuntary. The question of 'voluntary' versus 'involuntary' unemployment was already muddied by the fact that the notion of 'suitable' employment gave some scope for the 'voluntary' refusal of a job in circumstances where jobs on offer were in some way sub-standard. The question of voluntary unemployment does not in itself require that benefit be refused to

[55] ibid.

[56] Commonwealth of Australia, *Parliamentary Debates*, House of Representatives, 11 April 1972, 1403–05.

[57] The collective responsibility principle was not explicitly incorporated into the administration of the benefit scheme until 1979: see Social Services Amendment Act 1979 (Cth) and the discussion in JC Tham, 'Industrial Action and Unemployment Income Support' (2002) 15 *Australian Journal of Labour Law* 40, 44–47.

workers on strike if they are on strike because working conditions make their work somehow unsuitable.[58] Rather, the industrial dispute disqualification is best thought of as more clearly related to the issue of state neutrality than to that of voluntary unemployment.

The issue is further complicated where a union had imposed a black ban on certain work or where a 'go-slow' had been imposed. In the first case, Social Services determined that no benefit would be payable where the union had declared a job 'black' after men had been stood down. In the second case, men stood down because of the imposition of a 'go-slow' would be refused benefit because of 'misconduct' as workers.

So, for example, during a 'go-slow' campaign by workers at the Intercolonial Boring Company in Brisbane in late 1946, Social Services had decided that workers stood down for adopting 'go-slow' tactics 'were to be adjudged guilty of misconduct as workers and have payment of [unemployment] benefit postponed'. Further, the postponement was to continue as long as the work from which they had been stood down remained available to them at the normal rate and they refused it. In short, Social Services wanted the work test administered in such a way that workers would only be offered their old job and, on refusal, be denied benefit. This raised direct problems in the eyes of the CES. Funnell suggested to the Director-General of Social Services that such an approach

> appears to indicate some misapprehension on the part of your officers ... as to responsibility for application of the Works test and, apart from that, an attitude which, in my opinion, should not under any circumstances prevail. In application by officers of the CES ... the practice is to offer an applicant any work available consistent with his qualifications, experience, etc, ie, the offer is not limited to one particular job, but is extended to all suitable vacancies. Only if the applicant refuses to accept, without good and sufficient reason, such offers of employment does the question of penalty (ie, postponement etc) arise. It is clear to me that to limit opportunities of employment to only one job would not be in accordance with the spirit of the Act and would deny the applicant his lawful entitlements.[59]

The conflict presaged a more fundamental tension between the CES's work as a generalist placement agency and its role in administering a variety of welfare benefit. Manpower was eager that the Service operate on the basis that informed effective placement services worldwide: 'the referral to vacancies of only those applicants who are judged suitable, having regard to the employer's specifications for the vacancy'.[60] Any failure to follow this 'paramount principle' would bring 'disaster' to the CES, with the loss of confidence of employers using the Service and the progressive reduction in the number of vacancies notified to the Service.

---

[58] See L Lesser, 'Labor Disputes and Unemployment Compensation' (1945) 55 *Yale Law Journal* 167.

[59] Funnell to Rowe, 5 March 1947, National Archives of Australia, Series MP537/1, Item No 251/57/2, 'Unemployment and Sickness Benefits, Application of the Works Test 1946–1952'.

[60] Funnell to Rowe (Director-General of Social Services), 5 March 1947, ibid.

In short, it was vital that the CES follow the principles authorised by Manpower as to the placement of labour and avoid pressure from Social Services to apply the work test 'too much with a desire to reduce the number on benefit and at risk to the basic principle' enunciated above.[61]

***

There is a paradox lurking in this chapter. Australia developed an analytically and administratively sophisticated understanding of unemployment at precisely the time when there weren't that many 'unemployed' people around. For nearly three decades from the end of the Second World War Australia experienced unprecedented low rates of measured unemployment. With the exception of minor recessions in 1952/3 and 1961/2, the official unemployment rate did not exceed 2 per cent.

Perhaps this explains why scholars have shown scant interest in approaches to unemployment or the regulation of joblessness in the immediate post-war period. While commentators acknowledge the introduction of unemployment benefits in 1945 as a key moment in the development of the Australian welfare state,[62] most point to the prevailing low level of unemployment as the cause of a distinct policy inertia on the part of post-war governments. For example, Jill Roe observes that, with the exception of debates over the provision of health services, 'issues of social policy simply did not arise' due to the unprecedented industrial expansion of the time and the concomitant low take-up of unemployment benefit.[63] Similarly, Tom Kewley argues that the prevalence of full employment meant the rate of unemployment benefit remained 'of small consequence and of comparatively little political interest'.[64] In his survey of the development of Australian social security Terry Carney devotes coverage of the Menzies period overwhelmingly to a discussion of health services reform, observing that 'apart from the extension of health services ... the period to 1960 was one of mild consolidation and mild reform'.[65]

But as Martha Derthick has observed in the American context, policymaking is a combination of exciting and innovative events, *along with*

> not-so-exciting routines that are performed without widespread mobilisation, intense conflict or much awareness of what is going on except among the involved few ...

---

[61] Memo from NJ O'Heare (Deputy Director Manpower) to all District Employment Officers, 23 July 1947. As we will see, the conflict of principles would be exacerbated from the 1970s onwards when the collapse of full employment meant the simultaneous increase in the numbers of claimants requiring work testing and a decrease in job vacancies against which to test them.

[62] One of the best accounts remains R Watts, *The Foundations of the National Welfare State* (Sydney, Allen & Unwin, 1987).

[63] J Roe, 'Perspectives on the Present Day: A Postscript' in J Roe (ed), *Social Policy in Australia: Some Perspectives 1901–1975* (Sydney, Cassell Australia, 1976) 314.

[64] TH Kewley, *Social Security in Australia 1900–72* (Sydney, Sydney University Press, 1973), 281.

[65] T Carney, *Social Security Law and Policy* (Sydney, The Federation Press, 2006) 33.

[This] does not signify the absence of change, and what is routine, though it may not be interesting to analysts at a given moment, is cumulatively very important.[66]

The post-war decades were notable precisely because it was in this period that we see the emergence and consolidation in Australia of a rich and coherent discourse about unemployment – both how to define and measure it, and how to regulate the unemployed through a system of unemployment benefits. Underneath the prevailing narrative of 'not much happened', a momentous shift was taking place. And it was a shift worked out through the quite mundane practices of designing survey questions and administering an unemployment benefit scheme.

---

[66] M Derthick, *Policymaking For Social Security*, cited in P Pierson, 'The Study of Policy Development' (2005) 17 *Journal of Policy History* 34, 36.

6

Limiting Unemployment

The idea of unemployment that emerged across the twentieth century involved a regulatory two-step: distinguishing those in work from those out of work, then isolating those out of work who really wanted to work. But each step was fraught. Labour markets often tend to confound any easy distinction between working and not working, and there is no particular degree of desire for work that 'self-evidently distinguishes the unemployed from men and women who are simply not working'.[1] Writing in the British context, Noel Whiteside has made the observation that attempts to divide the labour force into two discrete categories – the 'employed' and the 'unemployed' – have often tended to ignore large numbers of people whose working lives do not allow them to be placed unproblematically in either category. She goes on to identify the post-war period as 'exceptional' precisely because such a bipolar taxonomy did manage to capture the experience of the bulk of labour market participants of that time.[2] But it could not capture everyone's experience. Bruce Curtis has similarly argued, with regard to the evolution of the Canadian census, that any statistical or administrative knowledge (such as the classification of people into the categories of 'employed' or 'unemployed') is always historically specific and, so, will be adequate for particular kinds of social formation and inadequate for others.[3] Curtis argues that statistics produce a way of knowing based on abstractions ('employed' and 'unemployed') that make it increasingly difficult to speak of the 'grounded and rich particularities of social lives'.[4] Whiteside's formulation suggests that such difficulties were minimised in the decades following the Second World War but not eliminated. These difficulties appear as essentially 'representational problems' within a particular statistical mode of knowing, as certain statistical or administrative categories struggle to

---

[1] A Keyssar, Out of Work: The First Century of Unemployment in Massachusetts (Cambridge, MA, Cambridge University Press, 1986) 342. The 2015 Canadian government manual for staff administering unemployment benefit referred to the 'sincerity' of a jobseeker's desire to end their period of unemployment as constituting 'probably the most difficult question to decide': J Grundy, Bureaucratic Manoeuvres: The Contested Administration of the Unemployed (Toronto, University of Toronto Press, 2019) 4.

[2] N Whiteside, Bad Times: Unemployment in British Social and Political History (London, Faber, 1991) 133.

[3] B Curtis, The Politics of Population: State Formation, Statistics and the Census of Canada, 1840–1875 (Toronto, University of Toronto Press, 2001) 308.

[4] ibid 309, citing Raymond Williams, The Country and the City (Oxford, Oxford University Press, 1973) 171.

grasp variations in social life that fall outside the dominant abstractions.[5] So a full account of the post-war period must be alert to these 'problems'.

So far I've suggested that post-war understandings of unemployment bounced off emerging ideas of labour market regulation and labour market organisation. One implication of this is that those people who were not fully integrated into, or who were in some way marginal to, those prevailing modes of regulation and organisation were also not easily integrated into post-war understandings of unemployment. Married women constitute one such group; remote area Aboriginal Australians another.

The Married Woman

Married women's labour market position up until the 1970s was determined by a formal juridical inequality within the Australian system of wage setting by arbitration. Wage setting was based on a notional 'family wage' whereby male workers were seen as breadwinners who needed to support a family and so were entitled to a higher wage than women. Women were presumed to be dependants and therefore regulation sanctioned a lower rate of pay: around 54 per cent of the male rate in the first half of the century. This was hedged with the proviso that in male-dominated occupations, women would receive the higher, male rate: this was meant to deter the substitution of lower-paid female labour for that of males and so protect male job security.[6] The disparity inherent in the 'family wage' not only delivered a lesser wage to single women. Its underlying impulse was to do away with the need for the employment of married women altogether, allowing them to devote themselves to full-time mothering.

This situation changed markedly during the Second World War. Women workers were needed in male-dominated occupations not just to address the shortage of labour caused by men being called up into the armed forces, but to more proactively release men from certain industries and make them available for placement elsewhere.[7] Between 1942 and 1944 women's pay was determined by a specially constituted wartime Women's Employment Board. Enterprises employing women in areas of traditionally male employment where no female rate had been set were required either to pay the women at the full male rate or to apply to the Board for a discounted rate (no less than 60 per cent of the male rate) that took into account 'the efficiency of females in the performance of the work and any

[5] Curtis, above n 3, 309.

[6] R Hunter, 'Women Workers and Federal Industrial Law: From *Harvester* to Comparable Worth' (1988) 1 *Australian Journal of Labour Law* 147; P Ryan and T Rowse, 'Women, Arbitration and the Family' (1975) 29 *Labour History* 15.

[7] C Fort, 'Developing a National Employment Policy, Australia 1939–45' (PhD Thesis, University of Adelaide, 2000) 189.

other special factors which may be likely to affect the productivity of their work on relation to males'.[8] It had long been possible for women to be paid at male rates for doing 'men's work'; it's just that prior to the war the number of such women was low. The real innovation of the wartime regulation, argues Carol Fort, was using 'efficiency' and 'productivity' as a yardstick for remuneration. This was a clear break with the 'family wage' principle that had justified gendered differentials in pay for the previous three decades, and it potentially opened the way for a more general policy of equal pay for work of equal worth.[9]

The wartime regulations meant women's pay in various occupations was adjusted to anything between 60 and 100 per cent of the going male rate – a reduced rate often justified as an offset to women's customarily higher rate of casual absence from work.[10] Yet women's movement into paid work was bolstered not merely by the promise of improved pay; it was also achieved via the direction of labour under the National Manpower Regulations, discussed in chapter three.

The wartime pressure to mobilise labour, both male and female, meant the idea that had begun to animate US labour force surveys in the 1930s – how to measure the gap between employers' demand for labour and the number of workers wanting to work – was effectively stymied. The primary concern now became the stock of available human resources and the estimation of potential labour *supply*. People's current labour market activity as indicative of their desire to work was irrelevant. Accordingly, the government began to focus on the registration and direction of 'economically inactive' prime age married women. By March 1942 every 'unemployed' person was required to register with their nearest National Service Office.[11] Wallace Wurth, Director-General of Manpower, admitted there was always 'some doubt as to the precise meaning to be accorded to the word "unemployed"'.[12] In explaining the administration of the regulations, Wurth referred to those who were 'technically unemployed', and distinguished these individuals from 'those who were not gainfully occupied, the latter group comprising relatively large numbers of females who were not actively seeking employment'.[13] This suggests an understanding of 'unemployment' as necessarily encompassing job-seeking activity, an idea that had perhaps percolated through to Australia from the work of US statisticians or from the British unemployment insurance scheme instigated in 1911. But the distinction Wurth made between the two categories did not seem to overly preoccupy him or his staff. The priority was to mobilise

[8] SR 146/1942, National Security (Employment of Women) Regulations.

[9] Fort, above n 7, 207–08.

[10] ibid 208. See also O Foenander, *Wartime Labour Developments in Australia: With Suggestions for Reform in the Post-war Regulation of Industrial Relations* (Melbourne, Melbourne University Press, 1943); Ryan and Rowse, above n 6.

[11] Statutory Rule No 113 of 1942.

[12] W Wurth, *Control of Manpower in Australia: A General Review of the Administration of the Manpower Directorate, February 1942–September 1944* (Sydney, Government Printer, 1944) 95.

[13] ibid 132.

all available labour – that is, to *efface* any distinction between the 'technically unemployed' and those available for work more generally.[14]

The immediate post-war period, though, was marked by a quite difference set of concerns. The Re-establishment and Employment Act of 1945 gave absolute preference to returned service men in employment. The government ceased subsidies to kindergartens and childcare which it had put in place to encourage married women's labour force participation during the war; media and church groups waged a campaign encouraging women to return to the home and care for their husbands during the transition from the horrors of war to post-war 'normality', and to increase the birth rate in line with the government's 'populate or perish' policy.[15] Married women would only be encouraged to enter the labour force when the labour market was so buoyant that they would not be competing for men's jobs.

The wartime desire to increase female labour market participation meant that 'unemployment', as determined by the Manpower Directorate, had been a very real possibility for married women, whether they were seeking work or not. In the post-war period, by contrast, it became difficult to imagine a married woman as unemployed. They tended to be viewed as either actually employed, or not in the labour force at all. The persistence of the 'family wage' implied that married women's primary role was in the home and, as Ann Porter has observed in the Canadian context,

> even those who had been engaged in wage work were not really considered unemployed when they lost their jobs. It was assumed that they would take up or intensify their activities within the home and that they would be supported by their husbands.[16]

She goes on to suggest that, as a result, married women's claims to be counted as 'unemployed' were often regarded as not legitimate. Indeed, William Beveridge thought that the 'genuinely seeking work' test inserted into the UK unemployment insurance scheme in the 1920s did not so much catch out the work shy or malingering man, but provided a weapon 'against claims by women who on marriage had practically retired from industry and were not wanted by employers, but tried, not unnaturally, to get something for nothing out of the fund'.[17] Post-war commentators in Australia exhibited a similar scepticism that married women might merely be representing themselves as unemployed when in fact they had withdrawn from the workforce, had no serious intention of working, and were not obliged by economic circumstances to find a job.[18]

---

[14] ibid.

[15] C Allport, 'Left off the Agenda: Women, Reconstruction, and New Order Housing' (1984) 46 *Labour History* 1, 19–20; Ryan and Rowse, above n 6, 27–29.

[16] A Porter, *Gendered States: Women, Unemployment Insurance, and the Political Economy of the Welfare State in Canada, 1945–1997* (Toronto, University of Toronto Press, 2003) 43.

[17] ibid 280.

[18] R Smee, '"Some Problems in the Measurement of Unemployment" – A Comment' (1969) 11 *Journal of Industrial Relations* 253. On Canada, see Porter, above n 16, 48.

In some ways, the labour force framework better captured married women's actual labour market activity than the old 'gainful worker' approach. But the focus on job search activity buttressed the post-war suspicion regarding married women's motivation and desire for work. Many married women demobilised from war industries may have considered themselves 'gainful workers' who were now 'unemployed', but unless they were actively seeking new work their 'unemployment' was effaced.

Statisticians had always expressed some unease that a rigid activity criteria – actually 'working' or 'seeking work' – was likely to 'yield an incomplete count of persons with jobs or in the market for jobs'.[19] So statisticians had turned their minds to the possibility of the 'inactive' unemployed. The two main groups in this category were those who wanted work but whose job search activity had been interrupted by temporary illness, and those who wanted work but had ceased job search in the belief that no work was available.

That latter group was usually identified as those 'stranded' in rural settlements or company towns where the person was pretty much aware of all possible sources of employment in the area and hence the futility of job search.[20] But writing in 1969, John Steinke observed that those not seeking work because of a belief that no work was available 'are likely to fluctuate greatly in number, be unevenly distributed, and may in some instances be very numerous'. Furthermore, it was 'among females, hedged about by legal and social restrictions on employment, that hidden unemployment seems most likely to occur'.[21] He referred to a 1964 survey undertaken to discover the extent of female 'unemployment' in Wollongong, and which was designed specifically to discover the reasons for female labour market inactivity. Whereas 12 per cent of women were unemployed and actively looking for work, 14 per cent were out of work and did not look for work because they believed no work was available.

Judith Innes, contrasting US practice in the 1930s with the post-war period, observes that statisticians' willingness to include 'discouraged' workers in the count of unemployed persons varies according to labour market conditions: that is, whether their numbers are significant and their discouragement considered reasonable.[22] Whereas the number of 'discouraged' married women workers may have been significant, for many commentators their discouragement was not reasonable. Rather than see a failure of the labour force framework to adequately grasp married women's labour market experience, commentators sheeted the

[19] G Bancroft, *The American Labor Force: Its Growth and Changing Composition* (New York, John Wiley and Sons, 1958) 192; see also P Hauser, 'The Labour Force and Gainful Workers: Concept, Measurement and Comparability' (1949) 54 *American Journal of Sociology* 341.

[20] G Palmer, *A Guide to Australian Economic Statistics* (Melbourne, Macmillan, 1963) 82; Bancroft, ibid.

[21] J Steinke, 'Some Problems in the Measurement of Unemployment' (1969) 11 *Journal of Industrial Relations* 39, 43.

[22] J Innes, *Knowledge and Public Policy: The Search for Meaningful Indicators*, 2nd edn (New Brunswick, Transaction Publishers, 1990) 186.

blame home to married women themselves: only 'marginally available' for work, the problem was their '"chameleon"-like appearance in respect to their attitude toward work'.[23] This 'chameleon-like' attitude could not be captured by the prevailing labour force framework: married women could not satisfy the strictures of the labour force framework that made consistent searching for any job whatsoever central to its enquiry. Instead, married women were 'more particular' in the job package they desired and had a marked preference for part-time work[24] – and at a time when 'opportunities to work part-time are extremely limited'.[25]

This group was seen as part of a larger group that commentators called the 'hidden unemployed',[26] although that term lacked the imprimatur of either the Australian Bureau of Statistics (ABS) or the International Labour Organization's (ILO) Conference of Labour Statisticians. The ABS would go on to institutionalise a measure of the 'hidden unemployed' that modified the strictures of the activity requirement. From 1983, following resolutions of the ILO's Conference of Labour Statisticians, the Bureau began to make reference to those 'not in the labour force' but 'marginally attached' to the labour force: that is, those who were out of work and desiring work, and were either looking for work while not available, or available for work but not looking. That last category included 'discouraged' jobseekers whose reason for not looking involved 'labour market reasons': for example, the belief that no work was available given a jobseeker's particular characteristics or preferences. More recently, the ILO has favoured the term 'potential labour force' rather than 'marginally attached', with the category comprising 'unavailable jobseekers' along with 'available potential jobseekers' (the latter including the old category of 'discouraged' jobseekers).[27]

In the post-war period, married women's preference for part-time work also meant their willingness to work was hidden by the Commonwealth Employment Service (CES) figures of registered out-of-work jobseekers, as those figures were restricted to those seeking full-time work.[28] Further, married women, even if seeking full-time work, had less incentive than a man to register at the CES because they were generally unable to receive the new unemployment benefit. The 1944 Act simply debarred married women claiming unemployment benefit in their own right unless it was not 'reasonable for her husband to maintain her'.[29] This could be seen as a necessary complement to the institution of the family wage enshrined

---

[23] Smee, above n 18, 253.

[24] B Merrilees, 'Hidden Unemployment of Women in Australia' (1977) 19 *Journal of Industrial Relations* 50, 53.

[25] Smee, above n 18, 253 (emphasis in the original).

[26] See, eg, Merrilees, above n 24; P Stricker and P Sheehan, *Hidden Unemployment: The Australian Experience* (Parkville, Institute of Applied Economic and Social Research, University of Melbourne, 1981).

[27] See ABS, *Labour Statistics: Concepts, Sources and Methods*, Cat no 6102.0.55.001, February 2018. I am indebted to Judith Willis's research on the evolution of these classifications.

[28] S Stevens, 'Problems in the Interpretation of Australian Statistics of Unemployment' (1963) 39 *Economic Record* 142, 144.

[29] Unemployment and Sickness Benefit Act 1944 (Cth) s 18.

in arbitral practice. Nevertheless, the stark legislative evocation of married women as dependent appears anomalous given the numbers of married women working in war industries at parity or near parity wages with men at the very time the legislation was enacted. Looking to the future, though, Labor MP Arthur Calwell assured Parliament that women's wartime labour activity was a 'passing phase'.[30] In any case, the blanket exclusion was largely unnecessary: entitlement to benefit was tested against household income which meant a married woman with a husband even in low-waged work would invariably be denied benefit – and, indeed, the provision was removed when the unemployment benefits legislation was consolidated with other social security legislation in 1947. In the case of a woman married to an out-of-work man, the male unemployment benefit included an additional benefit for a dependent wife. Even in the absence of a wage, the male's role as 'breadwinner' was maintained.

The Remote-Area Aboriginal Australian

The situation of some groups of Aboriginal people was even more marginal. Section 127 of the Commonwealth Constitution meant that prior to 1967 'full blood' Aboriginals were not enumerated in the census at all, and so had no labour force status for the purpose of the census categories. 'Aboriginal natives' were also excluded from Australia's original old age and invalid pension schemes.[31]

However, from 1941 new welfare legislation covering child endowment and widows' pensions made a qualified inclusion of Aboriginal Australians, relying on socio-cultural markers of eligibility rather than the biological marker of caste.[32] Commonwealth child endowment legislation introduced in 1941 excluded Aboriginal peoples who were 'nomadic' or 'wholly or mainly dependent on the Commonwealth or state',[33] but the government wished to extend endowment to those Aborigines 'living at European standards'.[34] The parliamentary Joint Committee on Social Security also recommended extending pensions to non-nomadic Aborigines and those living under conditions 'reasonably comparable to Australian living standards'.[35] On this basis, the Labor government in 1942 amended the Invalid and Old Age Pensions Act 1908 (Cth) to extend coverage to those Aborigines 'exempt from the provision of the law ... relating to the control

[30] J Murphy, *A Decent Provision: Australia Welfare Policy, 1870 to 1949* (Farnham, Ashgate, 2011) 215.

[31] Old Age Pensions Act 1908 (Cth) ss 16(1)(c) and 21(1)(b).

[32] J Murphy, 'Conditional Inclusion: Aborigines and Welfare Rights in Australia, 1900–1947' (2013) 44 *Australian Historical Studies* 206.

[33] Child Endowment Act 1941 (Cth) s 15.

[34] Treasury adviser Roland Wilson, quoted in Murphy, 'Conditional Inclusion', above n 32, 218.

[35] Commonwealth of Australia, Joint Committee on Social Security, *Interim Report*, Parl Paper No 48 (1940–43) para 21.

of aboriginal natives'.[36] This was a reference to those States that had protective reserve schemes for Aborigines and issued certificates of exemption from protective laws: Queensland, Western Australia, Northern Territory and South Australia (NSW introduced a system in 1943, after passage of the Act). Eligibility for the Commonwealth's new widows' pension, introduced in 1942, was set on the same terms.[37] The fact that States' exemption systems became the proxy for eligibility meant that responsibility for determining Aborigines' access to Commonwealth social security effectively passed from the Commonwealth to the States.[38] In those States without a certificate of exemption system, eligibility would depend on the 'character, standard of intelligence and development of the aboriginal native'.[39]

The 1944 unemployment benefit legislation reflected this qualified inclusion: Aboriginal applicants were entitled to the benefit if the Director-General of Social Services was satisfied that it was 'reasonable' that the applicant receive it.[40] John Murphy characterises this as a 'step backwards' as there was no reference to the States' exemption systems and so entitlement relied solely on the highly discretionary judgement of the Director-General.[41] But State-based exemption systems were themselves already highly discretionary, based on socio-cultural classifications that were always 'more fluid than the rigidities of caste, and consequently more imprecise … in their application'.[42] It was the Commonwealth jurisdiction that had insisted, more than any other, on the importance of the biological distinction between 'full-blood' and 'half-caste', and that distinction had been entrenched – not without problems – in official Commonwealth statistics.[43] Some administrators did hold the belief that character and outlook 'were closely correlated with, and substantially determined by, genetic make-up'.[44] But in many of the States the apparently biological terminology of full-blood and half-caste simply served to summarise a more or less sociological distinction between tribal and detribalised Aboriginal Australians. The administrative practices of the various State authorities meant that 'Aboriginal' was already a fairly 'ad hoc classification of people by skin colour, way of life, associations and dependency'.[45]

[36] Old Age and Invalid Pensions Amendment Act 1942 (Cth) s 4, inserting new s 16(1A)(a)(i) in the principal act.

[37] Widows' Pensions Act 1942 (Cth) ss 14(1)(g), 14(5).

[38] Murphy, 'Conditional Inclusion', above n 32, 223. As Murphy points out, State exemption certificates were revocable, making them a potent form of surveillance and policing of Aboriginal Australians' behaviour.

[39] Old Age and Invalid Pensions Amendment Act 1942 (Cth) s 4, inserting new s 16(1A)(a)(ii) in the principal act.

[40] Unemployment and Sickness Benefit Act 1944 (Cth) s 19.

[41] Murphy, 'Conditional Inclusion', above n 32, 224.

[42] ibid 210.

[43] T Rowse, *Indigenous and Other Australians Since 1901* (Sydney, NewSouth, 2017) 193. The distinction was made central to the interpretation of s 127 of the Constitution by the then Attorney-General, Alfred Deakin, in 1901: ibid, 136.

[44] ibid 193.

[45] ibid 136, 186.

In the case of unemployment benefit, the 'reasonableness' of the claim was to be judged according to the Aborigine's character, standard of intelligence and social development, and an Aborigine who was ordinarily engaged in waged work was automatically considered eligible.[46] In 1959 the Social Security Act was amended to extend all benefits and pensions to Aboriginal Australians who were not 'nomadic or primitive'.[47] This severed any connection between eligibility and State-based exemption certificates, but given payment of unemployment benefit had always rested on a broader discretion, the amendment was probably of little effect. In 1966 all exclusionary references to Aborigines were removed.[48]

The original statutory qualification on access to unemployment benefits nevertheless established a de facto hierarchy of eligibility structured by race. It was a throwback to a gainful worker approach whereby an Aboriginal Australian who *usually* worked could be considered as 'in the labour force' and hence unemployed. Previous employment indicated a commitment to wage labour and thus demonstrated the genuineness of a person's availability for work. If an Aboriginal person did not have a history of work, any claim for benefit was viewed with suspicion; actively seeking work, on its own, was often not enough. Clearly, what it meant to demonstrate 'availability for work' differed as between whites and blacks.

Even for those Aboriginal Australians who did qualify, there was no guarantee that they would actually receive the benefit. The 1959 amendments altered the principal legislation so as not to just allow payment to 'persons' other than the pensioner or beneficiary, but also payment to an 'institution or authority on behalf' of the claimant.[49] This enlarged dispensation seemed designed to accommodate a new class of claimants envisaged by the amending act: Aborigines not 'nomadic or primitive' but still under protection laws. State protection laws already exhibited a scepticism regarding Aborigines' capacity to manage money, allowing for employers of protected persons to pay some or all of their wages into government trust funds, thereby enabling protectors to regulate the spending of individuals.[50] Now, Commonwealth social security payments could also be paid en masse to institutions or State native welfare authorities, rather than individual claimants, which in turn could distribute the income as they chose.[51]

But aside from these explicit statutory provisions, the capacity of remote area Aboriginal Australians to be 'unemployed' depended on how the operation of the work test interacted with a particular racialised labour market and its system of regulation.

---

[46] TH Kewley, *Social Security in Australia, 1900–72* (Sydney, Sydney University Press, 1973) 266.

[47] Social Services Amendment Act 1959, inserting a new s 137A in the principal act.

[48] Social Services Act Amendment Act 1966 (Cth) s 29.

[49] For unemployment benefit, see s 23 of the amended Social Services Act Amendment Act 1966 (Cth). Similar amendments were made regarding pensions, child endowment and maternity allowance. The Old Age and Invalid Pensions Amendment Act 1942 (Cth) s 13, had already made provision for this type of arrangement.

[50] Rowse, *Indigenous and Other Australians*, above n 43, 228.

[51] J Chesterman, 'Defending Australia's Reputation: How Indigenous Australians Won Civil Rights, Part One' (2001) 32 *Australian Historical Studies* 20, 31.

In the first half of the twentieth century, the employment of Aboriginal Australians on government settlements, missions and pastoral stations in the Northern Territory was governed by a series of ordinances made under the Northern Territory Aboriginals Act 1910 (Cth). Employers of Aboriginal labour were required to obtain a licence, but the initial ordinances prescribed no particular wage rate for Aboriginal employees. Later they set down a minimum wage, but part of that wage was to be paid into a trust fund administered by the Protector of Aborigines, and in the immediate post-war period pastoralists who could show that they were maintaining an Aboriginal employee's relatives and dependants could pay the employee in rations and clothing rather wages.[52] A revision to the Ordinance in 1949 set out a minimum wage well below award minimum wages, and where a pastoralist and the protector agreed that an Aboriginal worker was not sufficiently 'competent' for a particular job, a lesser rate could be paid.[53]

On pastoral stations, station owners (that is, the holders of pastoral leases) paid the prescribed low wages plus 'rations and upkeep' to Aboriginal male workers. These were meant to cover the basic needs of the worker, his first wife and first child. The Territory administration then subsidised the pastoralist for providing rations to maintain the worker's other dependants. This meant entire Aboriginal extended families and groups could remain on the station and maintain their links to their traditional country. Tim Rowse refers to this as 'unresolved dispossession': indigenous people had no choice but to accommodate pastoralists' use of their country, but themselves were not prohibited access to it.[54] But this type of labour market did not generate 'unemployment' in the way that post-war administrators had come to understand it. First, the pastoral industry's 'inconstant demand for labour blurred the boundary between working and non-working adult males: a lot of men occasionally worked'.[55] Secondly, subsidised rations for non-working members of the group were freely available. This confounded what the post-war administrative and regulatory project around unemployment – especially the provision of unemployment benefits – was trying to do: divide the population into a group of people 'in the labour force' (ie, largely subsistent on wage labour) and a group legitimately excused from wage labour; and to further divide that first group into those employed and to have the remainder look for work. And ideally, this last set of 'unemployed' would be willing to sell their labour wherever it was in demand. But as long as work remained intermittent and station residents were able to share in rations, in goods purchased with workers' cash, and in food hunted on the station, it was impossible to point to a clearly defined group of wage-subsistent able-bodied men.[56] And as long as the indigenous groups remained

---

[52] S Gray, 'The Elephant in the Drawing Room: Slavery and the Stolen Wages Debate' (2007) 11 *Australian Indigenous Law Review* 30, 43.

[53] ibid 44.

[54] T Rowse, *White Flour, White Power: From Rations to Citizenship in Central Australia* (Melbourne, Cambridge University Press, 1998) 140.

[55] ibid 136.

[56] ibid 135.

bound to country, rather than mobile and attracted to job prospects in other areas, they would fail the availability-for-work test. The twin factors of what Rowse calls 'Indigenous territoriality' and 'distributional entitlement' thwarted the emergence of 'unemployment' as understood in the wider post-war context.[57]

As Aboriginal workers were increasingly integrated into a regulated, wage-based labour market, their capacity to be counted among the 'unemployed' grew. In 1959, the year the exclusionary provisions regarding unemployment benefit were loosened, a new Welfare Ordinance took effect. The Ordinance was enacted in 1953 but not proclaimed until six years later. It carried what Russell McGregor calls the rather 'coy' subtitle: 'An ordinance to provide for the care and assistance of certain persons'.[58] It made no reference to 'full blood' Aborigines but simply referred instead to 'wards' under the guardianship of a Director of Welfare. These 'wards' were people judged to be in need of special care and assistance, whether by reason of not being able to manage their own affairs, their associations, manner of living and so on. Paul Hasluck, the federal Minister for Territories from 1951 to 1963, was insistent that the new regulation use racially neutral nomenclature. As with changes to eligibility for social security benefits, this fitted with the prevailing logic of assimilation and the move from an essentialist biological marker of race to a socio-cultural one based on a – possibly transient – need for care and protection.

The Northern Territory Legislative Council was sceptical, and would only pass the Ordinance if it were made clear that whites could not be included under the new proscriptions. So reference was made to the Territory's electoral regulations: a declaration of ward status was restricted to those ineligible for enrolment under the electoral regulations, making it impossible for a non-full-blood Aborigine to be declared a ward. And by reference in a schedule to the Queensland, South Australian and Western Australian protection Acts, Aboriginal Australians covered by those Acts were deemed to be wards if they entered the Territory. So despite the racially blind language of the Ordinance, it was in fact impossible for white people to be classified as wards. By contrast, when the Ordinance was gazetted in 1957, all but six full-blood Aborigines in the Territory were designated wards.[59] In effect, the new Welfare Ordinance did pretty much the same job that the previous ordinances did, allowing for the declaring and registering of 'full-blood' Aborigines as wards and subjecting them to the traditional restraints.[60]

The Welfare Ordinance provided the basis for the Wards' Employment Ordinance (WEO). The Regulations under the WEO laid down detailed wage

---

[57] ibid 142.

[58] R McGregor, *Indifferent Inclusion: Aboriginal People and the Australian Nation* (Acton, Aboriginal Studies Press, 2011) 82.

[59] ibid 85. The gazetting of a Register of Wards required a complete census of all Aboriginal peoples in the Territory, which took four years to complete: see H Douglas and J Chesterman, 'Creating a Legal Identity: Aboriginal People and the Assimilation Census' (2008) 32 *Journal of Australian Studies* 375.

[60] C Rowley, *The Remote Aborigines* (Canberra, ANU Press, 1971) 297. Similarly, the grounds on which an Indigenous person could claim revocation of ward status were essentially the same as those on which they could claim 'exemption' from earlier ordinances: McGregor, above n 58, 82–83.

rates – around 30 per cent of the Territory basic wage[61] – and other conditions of employment, including clothing allowances, accommodation, overtime and sick leave. Yet even this low wage was subject to several loopholes. An employer could employ a slow, aged or infirm ward at a lesser rate, provided the employer and welfare officer agreed on this designation. Missions employing Aboriginal labour pleaded financial hardship and were exempted from the Ordinance. The Ordinance also did not bind the Crown, so Aborigines living and working on government settlements were not covered.

Importantly, 'suitable work' for Aboriginal claimants of unemployment benefit meant employment available under the 'local conditions' applying to 'native labour': that is, any job offered under any industrial award including the WEO.[62] This was glossed by the Department of Social Services somewhat disingenuously as 'no different' from the normal operation of the work test as it applied to all claimants for unemployment benefit, but the existence of officially sanctioned below-award employment meant that indigenous claimants would find it more difficult to satisfy the work test than white workers.

In 1966, the year that all exclusionary references to Aborigines were removed from social security legislation, a decision of the Commonwealth Court of Conciliation and Arbitration saw Aboriginal pastoral workers fully integrated into the award system and granted equal pay with white workers. The removal of racially discriminatory provisions soon flowed on to other awards. The Commonwealth government, which had hitherto supported the exclusion of Aboriginal workers from award conditions, had intervened in the hearings in support of the unions' claim for equal pay, goaded by a mix of international pressure and domestic activism.[63] Once the Court's decision was implemented in 1968, Aboriginal workers enjoyed better rates of pay, but for shorter periods with substantial interspersed periods of joblessness. This was addressed by a procedure that made unemployment benefit available to stood-down workers provided the pastoralist vouched for the workers' continued availability for work on the station.[64] Even here, the effect was largely to extend access to benefit only to those Aboriginal workers who maintained a strong tie to an individual pastoralist, and the idea that Aboriginal Australians who did not have a history of employment were 'out of the workforce' and ineligible for benefit informed departmental decision-making well into the 1970s.[65]

---

[61] Rowse, *White Flour*, above n 54, 166. Evidence before the Commonwealth Conciliation and Arbitration Court in 1965 estimated the total cost of employing a ward was about half that of employing a stockman on award wages: Rowley, ibid, 301.

[62] W Sanders, 'The Politics of Unemployment Benefit for Aborigines: Some Consequences of Economic Marginalisation' in D Wade-Marshall and P Loveday (eds), *Employment and Unemployment: A Collection of Papers* (Darwin, ANU North Australian Research Unit, 1985) 139, 142.

[63] J Chesterman, 'Defending Australia's Reputation: How Indigenous Australians Won Civil Rights, Part Two' (2001) 32 *Australian Historical Studies* 201, 208–13.

[64] Sanders, above n 62, 141.

[65] ibid 142, 147.

The 'Dole Bludger'

It was the structural position of married women and Aboriginal Australians in the post-war labour market that made it difficult to think of them as genuinely 'unemployed'. Marginal to our mid-century understandings of the standard employment relationship, they ended up marginal to our understanding of unemployment as well. But suspicion as to the genuineness of claims for unemployment benefit extended more widely, and that suspicion was neatly summed up in an Australian vernacular term: the 'dole bludger'.

It was always recognised that 'full employment' would not mean that there would be no unemployed people. The assumption, though, was that the normal lag between jobs would be very short. The seven-day waiting period for unemployment benefits envisaged the existence of very short-term unemployment that was not in need of compensation. An efficient employment service would also keep any period of involuntary unemployment to a minimum.

In addition to this 'frictional' unemployment, a Commonwealth government report in 1970 recognised it was also 'inevitable ... that there will be some structural unemployment arising from an imbalance between the skill pattern and location of the unemployed on the one hand and the skill requirements and location of available job vacancies on the other'.[66] As we've seen, the work test was designed to address – at least in part – this phenomenon of structural unemployment, in that a claimant's 'willingness or ability' to undertake suitable work was judged against the willingness to change both occupation and residence.[67]

Finally, the Report went on, there were the 'hard-core unemployed': persons who would always find it difficult to obtain employment because of 'certain personal characteristics they possess', including 'serious physical or mental handicaps ... unsatisfactory work attitudes and records ... too old in relation to the work they are seeking'.[68] Using these classifications, the Report concluded that of those registered as unemployed in 1969, one-quarter were 'frictionally' unemployed; one-half 'structurally' unemployed; with the remainder principally the 'hard-core' unemployed.[69]

A government-sponsored survey of 'long-term unemployed people under conditions of full employment' undertaken by Alan Jordan in the early 1970s came up with an even more elaborate taxonomy. It divided the (albeit small) sample

---

[66] Department of Labour and National Service, *An Analysis of Full Employment in Australia*, Labour Market Studies No 2, Melbourne, 1970, 25.

[67] The Labour and National Service report acknowledged that structural unemployment was addressed by an immigration programme targeted towards trades and skills in short supply, and by specialised training schemes targeted at particular groups to acquire suitable skills. But while it referred to the 'willingness and ability' of a jobseeker to change residence or occupation, it did not consider the role of the work test in this regard.

[68] Department of Labour and National Service, *An Analysis of Full Employment in Australia*, above n 66, 2.

[69] ibid 3.

of long-term unemployed into 18 categories, and gave quite detailed qualitative analyses of each: their living arrangements and geographical mobility, personal handicaps, sub-culture and so on.[70] The categories ranged from young single women in areas of job shortage, through older married men, adults suffering from severe mental disorders, adult male seasonal workers, those with 'intellectual retardation', 'isolated and withdrawn' young men and so on.

Perhaps indicative of the times, the most extended analysis was given over not to the 'hard-core unemployed' or the seemingly unemployable, but to the category 'Young people without apparent disability'. Aged from their late teens to mid-twenties, of above average educational status, healthy, they were absorbed in avocational activities of one sort or another: one an aspiring film maker; another a leatherworker; a third actively involved in the women's liberation movement having already written three novels; another interested in oriental religion; another in street theatre. They were 'sorting themselves out, deciding who they were, what they wanted to do with their lives and for what reason'.[71] They didn't face the hurdles of the true 'unemployables' (although, their 'typical accommodation was old and somewhat run-down, brightened up with posters on the walls and often untidy to the point of apparent chaos').[72] Not suffering from any clear lack of educational or occupational skills, poor health, social isolation or immobility, or lack of local demand for labour, but in fact readily employable, they were of interest precisely because they presented the social security system 'with a critical test of its liberality'.[73]

Given the fundamental indeterminacy of the work test – taking 'reasonable steps' to find 'suitable work' – the genuineness of these people's claim was always up for grabs. Anxiety around too liberal an interpretation of the test became apparent at the start of the 1970s. In a climate of strong demand for labour, any application of the test that excused capable workers from presenting for work was anathema to employers eager to fill vacancies.[74] In October 1971 the Department of Social Services Manual was amended to state that the 'genuinely looking for work' test 'applies especially to: members of "Hippie" colonies; members of the "Surfie" element; new arrivals in the area whose apparent purpose other than to seek work' and that unemployment benefit would not generally be granted to young single persons falling into those categories.[75]

With the election of the Whitlam Labor government at the end of 1972, Bill Hayden became the minister responsible for social security. A member of Labor's

---

[70] A Jordan, *Long Term Unemployed People under Conditions of Full Employment*, Research Report, Commission of Inquiry into Poverty (Canberra, AGPS, 1975) ch 2.

[71] ibid 21.

[72] ibid 22.

[73] ibid 19.

[74] K Windschuttle, *Unemployment: A Social and Political Analysis of the Economic Crisis in Australia* (Ringwood, Penguin Books, 1979) 156.

[75] A Law, 'Surfing the Safety Net: "Dole Bludging", "Surfies" and Governmentaility in Australia' (2001) 36 *International Review for the Sociology of Sport* 24, 29.

left faction, he expressed the view that the administration of unemployment benefit had become unacceptably 'coercive' and 'authoritarian'.[76] Hayden removed the explicit references to surfers and hippies, and narrowed the range of jobs used for work testing (while also removing the postponement of benefits as punishment for failing the work test).[77] So although the late-1940s' direction required claimants be prepared to take up work outside their trade, the Labor government in May 1973 declared that claimants who were qualified for a certain kind of employment (either by formal qualification or experience) need not be required to take work of a lower status. Claimants were also no longer required to submit regular lists of employers approached, and unconventional dress and appearance of itself was not a reason for disqualification from benefit, even though some employers might reject the claimant for that reason.[78] This last dispensation was in fact a return to the policy originally adopted in the early days of the benefit scheme: that postponement or termination of benefit could not be justified 'on the grounds that a person unwilling to make himself presentable to employers is not taking reasonable steps to obtain work'.[79]

But this liberalising of the test met with opposition within Hayden's department, in the press, and from socially conservative left-wing members of Hayden's own party (including the Minister for Labour and National Service, Clyde Cameron).[80] With employers clamouring for labour in a full employment economy, the idea that the jobless could draw benefit while *not* presenting for work seemed unacceptable. Jordan thought that at the time his survey was taken, some of the long-term unemployed claimants 'were probably not strictly entitled to benefit under the current rules … [as] many could have been work tested by referral to jobs outside the area in which they worked but had not been'. But he also reported that some CES staff had formed the opinion that under the new guidelines it had become almost impossible to have a claimant removed from benefit.[81]

By mid-1974 Hayden was forced to backtrack. From April that year the definition of suitable work was amended to refer to 'work of a type or nature in which the person usually engages or in which the person's experience, qualifications and training could be used'.[82] In other words, a claimant's right of refusal of work was limited to vacancies in which their experience, qualifications and training *could not* be used, and they would be penalised if they sought 'only occupations for which they are not qualified or which are extremely rare … in their area of residence'.[83]

---

[76] ibid 31.

[77] ibid.

[78] Jordan, above n 70, 46.

[79] W Funnell (Director of Employment) to Director General of Social Services, 5 March 1947, National Archives of Australia, Series MP537/1, Item No 251/57/2, 'Unemployment and Sickness Benefits: Application of the Works Test 1946–1952'.

[80] Law, above n 75, 32–33.

[81] Jordan, above n 70, 46.

[82] Law, above n 75, 34.

[83] Jordan, above n 70, 46. Similarly, school leavers were to be referred to jobs 'in keeping with their personal preferences, as far as practicable and their abilities, aptitudes, or experience, qualifications and training': Law, above n 75, 34.

Claimants would also now fail the work test if they were to 'deliberately ... make themselves unavailable for work by moving to a location where no such work is available' or if they 'deliberately make themselves unacceptable to employers'.[84] The language wasn't as specific as the 1971 directive, but the first stricture clearly targeted 'surfies' who had moved to coastal towns, while the second was aimed at 'hippies' in urban centres. And making a judgement as to 'deliberateness' clearly returned a significant degree of discretion to CES staff in judging the genuineness of a claimant's unemployment.

It was this period – the tail end of the long boom, with full employment still ascendant – that saw the emergence of the uniquely Australian term 'dole bludger'.[85] Jordan's assessment of the surfer and hippy was more sanguine. The liberalisation of the work test, along with increases in benefit payment rates, had not been accompanied by any discernible increase in measured unemployment, and he thought the fear and anger directed at these people was unjustified. They appeared to be 'neither lazy parasites, nor morally subversive'. Although 'their ways of looking at things were arguable', Jordan concluded that

> [t]hey ... often had a groping honesty likely in time to bring them to a place in the community where they can make the creative contribution that many of them hope to make. We expect, as they do, that most will finish in comparatively conventional careers, perhaps all too conventional.[86]

Although 'dole bludging' emerged as a pathology of a buoyant, full-employment economy, it persisted as an object of concern as Australia slid into recession after the 1974 oil shock. Higher measured rates of unemployment and increased claims for unemployment benefit meant the 'bludger' now became the target for governments wanting to rein in spending. Hayden's work test was tightened by the incoming conservative Coalition government. Soon after taking office in December 1975, the Coalition government reviewed the operation of the work test. From January 1976 applicants would not be considered to be genuinely seeking work if they placed themselves 'in the situation where they will remain, or are likely to remain unemployed'. This included moving to a location where there were few employment prospects for the particular individual or where the move was for purposes other than seeking employment. The provisions regarding jobseekers' mobility now cut both ways. Recall that the original formulation of the work test envisaged 'suitable work' for males of 19 years or older as work that may involve moving away from home. The Coalition government emphasised it would reinvigorate this 'long-standing policy', and unemployment benefit would not generally

---

[84] Jordan, above n 70, 46.

[85] V Archer, 'Dole Bludgers, Tax Payers and the New Right: Constructing Discourses of Welfare in 1970s Australia' (2009) 96 *Labour History* 177.

[86] Jordan, above n 70, 24–25. Jordan did draw attention to one interviewee who lived in a shared household, was interested in oriental religion and meditation, and had no particular vocational interests. 'The interviewer was startled by his claim to be God', Jordan concedes, 'But ... [the interviewer] ... did not think he was "institutional material"': 23.

be available to single persons over 18 'who show unwillingness to move from an area where no employment exists to an area where employment is available'.[87] At the same time, Hayden's changes to the appearance guidelines were comprehensively reversed. Claimants making themselves 'unacceptable to employers by adopting a style of presentation ... which is clearly inappropriate to the type of employment sought or which would restrict their ability to secure a job' would now fail the work test.[88]

From March 1976 the definition of 'suitable work' was modified so that skilled workers who had not found an appropriate job within six weeks would be required to look for and accept unskilled work.[89] The personal lodgement of fortnightly claim forms was reinstated. School leavers were not to be eligible for benefits across the long summer vacation and would only be paid from the commencement of the next school year provided they did not return to education. Postponement or suspension of benefit for instances of 'voluntary' unemployment (dismissal for misconduct and refusal of a job offer) – a procedure sidelined under Hayden – was reinstated. The period of postponement and suspension remained at the Director-General's discretion, but amendments to the Act in 1979 would go on to impose a mandatory minimum and maximum period of six and 12 weeks respectively.[90]

The provision regarding school leavers was one of the first instances where the Commonwealth government's apparent freewheeling capacity to alter eligibility conditions by administrative fiat was successfully called out, when Hobart schoolgirl Karen Green took the Department to the High Court.[91] The Court determined the blanket exclusion of school leavers who otherwise satisfied the strictures of the work test was at odds with the eligibility criteria as laid down in the Act. The Department nevertheless found other grounds to deny Green her benefit across the summer vacation, and the government went on to amend the legislative provisions, inserting section 120A which imposed a six-week postponement on all school leavers from the date they finished their formal education.

Similarly, up to 1979 the work test was administered in a way that suggested benefit might only be lost through a failure to accept an offer of full-time work (whether or not the job was permanent), leaving people free to refuse offers of part-time work and remain eligible for benefit. In 1979 the rules were altered such that beneficiaries were expected to accept offers of casual, part-time and temporary work so as to satisfy the work test.[92]

These manipulations of the work test across the 1970s, within largely unchanging legislative parameters, occurred along two axes: first, as to what constituted 'reasonable steps' to secure suitable work; and secondly, as to what constituted 'suitable work'.

---

[87] Ministerial Statement, Hansard, 23 March 1976.

[88] Ministerial release, cited in Victorian Council of Social Service, *Workers' Rights and Unemployment* (Collingwood, VCOSS, 1976). Ministerial Statement, Hansard, 23 March 1976.

[89] Commonwealth of Australia, *Parliamentary Debates*, House of Representatives, 23 March 1976, 871–72.

[90] Social Services Amendment Act 1979 (Cth) s 41, amending s 120 of the principal Act.

[91] *Green v Daniels* (1977) 13 ALR 1.

[92] Commonwealth of Australia, *Commonwealth Record*, 4 July 1979.

And any definition of suitable work serves two purposes. It circumscribes the parameters of job search activity (that is, the range of jobs sought), which goes to the question of whether someone is taking 'reasonable steps' to find work. It also defines a particular instance of voluntary unemployment that in turn attracted a cancellation or postponement of benefit (that is, the refusal of an actual offer of suitable work).

That second purpose of the 'suitable work' criteria is likely to diminish as unemployment increases. By the second half of the 1970s, an excess of jobseekers over job vacancies, along with CES practice to refer multiple registrants to the one vacancy, simply meant fewer and fewer claimants were likely to receive an actual offer of suitable work in the first place. But then the relevance of 'suitable work' resurfaces, not so much in policing workers' acceptance or refusal of actual offers of work – the 'voluntariness' of their unemployment – but in monitoring the 'reasonableness' of their job search activity. That is, the unemployed are obliged to look for and apply for the range of jobs that fall within the definition of suitable work. In this climate it is more likely that a claimant's failure to qualify for benefit will flow from the 'unreasonableness' of their limiting the range of jobs they seek, within a more or less broad conception of what jobs are 'suitable' for them.[93] Of course, failing to register with the CES, failing to make independent approaches to employers, to attend interviews at the CES when requested, or to follow up referrals to vacancies could also all count as failures to take 'reasonable steps' to seek suitable work.

The preoccupations of the Coalition government of this period – claimants moving to areas of low employment, or 'sabotaging' a job interview by deliberately presenting poorly to prospective employers – could be seen as examples of 'voluntary' unemployment. But it is clear from the various ministerial statements that the government also saw these behaviours as a failure to take 'reasonable steps' to find work.

The distinction was sometimes lost in the contemporary analysis of the period. Graeme Brewer, writing in 1978 for the Brotherhood of St Laurence, a Melbourne-based charitable organisation, reduced the 'main provision of the work test' to the 'offer of suitable work and the acceptance or refusal of it'.[94] In fact, as I've indicated, by the late 1970s the administrative focus had clearly shifted to taking 'reasonable steps' as the prime marker of eligibility, rather than the refusal of actual job offers. Even more problematically, a Victorian Council of Social Service (VCOSS) publication suggested that the work test consisted of the CES making job offers to claimants.[95] But this is untenable: only an employer can make a job offer; the CES could only make referrals to enterprises where a vacancy of suitable work existed. How a claimant then responded to such a referral obviously went to the question of

---

[93] Beveridge had recognised similar problems with administering the work test should unemployment outstrip vacancies. In effect, high or full employment was a necessary condition for the operation of an effective unemployment benefits scheme: WH Beveridge, *Full Employment in a Free Society* (London, Allen & Unwin, 1944) 164.

[94] G Brewer, *Rough Justice: A Study of the Causes and Effects of the Termination of Unemployment Benefit* (Fitzroy, Brotherhood of St Laurence, 1978) 26.

[95] Victorian Council of Social Service, *Workers' Rights and Unemployment* (Collingwood, VCOSS, 1976) 10.

their willingness to work and whether they were taking reasonable steps to secure work. Failure to follow up a referral, or to follow up the referral but 'sabotage' the interview process by deliberately making oneself unacceptable to the prospective employer, is better thought of as a failure to take 'reasonable steps' rather than amounting to a refusal of a job offer.[96] Somewhat remarkably, David Myers, an academic appointed by the Fraser government to review the unemployment benefit scheme, also glossed the legislative provisions with the observation that 'the purpose of the work test is primarily to ensure that unemployment benefit is not paid to persons who decline to accept suitable employment *offered* to them',[97] again apparently restricting the focus to the refusal of actual job offers from employers rather than what it might mean to take 'reasonable steps' to find work.

In all this it's important to reiterate the continued role of discretionary judgement in the administration of the work test. As Brewer observed, the work test across this period was 'administered with harshness or leniency according to the prevailing view within an office as well as the predispositions of individual administrators'.[98]

The work test was subject to repeated critique over this period. Charity and welfare groups such as the Brotherhood of St Laurence and VCOSS were part of this chorus, but Jordan's report, commissioned by a government-appointed commission of inquiry into poverty, also criticised the test as merely an

> inference of a person's state of mind from very limited observation of his behaviour ... It can be difficult or impossible with much better information than is usually available to distinguish the person who is willing but unable to work from the person who is able but unwilling.[99]

Perhaps most tellingly, Myers, appointed by the government precisely for the purpose of reviewing the unemployment benefit system, expressed doubt about the desirability of the test, casting it as serving 'very little purpose and administratively objectionable'. Instead, he proposed replacing the work test as a routine measure for all claimants with a test only to be applied where circumstances warranted it.[100]

Yet despite this, the work test – contested, and subject to continued recalibration – remained central to the construction of unemployment under conditions of both full employment and rising joblessness.

---

[96] In the Brotherhood of St Laurence study of claimants' loss of benefit, it is unclear in all cases where claimants were refusing to follow up a CES referral to a potential job or refusing an actual offer of work: Brewer, above n 94.

[97] Commonwealth of Australia, *Unemployment Benefit Policy and Administration: Report of Inquiry*, Parl Paper No 243 (1977) 15, para 4.11.8 (emphasis added).

[98] Brewer, above n 94, 16.

[99] Jordan, above n 70, 46.

[100] Commonwealth of Australia, *Unemployment Benefit Policy and Administration*, paras 4.11.10–4.11.13.

7

Reinventing Unemployment

The project of dividing working-age people into mutually exclusive labour force categories – 'employed', 'unemployed', 'not in the labour force' – found purchase in the post-war period because it meshed with the lived experience and rhythms of most people's working lives and with the established mode of labour market regulation. The prevailing condition of 'full employment' – what the White Paper described as a tendency towards a shortage of men rather than a shortage of jobs – also oiled the operation of the 'work test'. It made it possible to test unemployment benefit claimants' willingness and readiness to work by direct reference to an actual job vacancy. But in the final three decades of the twentieth century, these conditions changed dramatically and, with them, so did the idea of unemployment as a coherent administrative and regulatory category.

The Demise of the Standard Employment Relationship

In previous chapters I've traced the consolidation of the post-war idea of unemployment against the arc of the standardisation of employment. That there was a post-war 'standard employment relationship', based around full-time employment contracts of indefinite duration, was perhaps only recognised in hindsight, most spoken about when commentators were lamenting its passing.[1] It had crept up on people, the result of regulatory accretion, trade union agitation and shifts in managerial strategy. And the word 'standard' was gesturing to at least three different notions: a normative and slightly paternalistic understanding of what was best for working households; an empirical judgement as to what was the most prevalent or typical form of employment relationship; and a regulatory argument about what types of workers were most in need of protection.[2]

On any of these three counts, what is notable about recent decades is the *de*-standardisation of employment. But 'non-standard' employment relationships can deviate from standard employment relationships along one or more dimensions.

---

[1] G Bosch, 'Towards a New Standard Employment Relationship in Western Europe' (2004) 42 *British Journal of Industrial Relations* 617.

[2] JC Tham, 'Towards an Understanding of Standard Employment Relationships Under Australian Labour Law' (2007) 20 *Australian Journal of Labour Law* 123, 124.

They include self-employment and independent contracting, part-time work, casual work, fixed-term work or agency-based work. These are forms of employment that are heterogeneous and not mutually exclusively. As the term *non*-standard implies, they are largely defined by what they are not.[3]

We're not necessarily witnessing a shift away from the contract of employment itself. Across the last three decades of the twentieth century, self-employment remained fairly constant as a proportion of total employment – around 15 per cent – and more recently has actually declined.[4] But the contract of employment can take many different forms. In Australian labour law, the 'standard' form of employment relationship that emerged mid-century was the open-ended, ongoing full-time contract, terminable by notice, to which various protections were attached and which attracted the jurisdiction of the arbitral tribunals. By the early 1970s something in the order of 90 per cent of Australian employees fell into this standard employment category.[5] Four decades later, ongoing, full-time contracts of employment accounted for the working arrangements of just over 50 per cent of all employed persons.[6]

Some employees maintain ongoing, open-ended contracts but on a part-time rather than a full-time basis. They generally have the same entitlements as full-time employees, but accrue them on a pro rata basis according to the fraction of a full-time week they are working. Ongoing part-time employment was relatively rare until the 1970s. Since then, it grew from 4 per cent of employees to around 9 per cent by the end of the century.[7] This measure of 'part-time' is based on the fairly arbitrary cut-off of less than 35 hours' work per week, and so captures a very wide dispersion of actual hours, and it only counts a worker's primary job, whereas it would be expected that most second jobs are short-hours part-time jobs. For several decades now, part-time work has counted for a disproportionate share of new jobs.

But the most significant group of employees falling outside the standard-form category are 'casual' employees. In chapter one, I explained how the problem of casual work lay at the heart of attempts to think about the link between joblessness and labour market organisation. What commentators had in mind when they spoke of casual employment was work that was characterised by intermittency or irregularity. As we saw in chapter one, in Australia these intermittent workers came to be paid an hourly rate with a 'loading' that was meant to ensure they received a similar annual income to a worker engaged

[3] L Vosko, 'Gender Differentiation and the Standard/Non-Standard Employment Distinction: A Genealogy of Policy Interventions in Canada' in D Juteau (ed), *Social Differentiation: Patterns and Process* (Toronto, University of Toronto Press, 2003).

[4] K Atalay, W Kim and S Whelan, 'The Decline of the Self-Employment Rate in Australia' (2014) 47 *Australian Economic Review* 472.

[5] A VandenHeuvel and M Wooden, *Casualisation and Outsourcing: Trends and Implications for Work-Related Training* (Adelaide, National Centre for Vocational Education Research, 1999) 10.

[6] Derived from ABS, *Forms of Employment, Australia*, Cat No 6359.0, November 2013.

[7] Australian Bureau of Statistics, *Australian Social Trends 2000*, Cat No 4102.0, 116.

in ongoing, uninterrupted employment.[8] Already, in the early decades of the twentieth century, the term 'casual' necessarily encompassed a wide diversity of work arrangements. These included those employees working for extended periods at the one trade which was seasonal in nature (for example, shearers, meat preservers, flour millers); those working for extended periods at the one trade but with a series of different employers such that the year was broken by periods of looking for the next job (for example, builders' labourers); and those working at the one trade in chronically overstocked trades and who were thus subject to the call system, not knowing from day to day whether they would be offered work (for example, waterside workers). As well, there was provision even in those trades considered regular, that 'casual hands' could be taken on to meet periods of increased demand (for example, coalminers, textile workers).[9] In effect, casual hire emerged as a catch-all term for most hiring systems other than weekly hire (although, in rural trades, the term 'seasonal' hire was common).

As ongoing employees were granted rights to various forms of leave – most notably annual leave – 'casual' employees were in turn denied these. The Arbitration Court's reason for this was simply that employees who were getting a casual loading to compensate for the 'intermittency' of their employment could hardly claim to also be in need of the rest and recuperation required by continuous or permanent employees, which annual leave was designed to provide.[10] In short, the casual loading didn't emerge as compensation for casual employees' inability to accrue paid leave. Rather, casual employees' inability to accrue annual leave emerged as a consequence of the existence of the casual loading. (Casual workers, falling outside the award category of weekly hire, were already denied access to the six days annual sick leave enjoyed by weekly hire workers since the early 1920s. Strictly speaking, sick leave under weekly hire award provisions was not an 'accrued' right, but represented an annual cap on what was otherwise a potentially open-ended common law entitlement of long-term or permanent employees to be paid wages during absences due to sickness.)

The result was that there arose a broad and heterogenous group of 'casual' workers, existing outside weekly hire provisions, defined largely by access to a casual loading and the absence of leave entitlements. Accordingly, from the early 1980s Australian labour force statistics distinguished between 'permanent' and

---

[8] The first example of the Arbitration Court's approach can be found in *Waterside Workers Award* (1914) 8 CAR 53.

[9] See Commonwealth of Australia, Royal Commission on National Insurance, *Second Progress Report: Unemployment*, Parl Paper No 79 (1926–28) 7–8; G Anderson, *Fixation of Wages in Australia* (Melbourne, Macmillan, 1929) 490. In *Doyle v Sydney Steel Company* (1936) 56 CLR 545 Evatt J drew a distinction between 'true' and other casuals· 'True' casuals were those who were employed irregularly in different trades and callings, whereas other casuals worked at the one trade or calling but, given the intermittent nature of the trade, their work was irregular or for multiple employers across time.

[10] *Ship Carpenters and Joiners Case* (1942) 48 CAR 279. When one week's annual leave was introduced in the 1930s, it was seen as accruing at one day for every two calendar months of service: see the *Commercial Printing Award* (1935) 36 CAR 760.

'casual' employees by measuring the presence or absence of leave entitlements. By the end of the twentieth century, around 25 per cent of Australian employees did not accrue annual and sick leave and were categorised by the Australian Bureau of Statistics (ABS) as casual for that reason alone, having risen from about 16 per cent in 1988.[11]

But industrial awards typically did not define the type of work undertaken by a casual employee, leaving it to an employer to designate whether the employee is casual or permanent. As a result, casual employment has come to encapsulate not only the intermittent and irregular workers who are colloquially associated with the idea of 'casual' employment, but also regular part-time and regular full-time workers who have simply been designated 'casual'. That means the designation 'casual' now tells us little about an employee's length of tenure or regularity of hours and income: 'casual' employment refers to what employees *get*, by way of leave entitlements, rather than what they *do*.[12] By the last decade of the twentieth century a significant proportion of 'casuals' were in fact working fairly stable and predictable hours for the one enterprise over long periods. Up to one-third of 'casual' employees had earnings that did not vary from week to week, and around 20 per cent also worked full-time weekly hours. In 1998, a quarter of the 'casual' cohort had been engaged by the one employer for longer than two years.[13]

This suggests that rather than using casual workers as supplementary labour in fluctuating periods of peak demand, employers in many sectors were making significant use of casual employment provisions even where the true nature of the contract might have been for regular part-time or full-time employment.[14] The growth in casual employment did partly reflect the growth in the fluctuating, intermittent demand for labour that characterised, say, the hospitality and retail industries. But the significant proportion of casuals working fairly stable and predictable hours for the one enterprise over long periods suggests many employers were not so much seeking to avoid long-term attachments to employees as seeking to avoid the regulatory obligations that went with such attachments.[15]

Then there are those workers who are on fixed-term contracts – that is, for a specified period or for the duration of a specific task. These represent a significant group in their own right. A survey conducted in 2008 found 3.6 per cent of all

---

[11] I Campbell and J Burgess, 'A New Estimate of Casual Employment?' (2001) 27 *Australian Bulletin of Labour* 85, 102.

[12] J Buchanan, 'Paradoxes of Significance: Australian Casualisation and Labour Productivity', paper presented to ACTU, RMIT, and *Age* Conference, *Work Interrupted: Casual and Insecure Employment in Australia* (Melbourne, 2 August 2004).

[13] See G Murtough and M Waite, 'The Diversity of Casual Contract Employment', Productivity Commission Staff Research Paper (Canberra, AusInfo, 2000).

[14] On the relationship between the award category of 'casual' and the underlying contract of employment, see the discussion in A O'Donnell, 'Non-Standard Workers in Australia: Counts and Controversies' (2004) 17 *Australian Journal of Labour Law* 89, 97–102.

[15] Buchanan, above n 12. See also R Owens, 'The "Long term or Permanent Casual": An Oxymoron or a "Well Enough Understood Australianism" in the Law?' (2001) 15 *Australian Bulletin of Labour* 118.

employees (or 2.9 per cent of all employed persons) to be fixed-term.[16] According to the data, the number of fixed-term employees increased from 1998 to 2001, then declined to 2004, and rose again to 2008.[17] Survey data from the late 1990s suggested that compared with ongoing employees, fixed-term employees were more likely to be female, young, and working in professional occupations in the education, health, and cultural and recreational services sectors and twice as likely as ongoing employees to be employed in the public sector.[18]

Some mention, too, needs be made of agency work. The use of agency 'temps' grew in the post-war labour market as a way of allowing enterprises to source holiday replacement workers. In this guise, the focus was often on secretarial or other white-collar work. Also, agency work has been common for a long time in other sectors, such as nursing and theatrical employment, and attempts to commercialise domestic service provision by hiring out daily domestic workers date back to the interwar period and have again become increasingly common.[19] The use of short-term agency work to provide enterprise flexibility both during temporary vacancies or when demand temporarily increases is still a major factor driving the use of labour hire arrangements, and agencies now offer a range of staff beyond the categories that originally dominated the agency sector. In the late 1980s specialist firms arose to offer contract labour as a replacement for existing employees in a number of highly unionised and dispute-prone industries such as building, construction and shearing.[20] By constructing the legal relationships between the worker and the agency on the one hand, and the host enterprise on the other, so that the worker was not an employee of either the agency or the host enterprise, agency labour could be used as a way of undermining union control and providing staff at highly competitive rates of pay.[21]

---

[16] A O'Donnell, 'Fixed Term Work in Australia' in H Nakakubo and T Araki (eds), *The Regulation of Fixed-Term Employment Contracts: A Comparative Overview* (The Hague, Kluwer Law International, 2010).

[17] The growth between 1998 and 2001 may be partially explained by the fact that the 1998 survey only enquired as to whether an employee's employment had a finishing *date*, whereas subsequent surveys have asked whether the employment has a finishing date *or event*. The survey goes on to ask whether the finishing date or event is less than five years away, and whether the reason for having a finishing date or event is that the employee is on a fixed-term contract.

[18] M Waite and L Will, 'Fixed-Term Employees in Australia: Incidence and Characteristics', Productivity Commission Staff Research Paper (Canberra, AusInfo, 2002).

[19] See B Higman, *Domestic Service in Australia* (Melbourne, Melbourne University Press, 2002) 108; G Meagher, *Friend or Flunkey? Paid Domestic Workers in the New Economy* (Sydney, UNSW Press, 2003).

[20] R Hall, 'Labour Hire in Australia: Motivation, Dynamics and Prospects' (2002) Australian Centre for Industrial Relations Research and Training, University of Sydney Working Paper No 76.

[21] *Building Workers Industrial Union of Australia v Odco* (1991) 29 FCR 104; C Fenwick, 'Shooting for Trouble? Contract Labour Hire in the Victorian Building Industry' (1992) 5 *Australian Journal of Labour Law* 237. In many instances, however, a person is engaged either as an ongoing, fixed-term or casual employee of an agency and is then on-hired by that agency under a commercial agreement to another business that then controls the conduct of that employee's work for its own ends. So although there is no formal employment relationship between the worker and the user or host enterprise, many

Some of these shifts in employment arrangements reflect demographic changes – in particular, the increased number of young people staying in post-compulsory education and the number of women returning to the workforce after childbirth. In 1966 fewer than a third of married women were in the labour market; by 1996 the figure was 62 per cent. But the increase in women's *full-time* labour force participation across those two decades was modest; the real surge was in part-time work. In 1966, 74 per cent of working women were employed full-time; by 1996 that had declined to 56 per cent. This reflected a new pattern whereby women withdrew from the labour force for some time when their children were young, and returned on a part-time (and, often, casual or fixed-term) basis when children reached school age.[22] For young women too, who are staying in post-compulsory education longer, the full-time labour force participation rate has fallen, in favour of increased part-time work combined with study.

But we shouldn't lose sight of the shift in employer strategy. And it is a shift that has been facilitated by Australian labour law. Employers can now more easily pick the obligations and rights regime they want (casual, independent contractor, fixed-term and so on) and then deem the jobs they offer as having that nature, regardless of the way labour is actually engaged in the production process.[23] For much of the twentieth century, Australian labour law discouraged and restricted such a strategy. It did this either through express limitations embodied in awards and agreements or by moderating the attraction of non-standard labour to employers through the imposition of loadings and penalties. As well as imposing a casual loading, many awards up until the 1980s specified proportional limits or quotas on the number of casual workers, confined casual employment to part-time hours, and sometimes set restrictions on how long and under what conditions casuals could be used. Awards were also used to restrict the proportion of fixed-term jobs relative to full-time, ongoing employment or to limit the maximum duration of fixed-term appointments.[24]

However, such restrictions on the use of casual and other forms of non-standard labour have become less common over the past 20 years or so. The removal of restrictions on the use of non-standard labour since the 1980s reflected the notion

agency workers are engaged by the agency on a casual rather than a permanent basis: NSW Department of Industrial Relations, *Labour Hire Task Force: Final Report*, 27. See also P Laplagne et al, 'The Growth of Labour Hire Employment in Australia (2005) Productivity Commission Staff Working Paper (Melbourne, Productivity Commission).

[22] J Pech and H Innes, 'Women in the Australian Labour Market 1966–96: The Impact of Change on the Social Security System' [1998] *Social Security Journal* 3.

[23] Buchanan, above n 12. Mark Freedland refers to this as an example of labour law allowing a fairly arbitrary 'segmentation of rights' by way of managerial fiat: 'The Segmentation of Workers' Rights and the Legal Analysis of Personal Work Relations' (2015) 36 *Comparative Labor Law & Policy Journal* 241.

[24] R Mitchell and A O'Donnell, 'Participation, Exchange, and Rights and Obligations in Labour Markets and Work Relationships' in C Arup et al (eds), *Labour Law and Labour Market Regulation* (Sydney, Federation Press, 2006); See the examples given in J Romeyn, *Flexible Working-Time Arrangements: Fixed-Term and Temporary Employment*, Industrial Relations Research Series, No 13, Department of Industrial Relations, 1994, 97–99.

that by giving enhanced flexibility to business, non-standard labour was useful for boosting competitiveness and efficiency, while also providing a mode of participation for those who would otherwise be excluded from the labour market. By the last decade of the century, both international competitiveness and the promotion of high employment and the elimination of discrimination in employment appeared as explicit objectives of the federal labour statute.[25]

In 1987 Australia moved towards a two-tier system of wage bargaining in which the second tier of wage increases was determined on an enterprise-by-enterprise basis according to restructuring and efficiency principles. Many of these second-tier agreements allowed for the increased use of non-standard employment and restrictions on the use of non-standard employment were relaxed or removed. In the first half of the 1990s the Labor government pressured the federal tribunal to adopt enterprise bargaining and legislated specifically for union- and *non*-union-based agreements in the 1993 amendments to the Industrial Relations Act (Cth). As a result there began a steady evolution of bargaining and agreement-making at the workplace level and enterprise agreements began to open up more flexible arrangements in the scheduling of work, the ordinary hours of work and the use of part-time, casual and fixed-term labour.

The award-making powers of the federal tribunal were substantially constrained by the Workplace Relations Act 1996 (Cth) enacted by the incoming Liberal/National Coalition government. 'Type of employment' remained one of 20 'allowable' award matters under the Act, but the federal tribunal was expressly precluded from using this provision to make an award limiting the 'number or proportion of employees that an employer could employ in a particular type of employment'.[26] It was left to enterprise-level collective agreements to attempt to regulate the circumstances in which non-standard contracts might be used. Depending on unions' bargaining strength, examples might include limits on the total period of employment under successive fixed-term contracts, provisions giving fixed-term or casual contract workers an option to convert to continuing employment, and attempts to set the terms and conditions of staff supplied to the enterprise through labour hire agencies.

Is this destandardisation of employment arrangements simply a return to the pre-war situation? As Iain Campbell has noted, there are clear parallels – 'similar processes driven by similar forces' – but there are also major differences between

---

[25] Workplace Relations Act 1996 (Cth) s 3(a), s 3(m).

[26] Workplace Relations Act 1996 (Cth) s 89A(4). So, eg, union claims for giving fixed-term employees the right to convert to continuing status; imposing limits on the circumstances in which fixed-term contracts could be utilised; and granting fixed-term employees' entitlement to notice and severance pay were allowable, but not union claims for the maintenance of an acceptable ratio of fixed-term to permanent employee: see *National Tertiary Education Industry Union v Australian Higher Education Industrial Association* (1997) 74 IR 326, cited in A Forsyth, 'The European Framework Agreement on Fixed-Term Work: An Australian Perspective' (1999) 15 *The International Journal of Comparative Labour Law and Industrial Relations* 161, 166.

more recent trends and the situation I explored in chapter one.[27] One distinctive feature of the contemporary era is that flows into and out of non-standard work are driven by life-cycle stages: the increased participation of married women with children in work and young people's extended stay in education. Similarly, although product market fluctuations play some role, employer strategy is also important – and, as I've pointed out, the erosion of certain labour standards has to some extent facilitated this.

The shift in work patterns put the labour force framework, with its attendant order of priorities, under strain. Or, rather, the headline unemployment rate (the number of 'unemployed' as a proportion of those 'in the labour force') began to provide a less than transparent window onto this changing labour market. The five-yearly censuses from 1966 to 1996 show that unemployment rates for males were 1.3, 1.5, 4.1, 5.5, 9, 12.3 and 9.9 per cent respectively, which supports the conventional story that things shifted dramatically around the middle of the 1970s. But *non*-employment rates for males aged 20–64 were 6.4 in 1966, 9.5 in 1971 and 11.5 in 1976 and by 1991 had reached 24 per cent. Commenting on these figures, Alan Jordan observed that the erosion of 'full employment' for males seems to have been well and truly underway by the late 1960s.[28] Labour force categories such as 'marginally attached' or 'underemployed' began to tell us more about the state of the labour market than a headline unemployment rate. A significant number of these jobless men, now designated as 'not in the labour force', may have been ready and willing to work but not seeking work. The conundrum presented by married women, outlined in chapter six, transitioning between 'employed' and 'not in the labour force' while skipping the statistical and juridical category of 'unemployed', seemed to become more generalised.

Shifts in labour force participation and the fluidity of people's engagement in the labour market associated with their life-cycle suggested the declining capacity of the labour force framework to adequately capture what was going on. As long as the notional 'labour force' remained the denominator of our unemployment rate, that rate on its own became less and less meaningful as an economic indicator.[29] We need at least to acknowledge that the 'labour force' is now a much more permeable and unstable category than post-war planners and statisticians envisaged. In Monica Threlfall's words,

> [w]hereas once 'labour force' was coterminous with an identifiable social category, today it is more like an unbounded space that a variety of people of different ages enter, leave and re-enter at a variety of rates.[30]

[27] I Campbell, 'A Historical Perspective on Insecure Work' (2013) 16 *Queensland Journal of Labour History* 6.

[28] A Jordan, 'Employment, Unemployment and Social Policy: Response to Structural Change' (unpublished manuscript, 2000).

[29] At the least, such a rate needs to be supplemented by figures of underemployment and discouraged workers if we want to reach a more encompassing labour 'underutilisation' rate.

[30] M Threlfall, 'A Critique of the Statistics that Support European Employment Policy' (2005) 88 *Radical Statistics* 22, 26.

Towards an 'Active Society'

The withdrawal of men from paid work was someway counterbalanced by women's increased labour supply across the same period. But increased female participation in paid employment did not fully compensate for decreased male participation at the level of individual households. That is, the rather rapid growth in women's employment across the last decades of the twentieth century overwhelmingly went to women with an employed partner and so didn't necessarily offset the household joblessness generated by men's loss of work.[31] Instead, there was an increase in households with no earners as well as an increase in households with two earners. This upset those intra-household resource flows on which the post-war Australian model of labour regulation had, implicitly, depended and which were entrenched in the idea of the family wage. So although the overall labour force participation rate remained relatively unchanged, joblessness became of increasing concern to policymakers because an increased proportion of the unemployed appeared to be concentrated within jobless *households* which were living in poverty and making increased claims on the income support system.[32]

The initial response of governments when confronted with persistently high unemployment in many Western economies in the second half of the 1970s was to try to reduce the labour supply and confine economic activity to a narrowing number of employees. This merely increased welfare costs through social security transfers to compensate the inactive, while also frustrating the desire of many groups for continued or increased labour market access. So attention shifted in the early 1980s towards either public sector job creation or private sector employment subsidies in an effort to at least temporarily increase employment opportunities. Again, the cost to government remained a concern, as did the limited effectiveness of such schemes in that they seemed to merely 'churn' participants through short-term placements rather than improve the position of excluded groups over time.[33]

By the mid-1980s the OECD was forced to confront the paradox that, due to higher educational attainment and the emancipation of women, more and more people were demanding access to paid employment at the same time as the labour market seemed to be stalling. The answer was to embrace the new, emerging forms of labour market participation outlined in my previous section. There was a strong need according to the OECD,

> not only for the highest possible rate of job-creating growth, but also for a rapid development of new forms of employment and for strengthening of the social fabric by

---

[31] A Jordan, 'A Generation of Growth in Female Employment, But How Much Change?' (1995) (December) *Social Security Journal* 78.

[32] Australian Bureau of Statistics, *Labour Force Status and Other Characteristics of Families*, Cat No 6224.0: Reference Group on Welfare Reform, *Participation Support for a More Equitable Society: Final Report* (Department of Family and Community Services, Canberra, 2000).

[33] OECD, 'The Path to Full Employment: Structural Adjustment for an Active Society', *OECD Employment Outlook* (Paris, Organisation for Economic Co-operation and Development, 1989) 8–9.

providing as many citizens as possible with an active role in society, both as a means of income and of self-identity. This aim goes beyond 'full employment' as traditionally described.[34]

The move beyond '"full employment" as traditionally described' had several dimensions. First, although there was an emphasis on job creation, it was recognised that many of the new jobs would be non-standard, likely to be in small private sector firms, and paying 'modest' wages. Governments were encouraged to pursue the removal of institutional impediments to non-standard work such as part-time work, weekend work, self-employment and independent contracting: 'The "permanent" job as an entitlement to a secure income in return for performing the same unchanging tasks is increasingly inappropriate in societies which seek to mobilise their full talents in response to evolving technologies and markets'.[35] Secondly, in the context of an increasingly flexible, volatile labour market, the importance of worker mobility and the transition between types of job assumed a new importance. The role for social assistance increasingly becomes one of facilitating 'adjustment':

> [R]educing individual hardship [via payment of unemployment benefit] lacks a dynamic, future-oriented element, and very often does not result in productive job search ... It is vital, therefore, to improve the productive capacity of displaced workers. A detailed assessment of potential skills, motivations and capabilities, and a training strategy tailored to individual needs, is in general the most appropriate approach to follow.[36]

This new approach to income support was glossed as involving 'active programmes' rather than 'passive support'.[37] An 'active' programme was one which made continued income support conditional on recipients undertaking activities to improve their 'readiness' for the labour market, rather than one which 'merely maintained [their] incomes'.[38] Social assistance had been generally perceived as support for a 'non-active' population. It was now being seen as something that impinged potentially on all citizens' lives. In a turbulent economy characterised by ongoing job creation, destruction, and technological change, social policy programmes should no longer be restricted to 'entitling particular classes of individuals to particular forms of income support' during periods when they cannot access standard full-time work.[39] Any clear dichotomy between being 'in work' or 'on welfare' was breaking down. Everyone was potentially an 'active' participant in economic life, and such participation was not only recognised as a valid aspiration but was seen as an economic good which would 'enhance the effective productivity of the

---

[34] OECD, 'Activity for All in Tomorrow's Society', *OECD Employment Outlook* (Paris, Organisation for Economic Co-operation and Development, 1987) 7.

[35] OECD, 'The Path to Full Employment', above n 33, 10.

[36] OECD, 'Activity for All in Tomorrow's Society', above n 34, 14.

[37] OECD, 'The Path to Full Employment', above n 33, 10.

[38] ibid 10.

[39] ibid 11.

population as a whole by drawing on previously-unused talents, and harnessing them in a more effective and comprehensive division of labour.[40]

The OECD idea of the 'Active Society' was to prove influential in the slew of reforms that overtook Australian unemployment assistance in the late 1980s and early 1990s. In December 1985, Brian Howe, the Minister for Social Security in the Hawke Labor government, announced a major review of the Australian system of social security. Howe, like Hayden, was a member of the Australian Labor Party's left faction, and had a long history of engagement with welfare issues dating back to his days as an activist Methodist minister in inner-urban Melbourne in the early 1970s. His Social Security Review looked at three main aspects of the social security system: income support for people of workforce age (including the unemployed, people with disabilities and single parents), for families with children, and for the aged. The Review was chaired by Bettina Cass, a social policy academic who worked closely with the research and policy staff at the Department of Social Security.

The influence of the OECD can be seen in the manner in which the Social Security Review combined consideration of income support for the unemployed, single parents and people with disabilities under the single rubric 'social security and the labour force'. Special reference was made to 'transition to work' issues,[41] mirroring the OECD's concern that social security policies needed to move beyond so-called 'passive support' to 'active' schemes that more fully mobilised claimants towards re-entry into the workforce. Now, if we were to take seriously this distinction, Australia in fact had operated an 'active' system since the inauguration of its unemployment benefit scheme in 1944, as active job search was explicitly built into the eligibility conditions. The Review recognised this,[42] but went on to suggest that despite unemployment benefit being directed towards 'active jobseekers', it had nevertheless 'acquired the stigma of encouraging "passivity" and dependence, rather than denoting the set of activities which it was intended to support'.[43]

Economic conditions since the mid-1970s had also revealed a troubling phenomenon that the government needed to address: chronic and long-term unemployment. The probability of finding work appeared to decrease according to the duration of unemployment, suggesting that the cohort of long-term unemployed did not necessarily benefit from a post-recession economic recovery as many recovery-based jobs were filled by new entrants to the labour force, including women partnered to working men, rather than by those displaced during recession. So, after each recession, unemployment fell, but generally not to pre-recession levels. There appeared to be a group of unemployed that was resistant to the normal prescription of economic recovery and growth.

[40] ibid 9.
[41] Commonwealth of Australia, Social Security Review, 'The Case for Review of Aspects of the Australian Social Security System', Background/Discussion Paper No 1 (Canberra, DSS, 1986) 11.
[42] Commonwealth of Australia, Social Security Review, 'Income Support for the Unemployed in Australia: Towards a More Active System', Issues Paper No 4 (Canberra, DSS, 1988) 270.
[43] ibid 290.

In the light of these concerns, the Review proposed linking an increase in the level of income support to both a restructured income test, to encourage greater labour force attachment, and an 'activity test' which would expand the work test to include activities that went beyond job search and acceptance of job offers.[44] Income support would be integrated with labour market programmes provided through the Commonwealth Employment Service (CES). The Review explicitly evoked the 'Swedish model' of 'an active income support policy integrated closely with labour market programmes'. The objective of this approach was

> to rectify the mismatch between labour supply and demand which structural change in the labour market produces, to increase the skill level of labour in line with industrial and occupational restructuring ... and to use income support as an integral component of a multi-faceted approach to job search and the activities required to sustain it.[45]

The Review also echoed the OECD's views about what an 'active society' might look like in terms of the future of work. It asked whether 'full-time [jobs], covering a working life-span of 49 years of uninterrupted workforce participation as traditionally expected of able-bodied men' provided the most appropriate model for the diverse groups of people now seeking work: mothers, older workers and people in education and training.[46]

Under the proposed 'activity test', claimants of unemployment benefit could prove their eligibility by undertaking a range of activities, other than the search for full-time work, that were likely to reduce labour market disadvantage. These activities included labour market programmes likely to improve their prospects of finding work, or developing a self-employment venture. The Review proposed disaggregating the unemployed and other jobseekers according to stage of working life, attachment to the labour market, and duration of unemployment. This would have resulted in a diversity of programmes and payment structures for jobseekers. The government had, in 1988, already abolished unemployment benefit for 16- and 17-year-olds and replaced it with a Job Search allowance (JSA), which carried with it a significantly expanded 'activities' test. The Review proposed extending this to 18–20 year-olds who had not had six months cumulative employment, while adding a Short-Term Employment Payment for prime-age people who would then transfer to a Long-term Adjustment Payment once they had been unemployed for at least 12 months (or who had been out of the labour force for 12 months before commencing active job search). Finally, a Transition Age Payment was proposed for long-term unemployed people aged between 55 and pension age. The Review also argued that payment rates for those programmes targeted at the long-term unemployed should maintain parity with the more generous rates payable to old age and disability pensioners.[47]

---

[44] ibid 267.
[45] ibid 271.
[46] ibid 273.
[47] ibid 267–98.

From Work Test to Activity Test

The full shift to an 'activation' paradigm was accomplished through an accumulation of legislative amendments over the following decade. Crucially, in enacting a new Social Security Act 1991, the government rejected the fourfold differentiated payment structure proposed by the Review. Instead, it moved to a dual structure based simply on duration of unemployment rather than stage of working life or labour market attachment. Unemployment benefit was abolished and JSA was extended to claimants over 18 years during the first 12 months of their unemployment. A Newstart Allowance (NSA) was put in place for those who had been unemployed for longer than 12 months.[48] The purpose of the JSA was 'to support and require active job search, combined with appropriate training or other job preparation activities where there is an identified risk of long-term unemployment'. The NSA recognised 'the special and intractable problems facing the long-term unemployed and the need for a different approach to client contact, assistance and obligations'.[49] And whereas the Social Security Review had envisaged an expanded 'activity test' for the *long-term* unemployed,[50] the government replaced the old 'work test' with an expanded 'activity test' for both JSA *and* NSA recipients.

At the core of the new test was the requirement that a claimant be willing to undertake suitable work and was 'actively seeking' such work. In 1994, this was amended slightly: the reference to 'suitable work' was changed to 'work other than that which is unsuitable' and the sort of work that was deemed unsuitable was spelled out in the legislation.[51] The test mirrored labour law notions of 'suitable work': that is, work subject to award standards (and occupational health and safety standards). As we've seen, 'suitable work' had always been given a fairly broad meaning in Australia compared with some countries in that generally people had to look for and accept any job they were qualified for, even if it meant working outside their normal trade or at a lesser level of skill. But as I indicated in chapter six, there was room for both the government of the day and/or front-line officers to tinker with the concept of 'suitable' work without any formal changes to the legislation, and thus increase or lessen the intensity of job search activity. The 1994 legislation more or less amounted to a codification of long-standing guidelines and thus lessened this 'discretional slippage'.[52]

The legislative specification of 'unsuitable work' has been narrowed over the subsequent years, suggesting that the range and intensity of job search by claimants would be correspondingly increased. For example, the original codification

---

[48] Social Security (Job Search and Newstart) Amendment Act 1991 (Cth).

[49] Department of Social Security (1991) 105.

[50] Social Security Review, 'Income Support for the Unemployed', above n 42, 288.

[51] Social Security (1994 Budget and White Paper) Amendment Act 1994 (Cth), inserting ss 522(2A) and 601(2B) into the main Act.

[52] T Carney and P Hanks, *Social Security in Australia* (Melbourne, Oxford University Press, 1994) 169.

defined work as 'unsuitable' where a person lacked the particular skills, experience or qualifications needed to perform the work. In 1996 this was amended with the addition 'and no training will be provided by the employer'. Where the original definition of unsuitable work referred to the claimant having 'an illness, disability or injury that would be aggravated by the work', in 1996 this required the production of medical evidence. Where the original classed self-employment as a form of unsuitable work, in 2005 self-employment was removed from the list.

But this apparent broadening of the job search requirement was partly offset by the shift from a 'taking reasonable steps' formula to one of 'actively seeking' suitable work. Initially, this shift was seen as not really altering the existing operation of the work test.[53] Yet the removal of the 'reasonableness' criterion did significantly alter the application of the test. The idea of 'reasonable steps' meant regard had to be had to both the range of jobs sought and to the realistic, objective prospect of success. The simple requirement to 'actively seek' suitable work in the new formulation meant these two elements were of less importance: whether someone was 'actively seeking' suitable work did not entail any consideration as to the range or likely success of their job search activity. For example, in one instance, the 'job search' activity involved the claimant campaigning for election to the New South Wales Parliament as a Greens Party candidate for Coffs Harbour. Although the campaigning did not allow him time to seek other work, and prospects of electoral success were slim, the claimant was found to have met the test.[54]

To some extent, then, the clearer bright-line and progressively tightened definition of 'suitable work' was undercut by the absence of any obligation to seek the full range of such suitable work. But crucially, the new activity test now extended beyond the core requirement of actively seeking work and incorporated the capacity for the Secretary to impose additional 'requirements' on claimants. These requirements could substantially expand the range of activity that may be demanded as a condition of receipt of benefit, and the determination of whether a claimant had taken 'reasonable steps' to comply with any such requirement merely reintroduced the discretionary element of 'reasonableness' that had been removed from the assessment of job search activity.[55]

The 'requirements' power was not entirely new. The original 1944 legislation enabled the Director-General to require a benefit recipient – of either sickness or unemployment benefit – to undergo training, a medical examination, or to work as a condition of receipt of benefit.[56] The Social Services Consolidation Act 1947 extended the power to cover pensioners as well as those in receipt of child endowment. In the 1980s the potential requirements, although still extending to all claimants and beneficiaries, were more closely aligned with labour

---

[53] See Explanatory memorandum for Social Security Act 1991 (Cth).

[54] *Spencer v Secretary, Department of Social Security* (1998) 83 FCR 306; see also *Castleman v Secretary, Department of Social Security* (1999) 29 AAR 458.

[55] Social Security Act 1991 (Cth) ss 522(3) JSA and 601(3) NSA.

[56] Unemployment and Sickness Benefits Act 1944 (Cth) s 45.

market programmes: for example, the requirement to undergo 'any course of training for the improvement of [a claimant's] physical or mental capacities' was replaced with a reference to courses of vocational training to which there had been a CES referral.[57] Further, whether a claimant was taking 'reasonable steps' to comply with such requirements was to be judged according the state of the labour market and whether such training would in fact improve the claimant's employment prospects.[58] Finally, the 1991 legislation further restricted the operation of the power to the imposition of those requirements likely to improve prospects of obtaining paid work or assisting in job search.[59]

The new focus on 'requirements' meant the ambit of the activity test was capable of significant expansion. The earliest example of this expansion was the power conferred on the Secretary of the Department of Social Security to require a recipient of either the NSA or the JSA to apply for a particular number of advertised job vacancies as part of the activity test.[60] In 1997, the Secretary of the Department of Social Security acquired an additional power to require recipients of the NSA to participate in an 'approved programme of work' – commonly known as the 'Work for the Dole' programme – as a condition of the activity test.[61] Work for the Dole reconfigured recipients' income support payments as a notional 'wage', at minimum award rates, for undertaking around 15 hours of work each week with community organisations. The requirement was initially directed at 18–24 year-olds who had been on NSA or Youth Allowance for six months or more. In 1999 it was extended to 25–34 year-olds who had been unemployed for 12 months. Work for the Dole was in fact just one possible activity under the Coalition government's 'Enhanced Mutual Obligation' requirements targeted at these groups. Others included voluntary work, literacy or numeracy training or job search training, but Work for the Dole became the largest programme and the default requirement for those who failed to commence an alternative activity in a specified time.[62]

So essentially, the new activity test kept aspects of the old work test at its core: a claimant had to be actively seeking and willing to undertake suitable paid work. But in addition, a claimant might be 'required' to take reasonable steps to comply with other specific obligations imposed by the Secretary, such as particular paid work, vocational training or labour market programmes likely to improve the prospects of finding work or assist in seeking work, or, where

---

[57] Social Security and Veterans' Entitlements Amendment Act (No 2) 1987 (Cth). The evolution of labour market programmes in this period is discussed in more detail in ch 8.

[58] *Secretary to DSS v Stanik* AAT No 6627, decided 7 February 1991.

[59] Social Security Act 1991 (Cth) ss 522(2) and 601(2).

[60] Social Security (Budget and Other Measures) Legislation Amendment Act 1993 (Cth).

[61] Social Security Legislation Amendment (Work for the Dole) Act 1997 (Cth).

[62] Although Work for the Dole had express legislative authorisation, the legal basis for the entire suite of Enhanced Mutual Obligation activities is less clear: see the discussion in T Carney and G Ramia, *From Rights to Management: Contract, New Public Management and Employment Services* (The Hague, Kluwer Law International, 2002) 93–95.

there is no accessible local labour market or training opportunities, some other activity suggested by the claimant and approved by the CES. Failure to take such reasonable steps meant the person was deemed to have failed the 'activity test' as a whole, regardless of whether his or her job search activity would have satisfied the old 'work test'.[63]

Making Agreements

An innovation of the 1991 legislative reforms was the introduction of 'Activity Agreements' for the long-term unemployed. Newstart Activity Agreements were negotiated between the claimant and the CES, focusing on appropriate job search and/or training activities, including measures designed to eliminate or reduce labour market disadvantage, or any other activity proposed by the claimant. A claimant's failure to negotiate an agreement or refusal to enter an agreement would lead to disqualification from the allowance.[64] That is, preparedness to enter an Activity Agreement itself became a condition of eligibility for NSA.[65] Apart from requiring the Secretary to the Department of Social Security to take into account the claimant's capacity to comply with the terms of the proposed agreement and his or her needs,[66] the legislation did not impose any express restriction on the content of these 'agreements'. There were, however, 'minimum-content' requirements.[67] Delay in negotiating an agreement entitled the CES to issue a notice that had the effect of deeming a person to have failed to enter an agreement.[68] This might occur where the person had unreasonably failed to attend the relevant appointment, to reply to correspondence about it, or to agree to the terms proposed.[69]

From March 1994, similar JSA 'Activity Agreements' were able to be incorporated into the 'requirements' limb of the JSA activity test.[70] With the introduction of the Coalition's Enhanced Mutual Obligation requirements for the young, long-term unemployed some years later, claimants would choose their activity and sign a 'Mutual Obligation Activity Agreement'. From 2000, all claimants for NSA had to

---

[63] Social Security Act 1991 (Cth) part 2.11, s 522 (JSA) and part 2.12, s 601 (NSA) as amended by Social Security (Job Search and Newstart) Amendment Act 1991 (Cth) s 7.

[64] Social Security Act 1991 (Cth) s 606 as amended by Social Security (Job Search and Newstart) Amendment Act 1991 (Cth) s 7.

[65] Social Security Act 1991 (Cth) s 593 as amended by Social Security (Job Search and Newstart) Amendment Act 1991 (Cth) s 7.

[66] Social Security Act 1991 (Cth) s 606(2)–(4).

[67] ibid s 606(1).

[68] ibid s 607.

[69] On procedural steps, see *Re Bartlett and Secretary, Department of Social Security* (1994) 19 AAR 398 [33 ALD 661].

[70] Social Security Act 1991 (Cth) ss 513, 522, as amended by Social Security (Budget and Other Measures) Legislation Amendment Act 1993 (Cth) ss 9, 12.

sign a 'Preparing for Work Agreement' at their initial claim interview before being eligible to receive any payment.[71]

This new focus on agreement-making represented both a 'personalisation' and 'contractualisation' of the relationship between the unemployed claimant and the Commonwealth government.[72]

The idea that the unemployed were not a homogenous group can be found in various taxonomies developed near the end of the post-war long boom and referred to in my previous chapter: distinctions between the 'frictional' and the 'hardcore' unemployed, for example, or Jordan's more elaborate taxonomy of the long-term unemployed. To the extent that there had been any administrative response to this, it was probably largely found in the exercise of discretion by front-line staff responding to what they saw as the particular needs of individual claimants. Any formal diversification of service delivery or assistance – access to certain labour market programmes, or the initial distinction between JSA and NSA – was usually made on the basis of target groups defined broadly according to duration of unemployment or certain social or demographic characteristics.[73] This type of categorisation still goes on, although through a complex – and partly automated – process of profiling and risk assessment using a lengthier and more finely grained set of social and demographic variables. In the next chapter I'll examine the restructuring of employment assistance and how this profiling and streaming of claimants into different levels of assistance intersects with the financial incentives provided to private operators of employment services to achieve particular outcomes.

Agreement-making, however, promised an even more radical individualisation of assistance. This was supported by the legislation, which indicated that in setting terms the CES delegate must have regard both to the claimant's capacity to comply and to the needs of the person, including their education, experience, skills, age, the state of the local labour market, available training and other factors relevant in the circumstances.[74]

The language of activation and individual agreement-making appears to put a fundamentally new cast on the regulation of the unemployed. But, to a large extent, genuine individualisation or 'personalisation' failed to materialise. Mutual Obligation Activity Agreements, for example, carried a range of around 15 activity options, signaling scope for tailoring activities to a claimant's particular

---

[71] Preparing for Work Agreements were 'Activity Agreements' for the purpose of the Social Security Act 1991. Claimants aged 18–24 and 25–34 had to also choose a Mutual Obligation activity at this initial interview, although they would not be required to commence the activity until they had been unemployed for six months or 12 months respectively: C Howard, 'The Promise and Performance of Mutual Obligation' in C Aspalter (ed), *Neoliberalism and the Australian Welfare State* (Taichung, Casa Verde, 2003) 131. At the time of writing, the nomenclature for such an agreement was a 'Job Plan'.

[72] M Freedland et al, *Public Employment Services and European Law* (Oxford, Oxford University Press, 2007) 313.

[73] ibid 315.

[74] Social Security Act 1991 (Cth) s 606(3)–(4).

circumstances, but many claimants were ineligible for, or did not require, many of the forms of assistance on offer. So they were left with a range of about five options to choose from in a 'tick a box' approach.[75] In 1995, 95 per cent of JSA recipients and 92 per cent of NSA recipients were undertaking job search as their 'activity';[76] by 2009, only 16 per cent of unemployment benefit recipients were meeting their activity requirements through activities other than job search, such as training, education or self-employment development.[77] The reasons for the relative lack of diversity in activity would probably vary as between the two dates mentioned. In 1995, Activity Agreements were formulated by public officials in the CES; by the later date, agreements were being brokered by independent advisers and case managers working in a privatised network of employment services. Bureaucratic inertia might explain the dominance of job search activity as the dominant activity in 1995.[78] The continued dominance of job search more than 10 years later is odder, particularly because one of the main rationales for moving to a privatised system was to encourage innovative and entrepreneurial responses to individuals' particular needs for assistance. I'll explore this further in chapter eight.

The use of agreements between claimants and the government, and the prospect of loss of benefit should the claimant 'breach' the agreement, also evokes the idea of there being some sort of contractual relationship between the claimant and the government. Yet these Activity Agreements have always sat uneasily with classical contract doctrine. They were not really negotiated arrangements that necessarily represented any 'meeting of minds': the government could simply impose the 'agreement' and largely prescribe, vary or suspend its terms, subject only to certain procedural requirements.[79] And as a British commentator has observed regarding that country's similar Jobseeker Agreements, even if there were some notional 'agreement', the 'institutional environment is one of compulsion and the principal policy objective that of labour market discipline'.[80]

What is more, the types of matters considered appropriate for NSA Activity Agreements more or less mirrored the 'requirements' that could be imposed on JSA claimants under the 1991 activity test reforms – and, indeed, these in turn mirrored some aspects of the conditionality that had been imposed by ministerial fiat under the preceding legislation.[81] Given that increased conditionality can be

---

[75] Howard, above n 71, 139–40. For example, the Community Development Employment Program was for Indigenous Australians; Advanced English for Migrants was for newly arrived migrants; participation in the Green Corps was subject to an age limit; and many people did not need literacy or numeracy training.

[76] J Powlay and K Rodgers, 'What's Happened to the Work Test?' [1995] *Social Security Journal* 67, 70.

[77] P Davidson and P Whiteford, *An Overview of Australia's System of Income and Employment Assistance for the Unemployed* (Paris, OECD, 2012) 25.

[78] Powlay and Rodgers, above n 76, 71.

[79] Social Security Act 1991, s 606(2), (4)–(5).

[80] P Vincent-Jones, *The New Public Contracting: Regulation, Responsiveness, Rationality* (Oxford, Oxford University Press, 2006) 244.

[81] In the case of Mutual Obligation Agreements this may reflect the fact that no amending legislation was enacted to establish them, thus the legal validity of the agreements must derive from pre-existing powers of the Director and reflect those powers: see Carney and Ramia, above n 62, 93–95.

achieved simply through the imposition of 'requirements' as part of an expanded activity test, any move to greater conditionality and coercion need not be associated wholly with the apparently 'contractual' nature of the rules.[82] As we've seen, dating from the 1944 legislation there was already a power to impose individualised 'requirements' as to training, work and medical examinations, and that power existed independently of any activity 'agreement'. These requirements now simply became clothed in contractual form. Paul Davies and Mark Freedland conclude with regard to similar developments in Britain:

> The choice between rule-making which takes an apparently contractual form and rule-making of a more traditional administrative character is mainly a matter of choice on the part of the government, with little significant importance beyond the rhetorical or psychological.[83]

This is an important point, although I'd question the somewhat blithe bracketing off of the agreement's 'rhetorical' and 'psychological' force. Hugh Collins observes that it is precisely the rhetorical or psychological force of contract that gives the intensified bureaucratic control of claimants 'a new legitimacy' based on a purported respect for the individual.[84]

The idea that assistance has been tailored to meet individual needs certainly bestows a legitimacy on administrative interventions – although, as I just noted, whether genuine individualisation of assistance was actually proceeding is doubtful. But the new legitimacy is also grounded in contract's 'logic of reciprocity'.[85] This logic was nascent in the approach of the Social Security Review. The Review referred to the already existing work test as based on a 'reciprocal obligation': that is, 'an unemployed person is required to actively look for work and in return society accepts an obligation to pay income support'.[86] This recognised the 'active' nature of Australia's system of unemployment benefits, but up until this point the activity in question had rarely, if ever, been constructed as some sort of quid pro quo or social 'compact' in the manner suggested. Rather, as I've explored in earlier chapters, the activity requirement – taking reasonable steps to obtain suitable work – was meant to serve a number of other functions. It was central to a categorical system of assistance, necessary to define the 'unemployed' as a group separate from other claimant groups (the retired, the widowed, the disabled and so on).[87] Also, the work test was used to render the unemployed occupationally and geographically mobile for the purposes of post-war national development.

---

[82] P Davies and M Freedland, *Towards a Flexible Labour Market: Labour Legislation and Regulation Since the 1990s* (Oxford, Oxford University Press, 2007) 173.

[83] ibid.

[84] H Collins, *Regulating Contracts* (Oxford, Oxford University Press, 1999) 20.

[85] Freedland et al, above n 72, 325.

[86] Social Security Review, 'Income Support for the Unemployed', above n 42, 152.

[87] See also A Jordan, *Work-Test Failure: A Sample Survey of Terminations of Unemployment Benefit* (Canberra, Department of Social Security, 1981) 33; Social Security Review, 'Income Support for the Unemployed', above n 42, 145–46.

To the extent that it went to questions of desert, the work test aimed to guard against the moral hazard of persons claiming benefit when they were responsible for their current circumstances and their continuation.[88] Notably, even the Review's own argument for retention of the work test had not referred to this notion of reciprocal obligation.[89]

But by reconfiguring claimants' activity under the work test as a quid pro quo for benefit, the Review signalled an important staging-post on a path to justifying an expanded activity test. The Review's main concern was with the long-term unemployed and those with low prospects of finding work. For these people, the Review asked: should there be an additional obligation to participate in suitable and appropriate training? Any such obligation, though, carried with it the 'reciprocal obligation on society (which includes government and the private sector) to provide training and retraining programmes' for those expected to meet such an expanded activity test.[90] The same notion of reciprocal obligation – an increase in the obligations of the unemployed matched by an increase in the obligations of the government – found its way into the Minister's second reading speech for the legislation introducing NSA Activity Agreements.[91] It reached its apogee with the Labor government's 'Job Compact' announced in 1994 as part of its *Working Nation* policy. This imposed a 'reciprocal obligation' on the government and the long-term unemployed: those unemployed for longer than 18 months were put under an obligation to accept any such reasonable offer of a job, or otherwise lose their entitlement to income support; the government in turn assumed responsibility to provide a job offer.[92]

With the election of a conservative Coalition government in 1996, the idea of 'reciprocal obligation' was reconfigured as one of 'mutual obligation'. In practice, this meant the obligations imposed on unemployed beneficiaries were intensified while government spending on wage subsidies and labour market programmes was wound back. Under the idea of 'reciprocal obligation', increased requirements were imposed on claimants in exchange for assistance directly related to improving their employment prospects. In contrast, the centrepiece of 'mutual obligation' – the 'Work for the Dole' programme – imposed work obligations that were less packaged as a form of labour market assistance and more as simply claimants 'giving something back' in return for nothing other than basic income support.[93] Some commentators continued to see 'mutual

---

[88] Jordan, *Work-Test Failure*, ibid.

[89] Social Security Review, 'Income Support for the Unemployed', above n 42.

[90] ibid, 152.

[91] House of Representatives, Hansard, 18 April 1991, 3020–21.

[92] Commonwealth of Australia, *Working Nation: Policies and Programs* (Canberra, AGPS, 1994) 116.

[93] M Raper, 'Examining the Assumptions Behind the Welfare Review' in P Saunders (ed), *Reforming the Australian Welfare State* (Melbourne, Australian Institute of Family Studies, 2000) 263. Subsequent evaluations of the Work for the Dole scheme showed that the scheme in fact had substantial *adverse* effects on participants' successful transition out of unemployment, presumably through suppressing actual job search activity: J Borland and Y Tseng, 'Does "Work for the Dole" Work?' (unpublished paper, Department of Family and Community Services, 2003).

obligation' as a worthwhile project because it had the potential to enhance self-reliance while placing an onus on government to make credible commitments to assisting the unemployed.[94] But it is clear that the lived experience of Mutual Obligation Agreements under the Coalition government was overwhelmingly an intensification of activity in return simply for basic income support. Indeed, even this minimal obligation on the part of the government to pay income support, although founded in the legislation, was not to be found in Mutual Obligation Activity Agreements themselves, which were concerned solely with the obligations taken on by the claimant.[95]

Thus the contractual logic of reciprocal or mutual obligations came to legitimate the system of unemployment assistance as a whole, although how this played out varied markedly as between the Social Security Review, the Labor government's Working Nation scheme, and the Coalition government's Mutual Obligation initiative. It was agreement-making – Newstart Activity Agreements for the long-term unemployed, Case Management Activity Agreements for claimants under the Job Compact, Mutual Obligation Activity Agreements, and later Preparing for Work Agreements – that took this system-wide 'logic of reciprocity' and embodied it at the level of the individual claimant.

Enforcing Compliance

This movement of claimants' obligations into quasi-contractual form was meant to achieve another purpose. Pioneered in social work practice in the 1970s, agreement-making evokes a voluntaristic ethos that promotes what Vincent-Jones calls 'responsibilisation'.[96] That is, a claimant's obligations are more likely to be honoured where those obligations have the appearance of being negotiated and agreed.[97] This contractual ethos of choice and consent is meant to enhance claimants' sense of agency. But not only might a claimant feel more responsible for taking the steps designed to get them out of their predicament, they might also feel more responsible for the consequences that flow from their failure to take those steps. The sanctions actually derive from the legislation rather than from any truly 'contractual' breach, but the rhetorical and psychological force of the 'contract' may render any sanction more acceptable and legitimate, both to the jobseeker and to the public at large.[98] Whereas the sanctions – such as suspension or cancellation of benefit – are still imposed unilaterally, agreement-making

---

[94] A Yeatman, 'Mutual Obligation: What Kind of Contract Is This?' in P Saunders (ed), *Reforming the Australian Welfare State* (Melbourne, Australian Institute of Family Studies, 2000).

[95] Howard, above n 71.

[96] Vincent-Jones, above n 80, 133. On the social work antecedents of agreement-making, see J Corden, 'Contracts in Social Work Practice' (1980) 10 *British Journal of Social Work* 143.

[97] Vincent-Jones, ibid, 80.

[98] Freedland et al, above n 72, 331.

means 'they can now be regarded as having the prior consent of the person who is subject to them … as a matter of individual psychology … it is supposed to secure a readier acceptance by the client of the requirements'[99] – and hence of the sanctions themselves.

Let's consider the juridical basis for these sanctions a bit more closely. Since the inception of the unemployment benefit scheme, it was possible for the government to postpone an application for benefit where a claimant's acts had, in some way, contributed to their own joblessness: that is, where previous employment was lost through misconduct; where unemployment was due to a voluntary act without sufficient reason; or where the claimant refused an offer of suitable paid work; and, more recently, where the claimant moved to a new place of residence that resulted in reduced job prospects. But the relationship between the failure to satisfy eligibility conditions set out in the 'work test' on the one hand, and the postponement or suspension penalties for reasons of voluntary unemployment on the other, was never entirely clear. Someone who failed the work test was disqualified from benefit and presumably the duration of the disqualification was for as long as the qualifying conditions remained unmet. So refusal of a job offer, for example, could be sanctioned by cancellation or refusal of benefit (that is a failure of the work test) or seen as grounds for postponement or suspension of benefit. Refusal of a job offer was treated as an occasion for imposing a double penalty: termination of benefit for breach of the work test, followed by a postponement on any subsequent claim.[100] In contrast, failure to follow up a referral does not amount to a refusal of an offer of employment, but could be construed as a voluntary act contributing to a person's unemployment, although in the mid-1980s the departmental guidelines made it clear that the latter example would result in cancellation as a breach of the work test. In addition, section 35 of the 1944 Act and section 131 of the 1947 Act gave the Director-General power to suspend or vary the rate of benefit on the grounds of fluctuations in income, change in circumstance or 'for any other reason'. Carney and Hanks thought this final, broad dispensation did not confer a power of suspension of payment 'at large' (for example, for failure to attend a CES interview, declining an isolated job referral and so on). Rather, the provision must be interpreted as advancing the purposes of the work test and the postponement grounds then contained in sections 107 and 120 of the 1947 legislation.[101]

The suspension and postponement provisions were briefly ignored in the mid-1970s, with Australian Labor Party Social Security Minister Bill Hayden declaring that the administrative discretion allowing for the suspension of benefits was

---

[99] ibid.

[100] See generally the discussion in T Carney and P Hanks, *Australian Social Security Law, Policy and Administration* (Melbourne, Oxford University Press, 1986) 110–14.

[101] ibid 113. Thus, the postponement provision of s 120 could be invoked for a new claimant not already in receipt of benefit, while the suspension provision of s 131 could be invoked to suspend the benefit of someone whose benefit was current but who had breached the provisions of s 120.

'arbitrary, coercive and in its nature authoritarian'.[102] Generally, by the mid-1980s any suspensions of payment were capped at six weeks, except in extreme cases. The full circumstances of the claimant's breach were to be taken into account including financial circumstances, extenuating circumstances and so on, and discretion exercised, with the departmental manual recommending a warning for a first breach, two to four weeks' suspension for a second, and five to six weeks for third and subsequent breaches.[103]

But by widening the behaviours and activities required for compliance – meeting job application targets, filling out job search 'diaries', attending a labour market programme and so on – the areas of sanctionable conduct are increased.[104] With the move to activation, breaches of the activity test attracted an automatic penalty, staged between two weeks and 12 weeks. In addition, breach of co-operation or administrative requirements – such as failure to attend a CES interview or respond to a letter – also attracted a penalty. From 2006, mandated suspension periods for particular breaches were replaced with the suspension of payments until compliance resumed. In either case, the actual operation of the sanctions regime has been complicated since the delivery of employment services – and hence the monitoring of compliance with requirements – was outsourced to private providers after 1998.

Unemployment Benefit or Basic Income?
Manipulating the Means Test

A final piece of the activation puzzle is the manipulation of the means test for unemployed claimants. It's useful to think of access to unemployment benefit as a question of both *eligibility* and *entitlement*. The work test addresses the first of these: is the claimant eligible for benefit? Then, if they are eligible, what are they entitled to receive in any fortnightly pay period? This is an important distinction in a means-tested system. A person might satisfy the eligibility requirements of a benefit category, but their household income might deny them entitlement across any given pay period.

Under the post-war benefit regime, unemployment was conceived as total severance from a job and hence entailing more or less absolute loss of earned income. Conversely, any claimant moving into work was assumed to be taking up a full-time job at award wages and would have no need of benefit payment. And not only was there no expectation that a claimant would take on less than

---

[102] A Law, 'Surfing the Safety Net: "Dole Bludging", "Surfies" and Governmentality in Australia' (2001) 36 *International Review for the Sociology of Sport* 24, 31.
[103] Carney and Hanks, *Australian Social Security Law, Policy and Administration*, above n 100, 110, citing the 1985 departmental manual, para 10.256.
[104] T Carney, *Social Security Law and Policy* (Sydney, The Federation Press, 2006) 139.

full-time work, there was also no monetary incentive to do so. The means test allowed only a very small 'free area' of allowable income and no tapered withdrawal of benefit as income increased, so earnings from even a minimal amount of part-time work would usually mean foregoing the entire unemployment benefit. In 1969, the means test was altered, with the allowable income raised from $2 to $6 per week.[105] The legislation was also amended to make some concession for those in episodic work – or 'recurrent unemployment' – by removing the seven-day waiting period for those who again became eligible for benefit after having served the waiting period during the previous 13 weeks.[106]

Changes to the income test in the first half of the 1990s resulted in a far more liberal allowance for claimants in part-time or episodic work. There were changes to the free area or 'earnings disregard' threshold, which governed the amount a person could earn before the income test was applied; the taper or rate at which the benefit was withdrawn as earned income increased; and an earnings credit scheme (subsequently abolished by the Coalition government then reinstated under the new name of 'transition bank') allowing beneficiaries to build up a bank of their fortnightly unused free areas over time that could then be offset against casual earnings in a subsequent payment period.[107] All this was meant to address the sometimes anomalous effects on entitlement that resulted from fortnightly income testing when beneficiaries took up casual or intermittent work.[108]

The aims of encouraging claimants to access part-time and casual work without losing their entire benefit were threefold. One was to reduce entitlement (and hence government outlays); another was to increase claimant's disposable income (and hence reduce their risk of poverty); a third was to maintain claimants' labour market attachment (and so, supposedly, increase the probability of them finding full-time work and leaving the benefit system entirely). But the actual behavioural impact of the apparent financial incentives that arose from changes to the means test has been disputed. Australian and British studies showed that many claimants were unaware of how income tests actually worked (and generally perceived them as harsher than they actually were). In particular, claimants' attachment to the labour force tended to be based primarily on their preference for certain types of work and, for lone parents, on the significance attached to the parenting role rather than calculations of income.[109] Claimants also tended to place more

---

[105] TH Kewley, *Social Security in Australia 1900–72* (Sydney, Sydney University Press, 1973) 458.

[106] ibid 459.

[107] Social Security Act 1991 (Cth) Pt 3.10 Division 5 as amended by Social Security (Budget and Other Measures) Legislation Amendment Act 1993 (Cth) s 7.

[108] See Social Security Review, 'Income Support for the Unemployed', above n 42, 122–24.

[109] See, eg, A Puniard and C Harrington, 'Working Through the Poverty Traps: Results of a Survey of Sole Parent Pensioners and Unemployment Beneficiaries' (1993) (December) *Social Security Journal* 1; S Cowling, 'Understanding Behavioural Responses to Tax and Transfer Changes: A Survey of Low-Income Households' (1998) Melbourne Institute of Applied and Economic Research, University of Melbourne Working Paper No 15/98; S Duncan and R Edwards, *Lone Mothers, Paid Work and Gendered Moral Rationalities* (Basingstoke, Macmillan, 1999).

importance on the perceived sense of financial stability provided by benefits than the higher but unstable income that may come from accepting short-term or casual work.[110]

To some extent, the debate about financial incentives is a replay of the old 'lesser eligibility' debate: the idea that no one should be better off on benefit than they would be in work. But the increasing variation in the rewards from different types of wage labour, the complex stacking of different welfare payments, supplements and concessions, and the differing costs associated with entering waged employment all meant the actual incentive to take up short-term work for any individual depended on an intricate web of personal circumstance. Yet individuals' actual patterns of behaviour were never really the focus. Rather, the debate was shaped by economists who constructed models to see, in Paul Spicker's words, 'whether anyone on benefit, anywhere, is better off than the lowest paid worker, anywhere'. And of course, as he observes, such an outcome was bound to happen.[111]

The government's wish that claimants be allowed to combine receipt of benefit with some part-time or intermittent waged work necessitated a legislative dispensation to the requirement that a claimant be 'unemployed' as a precondition of receiving benefit. This was achieved through a 1979 amendment whereby the Director-General was given the discretion to disregard paid work that would otherwise deprive a period to be classified as one of 'unemployment' and thereby allow the working claimant to be deemed to be 'unemployed'.[112]

So a liberalised means test, together with the legislative dispensation as to who counted as 'unemployed', clearly envisaged claimants combining income from part-time work with receipt of part payment of unemployment benefit. As I've noted, a key justification for this approach was the belief that some work would lead to more work and, eventually, to a claimant's exit from the benefit system. There was some evidence that receipt of part benefit along with earnings from part-time work increased the likelihood of ultimate exit from benefit.[113] Yet while it was clear that finding work was likely to initially involve work that was seasonal, casual or part-time, it was unclear under what circumstances this would then lead to a transition to full-time work. The extent to which the move from unemployment to part-time work constituted a pathway to full-time work, argued Jordan, remained untested:

> The idea that large numbers of people can make a transition from unemployment through casual or part-time to full-time work, attractive though it may be, should be

[110] E McLaughlin, 'Work and Welfare Benefits: Social Security, Employment and Unemployment in the 1990s' (1991) 20 *Journal of Social Policy* 485.

[111] P Spicker, *What's Wrong With Social Security Benefits?* (Bristol, Policy Press, 2017) 22.

[112] Social Services Amendment Act 1979 s 35, inserting a new sub-section (3) into s 107 of the principal Act. The provision can now be found in s 595 of the 1991 Act.

[113] P Flatau and M Dockery, 'How Do Income Support Recipients Engage with the Labour Market?', Policy Research Paper No 12 (Canberra, Department of Family and Community Services, 2001).

regarded with some scepticism. Too little is known of the circumstances under which it occurs. The strongest justification for encouraging employment that provides less than a full livelihood is that for many it may be the only alternative to complete and permanent unemployment.[114]

If this was the case, then the retained unemployment benefit was not compensation for unemployment, but compensation for *under*employment. And perhaps one reading of the OECD's prescription of an 'active society' that went beyond 'full employment as traditionally defined' was that people could package a more or less stable income from combinations of part-time work and part payment of a social security benefit.

This is arguably what happened with lone parents under the Australian system. Lone parents increased their rate of part-time employment over the last two decades of the twentieth century and increased their active job search.[115] This was done in the context of a sole parent pension means test even more generous than that applied to unemployed claimants. By 2003, it was possible for lone parents to earn up to $550 or $600 per week and still stay 'on welfare'.[116]

Notably, though, claimants of sole parent pension across this period were not subject to the strictures of an activity test.[117] For the unemployed, the scope for ongoing income packaging – in effect, using benefit to 'top up' inadequate earned incomes to some sort of acceptable minimum income – was less clear. Did someone working part-time and drawing part payment of unemployment benefit *and who wished to remain so* satisfy the activity test? The answer seemed to be 'no'. While it was true that the activity test recognised a wider range of activities than the old work test, it appeared that someone combining ongoing part-time work with part payment of benefits could still fall foul of the test. That is, their readiness and willingness to undertake suitable work could only be shown by their stating that they would accept any suitable offer of *full-time* work: that is, by a willingness to surrender secure, ongoing part-time employment for insecure full-time employment.[118] Reflecting this, the legislative discretion of the Director-General to deem someone in work as 'unemployed' was to be exercised conservatively,

[114] A Jordan, 'Labour Market Programs and Social Security Payments' (1994) (December) *Social Security Journal* 60, 71.

[115] M Gray et al, 'Changes in the Labour Force Status of Lone and Couple Mothers, 1983–2002', Research Paper No 33 (Melbourne, Australian Institute of Family Studies, 2003).

[116] RG Gregory, E Klug and PJ Thapa, 'Lone Mothers Work and Welfare: An Assessment of the Impact of Taper Rate Reduction and Related Reforms', paper prepared for the Social Policy Evaluation and Analysis Centre, Research School of Social Sciences, Australian National University, mimeo, 2005.

[117] An activity test was eventually imposed on lone parents of school-age children in 2005. This was achieved by transferring them to NSA – but, interestingly, unemployed lone parents under this new regime became subject to a test that prioritised the search for part-time rather than full-time work: Employment and Workplace Relations Legislation Amendment (Welfare to Work and Other Measures) Act 2005 (Cth).

[118] Commonwealth of Australia, Department of Social Security, 'Meeting the Challenge: Labour Market Trends and the Income Support System', Policy Discussion Paper No 3 (Canberra, DSS, 1993) 20.

a position reinforced by an Administrative Appeals Tribunal standpoint that 'the most common cases where the discretion is exercised would probably be where a person earns a small amount of money by casual part-time work *while looking for full-time work*'.[119] Later tribunal decisions also glossed the discretion as applying to 'unusual sporadic' paid work.[120]

There seemed a clear policy tension between the recognition of labour market trends through changes to the means test and the continued emphasis on full-time work in the activity test.[121] The system perhaps edged closest to a form of guaranteed basic income for the jobless in those instances where the activity test surrendered its preoccupation with the search for full-time work by claimants living in remote areas or long-term claimants over 50 who were undertaking 15 hours per week of voluntary or paid work (including self-employment).[122] But these concessions were tightly targeted, made for groups of people – especially the mature-aged long-term unemployed – whose probability of returning to full-time work was regarded as low. This less conditional access to income support was more an acknowledgement of labour market failure than any sort of basic or 'participation' income.

Nevertheless, by the end of the twentieth century there appeared to be a high degree of workers churning between intermittent employment – often characterised by low pay – and joblessness.[123] This suggested that the easing of means tests or other measures that facilitated a combination of part-payment of social security benefit and income from part-time and irregular work represented not merely support for once-off welfare-to-work transitions but had the potential to transform basic income support payments into a new form of in-work benefit, *over time*, for workers stuck in episodic or intermittent employment – as long as they were able to meet the demands of the activity test and demonstrate their willingness to take up full-time, permanent work.

* * *

In 1996 William Walters published an article about active welfare policies presciently titled 'The Demise of Unemployment?'[124] He was not arguing that activation policies had in fact been successful in addressing joblessness. Indeed, other

---

[119] *Re Waller* (1985) 8 ALD 26, emphasis added.

[120] P Sutherland, with A Anforth, *Social Security and Family Assistance Law* (Sydney, The Federation Press and Welfare Rights Centre, 2001) 335–36.

[121] P Saunders, 'Improving Work Incentives in a Means-Tested Welfare System: The 1994 Australian Social Security Reforms', Discussion Paper No 56 (Sydney, Social Policy Research Centre UNSW, 1995) 28.

[122] Social Security Act 1991 (Cth) ss 603(2), 602.

[123] A Le and P Miller, 'Job Quality and Churning of the Pool of the Unemployed', ABS Occasional Paper Cat No 6293.0.00.003 (Canberra, Australian Bureau of Statistics, 1999); Y Dunlop, 'Labour Market Outcomes of Low Paid Adult Workers', ABS Occasional Paper Cat No 6293.0.00.005 (Canberra, Australian Bureau of Statistics, 2000).

[124] W Walters, 'The Demise of Unemployment?' (1996) 24 *Politics & Society* 197.

scholars working in the same vein as Walters have highlighted what they see as the congenital failure of the activation paradigm.[125] Rather, Walters was suggesting that activation had effectively undone 'unemployment' as a robust regulatory category. Claimants of unemployment benefit were being activated in a way that made them look less and less like the unemployed claimants of the post-war period. At the same time, jobless people who would once have fallen outside the remit of any unemployment benefit scheme – lone parents of school-age children; the disabled – were increasingly subject to the same demands and strictures as unemployed claimants. In Australia, the two tendencies were mutually reinforcing. People deemed to have a partial capacity for work – lone parents and the disabled – were brought on to NSA, but could then satisfy the activity test by actually engaging in part-time work. At once, the pool of NSA claimants grew, but the proportion who were actively seeking suitable work diminished.

So the relationship between statistical definitions of unemployment and eligibility for unemployment benefit has been recast. As outlined in chapter five, regulatory understandings of unemployment – who was eligible for benefit – tended in the post-war period to track fairly closely emerging statistical definitions. Both approaches relied on an activity-based or behavioural definition of unemployment. But the number of unemployed persons delineated by each approach did not map seamlessly one onto the other. The activity in question – 'seeking work' – was defined much more broadly in the survey and census approach, whereas eligibility for unemployment benefit was confined to those who sought work in a particular way: that is, by registering with the CES. Registering with the CES was a prerequisite to obtaining unemployment benefit, but those unemployed persons who would be disentitled to benefit due to operation of the means test or the proscriptions against 'voluntary' unemployment, or who simply expected to find work fairly quickly, had little incentive to register with the CES. They could seek work in other ways and still be captured by the survey definition of unemployment while not showing up on CES statistics. Conversely, some people might have registered as unemployed and sought full-time work with the CES but may either have found a job and not notified the CES, or be engaged in small amounts of part-time work while looking for full-time work through the CES, and so would not be considered unemployed for the purposes of the labour force survey. All these things considered, it was reasonable to think that the number of jobseekers registered at the CES tracked the number of statistically unemployed, but came in slightly lower. The number of people actually eligible for unemployment benefit would have been lower still.[126]

[125] J Grundy, *Bureaucratic Manoeuvres: The Contested Administration of the Unemployed* (Toronto, University of Toronto Press, 2019).

[126] J Steinke, 'Some Problems in the Measurement of Unemployment' (1969) 11 *Journal of Industrial Relations* 39, 39–40; SP Stevens, 'Problems in the Interpretation of Australian Statistics of Unemployment' (1963) 39 *Economic Record* 142, 145–46; P Sheehan and P Stricker, 'The Collapse of Full Employment 1974 to 1978' in R Scotton and H Ferber (eds), *Public Expenditure and Social*

With the rise of activation, this pattern of correlation changed. Since 1993, claimants of unemployment benefit have generally outnumbered those who met the statistical definition of unemployed. There would still have been a significant number of out-of-work jobseekers who did not claim benefit, but this was more than offset by the substantial number of benefit claimants who were either working more than one hour a week and/or were not searching for work. By 2009, out of a claimant pool of around 565,000, only around 340,000 were jobseekers. A further 125,000 claimants of benefit were satisfying their activity requirements through activities other than job search. They were working part-time, or undertaking voluntary work, training, or the development of a self-employment venture.[127] If our starting point is the mid-century definition of unemployment – someone who is without any work whatsoever but looking for work – then NSA had, to a large extent, ceased to be an 'unemployment' benefit.

All in all, reforms to both the work test and the means test from the late 1980s indicated a pragmatic recognition of labour market change, especially the fact that most new jobs were part-time and that there was a decline in the probability of leaving unemployment for full-time work and an increase in the probability of leaving unemployment for part-time or temporary work. This was not only due to the increase in part-time or temporary jobs in the labour market at large. Rather, the profile of employment opportunities available to social security claimants was more likely to be dominated by casual, part-time and temporary jobs precisely because those jobs turned over more frequently than those in the permanent sector. And welfare recipients weren't merely reacting to those new labour market opportunities. Their take-up of such options was being encouraged by a more flexible income test as well as the requirement that claimants take up the first 'suitable' job offered, with 'suitability' increasingly broadly defined (or, rather, 'not suitable' fairly narrowly defined).

And there might be a symbiotic relationship between new directions in unemployment policy and prevailing employment trends such as the proliferation of casual or short-hours part-time work. At least, as Jamie Peck and Nik Theodore have pointed out in the context of similar welfare policies pursued by the British and US governments, activation approaches have tended to work with the grain of prevailing labour market trends and have accepted as given established systems of recruitment and labour management.[128]

The result has been the avoidance of any positive action to reconstruct recruitment practices and the distribution of work – whereas the reconstruction of recruitment practices and the decasualisation of hiring was, precisely, Beveridge's

---

Policy in Australia Volume II: The First Fraser Years 1976–78 (Melbourne, Longman Cheshire, 1980); F Di Giorgio and A Endres, 'The Changing Fortunes of CES Unemployment Statistics' (1983) 55 *The Australian Quarterly* 307, 313–14.

[127] Davidson and Whiteford, above n 77, 24.

[128] J Peck and N Theodore, '"Workfirst": Workfare and the Regulation of Contingent Labour Markets' (2000) 24 *Cambridge Journal of Economics* 119.

vision for the labour exchange and the 'organisation' of the labour market. Instead, in the late twentieth century, employer definitions of what was appropriate employment and what were appropriate attitudes to employment among welfare recipients began to permeate the labour market. Echoing Peck and Theodore's summing up of US welfare-to-work programmes, activation programmes not only exploited conditions found in contingent and insecure labour markets, they contributed to the regulation and reproduction of such markets. They most obviously did this by constructing a continuously job-ready, pre-processed secure labour supply for insecure work. In short, the new unemployment policy operated to help 'make flexible labour markets work'.[129]

This was Walters' point: the turn to activation clearly had implications for how we thought of unemployment as a regulatory category. The claimant drawing the modern day equivalent of unemployment benefit could be undertaking a range of activities – most notably, intermittent or casual work, but also training or self-employment – that would have once been seen as incompatible with our understanding of unemployment.

But once we delve beneath the rhetoric of activation, we also find a surprising continuity in the regulatory architecture underpinning Australia's unemployment benefit system. And it is perhaps this continuity from the 1940s through to the 1970s – that jobseekers engage in activity to prove their deservingness; that the activity can be modified by the imposition of requirements at the whim of the government; that entitlement was determined by minimalist statutory rights awash in a sea of ministerial discretion – that made Australia particularly receptive to the imposition of further discipline and conditionality on claimants, glossed now by the rhetoric of faux reciprocity.

---

[129] ibid 123.

8

Marketing Unemployment

In 1888 the social wing of the Salvation Army in Britain had begun an ambitious programme for social reform and spiritual revival focusing on the disciplining and retraining of the unemployed. City workshops in London gave unemployed workmen board and lodgings in return for eight hours work a day. Efficiency, deportment and cleanliness were rewarded by increases in food rations and eventually men were given a cash allowance. Attached to the workshops was a labour bureau that would put men in touch with potential employers. In 1905 the *Liberal Magazine* suggested that the Army be given a government contract to deal with the unemployed and, four years later, the Minority Report of the Poor Law Commission recommended that public authorities work in conjunction with religious organisations in training and reforming the recalcitrant unemployed.

Reflecting on this history in 1972, José Harris concluded that

> it is difficult to see how any government of the period could have justified the delegation of coercive or administrative powers over unemployed workmen to any unestablished religious sect … [W]hat is perhaps most surprising about proposals for making the Army an organ of public administration is … that they should have been considered at all.[1]

By 1998, however, Australia's Commonwealth Employment Service had been disbanded and replaced by a 'Job Network' of private providers of employment services to unemployed workers. As a result of a second round of tenders concluded in late 1999, the two largest providers of labour exchange services contracted by the Commonwealth government were religious organisations, including the Salvation Army.[2]

The Commonwealth Employment Service (CES) had grown up alongside Australia's post-war unemployment benefit scheme. While the Service had ambitions to be a generalist labour exchange, it importantly secured the authority to adjudicate the genuineness of individuals' claims to unemployment benefit. These two roles – generalist exchange and 'dole office' – had an uneasy coexistence,

---

[1] J Harris, *Unemployment and Politics: A Study in English Social Policy 1886–1914* (Oxford, Oxford University Press, 1972) 133–34.

[2] T Eardley, D Abello and H Macdonald, 'Is the Job Network Benefitting Disadvantaged Jobseekers? Preliminary Evidence from a Study of Non-Profit Employment Services' (2001) Social Policy Research Centre, University of New South Wales Discussion Paper No 111.

but through its administration of the 'work test' the CES became central to the way unemployment was constructed in the post-war period. The transformed unemployment benefit of the last decades of the twentieth century, outlined in chapter seven, would also require a means to adjudicate claims: to sort out the 'active' jobseeker from the 'passive', the person taking on their mutual obligations from those shunning them. The end of the twentieth century appears as a watershed not only in terms of what jobless people were entitled to (a benefit now hedged with increasingly onerous conditions, wrapped in the language of 'agreement-making'), but also in the way that benefit was administered. Any complete account of how Australia has constructed unemployment must include an account of this administrative transformation: in short, an account of the rise and fall of the CES.

The CES in the Post-War Labour Market

The ambition of those social reformers discussed in chapter one was that a national labour exchange could organise the labour market around full-time contracts of permanent employment. The more modest task envisaged by the drafters of the White Paper was that the exchange could meaningfully facilitate the mobility of labour. In either case, the exchange would need to exercise control over all or most labour hiring. And in the back-and-forth between Manpower and Post-war Reconstruction over the role of the CES, this became a key concern: could a Commonwealth employment service secure sufficient market share to operate effectively as a tool of both labour organisation and mobility?

The war years gave the Commonwealth government a taste of this type of control. A disparate collection of State bureaux, traditionally used to administer relief work for the unemployed, was transformed into a national, Commonwealth controlled operation for the placement of all grades of labour. By 1943, the International Labour Office (ILO) had recognised that manpower planning for wartime needs had substantially altered the role and public perceptions of national labour exchanges:

> A much broader conception of the service's place in national economic life has grown up because of the important task the service has performed in building the war economy ... The wider contacts of this machinery with management and labour throughout industry have in turn brought it into a position that enables it to solve their employment problems far more effectively than before.[3]

However, the ILO's optimistic diagnosis that government employment services would emerge from the war with enhanced capacity and prestige considerably undersold the problems faced by the CES in peacetime. The Manpower Directorate had indeed exercised unprecedented command over the engagement of labour

---

[3] ILO, *Man-power Mobilisation for Peace* (Montreal, International Labour Office, 1943) 73.

in the emergency circumstances of the Second World War, but that command was politically contested and often resented as a form of 'industrial conscription'.[4] Some European public employment services would go on to secure this sort of control in the post-war period, but it was difficult to imagine a peacetime post-war service retaining such powers in Australia.

For William Funnell, Director of Manpower at war's end, early drafts of the White Paper gave merely the 'faint suggestion' that it would be a good thing if employers were to notify the CES in advance of any changes in employment and generally co-operate with the Service. He was looking for stronger tools to ensure the new Service could do its job. Given the White Paper envisaged the temporary maintenance of wartime controls over prices and private overseas transactions, his first suggestion was that labour wartime labour controls also not be immediately discarded at the close of hostilities. While the direction and registration of all labour could be relaxed, 'we may want a power to control engagements of labour by certain industries or for employment in certain occupations'.[5] HC Coombs, Director of Postwar Reconstruction, sidestepped this issue, saying the government should simply state its intention 'to build up a thoroughly efficient and up-to-date service, which by its very quality can gain and hold a sufficiently influential position in the labour market'.[6]

The next opportunity for Manpower to secure greater influence for the Service was the introduction of the Re-establishment and Employment Bill in May 1945. It was Division 5, Part II of the Bill that established a Commonwealth Employment Service. But the notes to the Minister introducing the Bill simply reiterated Coombs' position that the CES should not enjoy any monopoly over placement services but would secure market share on the basis of the quality of its service. Echoing earlier concerns about disorganised hiring practices, the Minister's notes claimed the Service would be

> of such calibre ... as will attract employers by convincing them that better results in securing personnel for their requirements can be achieved through the employment service than by their own unco-ordinated separate and individual advertising or selection from gate pick-ups. Few employers can afford to, or are inclined to incorporate personnel selection divisions in their organisation. The object of the employment service is to provide this for the employer.[7]

In a full employment economy, the CES would also 'encourage workers already employed to use its facilities to find jobs even better suited to their abilities'. Pre-war labour exchanges, where they existed, were identified as catering largely

---

[4] On resistance to wartime labour controls, see generally C Fort, 'Developing a National Employment Policy, Australia 1939–45' (PhD thesis, University of Adelaide, 2000).

[5] Funnell to Coombs, 4 April 1945, National Archives of Australia, Series B551, Item No 45/78/12162, 'White Paper on Full Employment'.

[6] Coombs to Funnell, 7 April 1945, ibid.

[7] National Archives of Australia, Series B550, Item No 46/82B/310, 'Re-Establishment and Employment Act 1945'.

for the unemployed and unskilled worker. The aim of the new Service was to attract the 'skilled and professional classes as well as the artisan and clerical classes'.[8]

Manpower and its parent department, Labour and National Service, were less than satisfied with this approach. But the ILO provided them another weapon. On 17 May 1945 Funnell's principal adviser, Henry Bland, telegrammed Post-war Reconstruction to 'suggest you consider inserting in Bill power to prevent fee-charging employment agencies operating. We might base Commonwealth competence on Recommendations of International Labour Organisation on subject and external affairs power'. Bland followed this up with a letter nine days later, referring specifically to the ILO's 1933 Convention on Fee Charging Employ-ment Agencies that called for the regulation and eventual abolition of most forms of private employment agencies. He pointed out that certain State legislation, such as the New South Wales Industrial Arbitration Act, Part X, Division II, provided for close regulation of private agencies, but wondered whether it would be wiser 'in all the circumstances if power is simply given [to the Commonwealth] to make regulations to deal with these matters'. The issue hinged on whether the external affairs power of the Constitution could really give the Commonwealth a mandate to pass such legislation – that is, that it would allow not just the ratification of international conventions but also their implementation by the Commonwealth, even where the subject matter was normally constitutionally reserved to the States. Coombs responded to Bland on 11 June that there were 'differences of opinion' on the matter and the parliamentary draftsman was loath to place such a provision in the Re-Establishment and Employment Bill without further inves-tigation and discussion with the Attorney-General. By February the following year, the government had virtually conceded, on the advice of Professor Kenneth Bailey, that the High Court 'would reject any contention that the external affairs power gives [the Commonwealth] complete legislative coverage'.[9]

It appeared, then, that any labour market power the new CES wished to claim would have to be won by carving out a market share in competition with other labour market intermediaries. Here the CES faced problems precisely because of the broad scope of its wartime predecessor. A report commissioned from the J Walter Thompson advertising agency in March 1946 pointed out that the Manpower Directorate had been an unpopular instrumentality and, as a result, the CES was starting 'with a strong public relations handicap'. Many employers in particular, it observed, would still be smarting under recollections of inter-ventionist manpower directions during the war. The situation could not easily be repaired but required a 'continuous effort over several years' to 'make more friends and fewer enemies'. The Report recommended a comprehensive public relations

---

[8] ibid.

[9] ibid. In the early 1980s this cautious reading of the external affairs power was rejected by the High Court: see *Koowarta v Bjelke-Petersen* (1982) 153 CLR 168 and *Commonwealth v Tasmania* (1983) 158 CLR 1.

campaign, costed at £8,000 for the first three months, targeting press, radio and cinemas, carrying both employer and employee themes, overseen by a full-time public relations officer.[10]

The CES was able, at least, to partially exploit the ethos of post-war reconstruction. Appeals could be made to the goodwill of employers, urging them to hire ex-servicemen through the Service: 'He saved your home and business! Will You Help him now? If you have any employment vacancies contact the CES in your district'; 'Cheers and confetti will not rehabilitate him! Be practical – give him a job. For all your employment vacancies give the ex-serviceman the opportunity – contact the CES officer in your district'. And trade unionists probably did not have the same misgivings about the wartime direction of labour as did employers, as they had found their labour market position considerably enhanced under wartime conditions. Also, press comment on the new Service turned out to be largely positive, with some journalists praising it precisely because there was no compulsion to use its facilities.[11] Case studies and testimonials of successfully placed employees featured in *Pix* and *Women's Weekly*.

However, a tight post-war labour market meant jobseekers had little need for the Service. By the end of the 1940s, the Service acknowledged that 'the intense competition by employers for boys and girls makes it extremely easy to obtain employment without the assistance of our organisation'. Even government agencies and instrumentalities – such as the Postmaster-General's Department – were using their own employment offices rather than the CES to recruit staff.[12]

In retrospect, it is difficult to establish exactly what share of the placement market the CES captured in the immediate post-war period. The 1928 Report of the Development and Migration Commission on Unemployment and Business Stability had pinpointed 'diverse arrangements for the filling of vacancies' as contributing to labour market disorganisation. The Report listed private employment agencies, trade unions and State labour exchanges. Although the CES clearly displaced the State labour exchanges, it is unclear to what extent its operations displaced other arrangements. In 1960, the Victorian State government removed any licensing controls over private employment agencies on the grounds that the existence of the CES meant few manual workers – the target of the original licensing laws – were making use of such agencies. The continued existence of licensing arrangements for private bureaux in several other States, however, suggests that although the activities of private agencies were greatly constrained under the National Security (Manpower) Regulations during the war, they had regained some influence in the post-war labour market. Similarly, the use of trade

---

[10] 'The Commonwealth Employment Service and Its Public Relations', 5 March 1946, National Archives of Australia, Series B550/0, Item No 46/27A/112 Pt 1 – 'CES Publicity at inception and in immediate post war years'.

[11] *Canberra Times* (3 May 1946).

[12] NJ O'Heare (Deputy-Director of Manpower) to Funnell, 22 April 1949, National Archives of Australia, Series MP 1722/1, Item No 47/1/344 Pt 3, 'CES – Advertising'.

unions as de facto placement agencies persisted in certain industry sectors in the post-war period. Up to the mid-1950s there is evidence of trade unions being used as labour suppliers in furniture and liquor trades, in coal and metal mining, shearing and the motor vehicle industry.[13] A survey of 156 factories, employing a total of 85,000 workers, conducted in the early 1950s did list the CES as among the most common means of recruiting labour, but alongside advertisements in the metropolitan press, the recommendations of serving employees, and trade union contacts. While it found that some employers relied exclusively on the CES, it also observed that 'factories which recruited little labour and wanted mainly skilled tradesmen or employees with particular skills often relied solely on union contacts'.[14]

For some groups of workers, though, the CES did exercise considerable influence as a placement agency. At the end of the Second World War the Australian government had embarked on an ambitious immigration programme to meet projected post-war labour shortages, and by 1949 immigrants comprised the bulk of the CES's market.[15] Assisted Passage Agreements were concluded with Britain in 1946, Malta, Eire and the International Refugee Organization in 1948; the Netherlands and Italy in 1951; and West Germany in 1952. A General Assisted Passage Scheme for people from the United States, Switzerland, Denmark, Norway, Sweden and Finland was established in 1954. Selection of immigrants was initially made according to their suitability for rural work, nursing, and domestic work in hospitals and labour for reconstruction and developmental projects. The CES's role in the immigration programme consisted of, first, providing some of the labour market information to assist the government in setting its annual intake target and, secondly, interviewing immigrants on disembarkation and attempting to match them with the existing demand for labour, as well as providing transport to places of employment once placement had been finalised.[16] Assisted Passage Agreements up to 1952 involved immigrants signing an undertaking that allowed the government to 'direct' them to specific jobs. Such immigrants had to be engaged through the CES and CES officers were under instruction not to place newly arrived immigrants in employment for which suitable Australian workers were available or into situations that would lead to the displacement of Australian workers, and to ensure the immigrants would be

---

[13] P Weeks, *Trade Union Security Law: A Study of Preference and Compulsory Unionism* (Sydney, Federation Press, 1995) 18–19. Interestingly, on the docks, one of the areas where trade union administration of the labour pool was reasonable entrenched, the CES succeeded until 1951 in operating a pick-up centre in Melbourne for shipwrights, painters and dockers, displacing the trade union agency: R Morris, 'The Employer's Free Selection of Labour and the Waterfront Closed Shop' (1981) 23 *Journal of Industrial Relations* 49, 52.

[14] WP Butler, 'Recruitment and Selection Procedures in Australian Industry' (1954) 10 *Personnel Practice Bulletin* 34.

[15] T Sheridan, 'Planners and the Australian Labour Market 1945–1949' (1987) 53 *Labour History* 99, 113.

[16] JE Isaac, 'Manpower Planning in Australia' (1960) 82 *International Labour Review* 403, 424–25.

employed under conditions where they would receive not less than award rates and enjoy the same terms as would Australian workers undertaking the same work.[17] In this way, the CES played an important part in policing the conditions of newly arrived immigrants' employment and blunting the competitive edge that this influx of labour would otherwise have against the domestic workforce.

The other group of jobseekers that could not avoid the placement services of the CES were claimants of unemployment benefit. As noted in chapter four, Manpower was eager to link any post-war employment service with the administration of the new unemployment benefit scheme. So up until 1981, the CES carried out the task of registering claimants, issuing and receiving benefit claim forms and administering the 'work test'.[18] But the exact legal foundation for this arrangement remained unclear. Technically, the CES was only making recommendations to the Department of Social Services (after 1972, the Department of Social Security or DSS) as to whether any particular individual satisfied the work test: the Director-General of Social Services remained responsible in law for final decisions on benefit eligibility. At the same time, the objects of the CES set out in the 1945 Re-establishment and Employment Act 1945 (Cth) did not include any administrative responsibility for the unemployment benefit scheme. Nevertheless, the CES seems to have acted as agent for the government's major welfare department.[19] The Unemployment and Sickness Benefits Act 1944 (Cth) did enable the Director-General of Social Services to delegate powers and functions to Registrars,[20] and for reasons of 'administrative convenience' officers of, first, the Manpower Directorate and, after 1945, the CES, acted as Registrars.[21]

The job brokerage function of the CES obviously made it well placed for testing the willingness of beneficiaries to accept full-time employment, and hence the genuineness of their claim. Yet a 1977 review of the CES was highly critical of what it saw as a confusion of roles. It argued that there was a conflict between the Service, on the one hand, acting as provider to employers of people best qualified for the job in question and, on the other, administering a work test under which 'almost certainly unsuitable people will be referred to employers solely to test out unemployed people's attitude to employment'.[22] This in turn created concerns

---

[17] Commonwealth Employment Service, *District Office Manual,* January 1949, section 5711, National Archives of Australia, Series MP 243/2.

[18] For a period beginning in the late 1970s, beneficiaries were also required to attend the CES on a fortnightly basis to submit income statements: Commonwealth of Australia *Parliamentary Debates,* House of Representatives, 23 March 1976, 869–72.

[19] T Carney and P Hanks, *Australian Social Security Law, Policy and Administration* (Melbourne, Oxford University Press, 1986) 89.

[20] Unemployment and Sickness Benefits Act 1944 (Cth) ss 7–8.

[21] See Commonwealth of Australia, *Full Employment in Australia,* Parl Paper No 11 (1945) 7; Commonwealth of Australia, Commonwealth Bureau of Census and Statistics, *Labour Report No 35, 1945–46* (Melbourne, Commonwealth Government Printer, 1947) 124.

[22] Review of the Commonwealth Employment Service, *Report by Mr JD Norgard for the Minister for Employment and Industrial Relations,* Parl Paper No 177 (1978) 20.

in employers' minds that the Service was not effectively screening potential employees and at the same time hindered effective working relationships between CES officers and unemployed persons. Any involvement of the CES in administration of unemployment benefits on the DSS's behalf meant a continuing image in the eyes of many unemployed, employers and people who wanted to change jobs, that the CES was 'an unemployment office' or, even more disparagingly, 'the dole office'.[23] An inquiry into the unemployment benefit system carried out at the same time also noted that the Service's 'administrative responsibility ... contrast[ed] markedly with the legal responsibility for determining eligibility for unemployment benefit'.[24]

In response to these criticisms, during the 1980s the lodging of unemployment benefit claim forms, income statements and, later, fortnightly evidence of active job search, were transferred to the Department of Social Security, but registration with the CES remained a precondition for receiving unemployment benefits.[25]

Persistent and high unemployment throughout the late 1970s and 1980s, together with the CES's responsibilities regarding the provision of services for the unemployed saw the major focus of CES placement activity reoriented towards specified disadvantaged groups in the labour market, in particular assistance for the long-term unemployed. The Service's resources were increasingly channelled away from the day-to-day placement of workers for non-fee-paying customers.[26] A nationwide survey in 1996 of private sector firms found that the CES was more likely to be used to recruit blue-collar workers than white-collar workers and, within each of these categories, unskilled rather than skilled workers.[27] Between 1982 and 1997, the Service was instrumental in the successful job-match of around 10 per cent of out-of-work persons.[28]

Associated with this new orientation toward disadvantaged jobseekers, the CES took on responsibility for what became known as labour market programmes. In contrast to public employment services in a number of Western economies, the CES came relatively late to this role. The 1945 White Paper spoke of vocational retraining schemes for demobilised service personnel and suggested placing such schemes on a permanent basis, with special training plans to meet the need for workers in growing industries and to retrain workers forced to seek alternative occupations.[29] However, labour supply shortages and internal

[23] ibid 20–23.

[24] Commonwealth of Australia, Unemployment Benefit Policy and Administration: Report of Inquiry, Parl Paper No 243 (1977).

[25] Commonwealth of Australia, *Commonwealth Record*, 1 May 1981, vol 6, no 17.

[26] P Boreham, A Roan and G Whitehouse, 'The Regulation of Employment Services: Private Employment Agencies and Labour Market Policy' (1994) 29 *Australian Journal of Political Science* 541, 544.

[27] M Wooden and D Harding, 'Recruitment Practices in the Private Sector: Results from a National Survey of Employers' (1998) 36 *Asia Pacific Journal of Human Resources* 73.

[28] Australian Bureau of Statistics figures, cited in E Webster and G Harding, 'Outsourcing Public Employment Services: The Australian Experience' (2000) Melbourne Institute, University of Melbourne Working Paper No 4/00, 18.

[29] Commonwealth of Australia, *Full Employment in Australia*, above n 21, 10.

mobility requirements in the post-war period were met substantially through a large immigration programme. Labour market programmes remained underdeveloped in comparison with North American and northern European countries.[30]

The election of the Whitlam Labor government in 1972 signalled a major philosophical shift with regard to labour market policy. The government was committed to the Scandinavian model of using labour market programmes rather than immigration to allocate labour supplies.[31] The northern European programmes that the government was keen to adapt had been designed to improve labour market efficiency in times of full employment, and the Whitlam government instigated its own programmes, co-ordinated through the CES, in a year of low unemployment. The intention was to facilitate structural adjustment in the face of the government's tariff cuts and technological change.[32]

Because the programmes were intended to operate in a regime of full employment, it was assumed the number of participants would be low and the level of subsidy would remain high. For example, the Structural Adjustment Assistance Scheme provided up to six months of income support for workers displaced by the 25 per cent tariff cut of July 1973. It was later extended to cover workers displaced by other changes to levels of industry protection. The National Employment and Training (NEAT) scheme, introduced in October 1974, provided income support equal to the minimum adult award wage for formal full-time study and training to upgrade qualifications or to develop work-related skills in an occupation in demand. It initially targeted assistance to those who needed training because of tariff cuts, redundancy caused by structural change, residence in areas of limited employment opportunities, inadequate or inappropriate work skills, and domestic responsibilities or military service.[33] The Regional Employment Development Scheme (REDS), a direct job creation scheme modelled on a Canadian programme, financed the employment of jobseekers registered with the CES at award wages on locally initiated, socially useful, labour intensive projects in regions with relatively high unemployment rates.

As labour market conditions worsened at the end of 1974 it was seen as sensible to use REDS as a counter-cyclical measure to diminish growing national unemployment and the geographical targeting of the scheme was abandoned by February 1975.[34] Similarly, one year after its introduction, NEAT was restricted

---

[30] See PEF Kirby, 'An Overview of Australian Experience with Manpower Policies' in CE Baird et al (eds), *Youth Employment, Education and Training: Conference Papers* (Canberra, Centre for Economic Policy Research, ANU, 1982).

[31] B Chapman, 'Continuity and Change: Labour Market Programs and Education Expenditure' (1985) 18 *Australian Economic Review* 99. See Australian Interdepartmental Mission to Study Overseas Manpower and Industry Policies and Programmes, *Report* (Canberra, AGPS, 1974); Committee of Inquiry into Labour Market Training, *Labour Market Training in Australia* (Canberra, AGPS, 1974).

[32] A Stretton and B Chapman, 'An Analysis of Australian Labour Market Programs' (1990) Canberra, Centre for Economic Policy Research, Australian National University Discussion Paper No 247.

[33] Kirby, above n 30, para 4.13.

[34] Chapman, above n 31.

to the unemployed or those at risk of losing their job, while those with reasonable prospects of re-employment had to test the labour market for four months before becoming eligible for the scheme. But the shift from a buoyant labour market saw increasing numbers of displaced workers applying for assistance under all three schemes, resulting in a budget blowout at the same time as pressure increased on government to make anti-inflationary expenditure cuts.[35] CES managers began to express concern about 'the disproportionate share of office resources needed to service manpower programs ... to the detriment of the primary CES function of placement'.[36]

No sooner, then, had the CES taken on administrative responsibility for an expanding range of labour market programmes than it found that such programmes were being reoriented as predominantly 'welfare' programmes directed at a growing pool of disadvantaged or 'at risk' benefit claimants rather than at skill enhancement and labour mobility more generally. This reorientation was confirmed in the 1980s. In 1983 the Hawke Labor government instigated a committee of inquiry into labour market programmes, chaired by Peter Kirby. Reporting in 1985, the Committee argued that restoring the health of the labour market – and job creation in particular – depended on economic growth rather than labour market programmes. The appropriate role for such programmes was improving the long-term employment prospects of the unemployed and those facing severe disadvantage in the labour market.[37] As a result of the Committee's recommendations, and those of other government reviews,[38] the second half of the 1980s was characterised by a closer integration of labour market programmes and income support; continued targeting of programmes towards the long-term unemployed and disadvantaged; as well as a greater emphasis on training rather than short-term job creation and the integration of individual programmes to reduce their number but increase the flexibility of their delivery.[39]

The CES's involvement with unemployment benefit in the 1970s had raised the danger of its being seen as a 'dole office'. This was partly circumvented by a reallocation of administrative duties to DSS, but the Service's continued involvement from the second half of the 1980s with labour market programmes directed at the disadvantaged (and integrated with the unemployment benefit system)

---

[35] Stretton and Chapman, above n 32, 20–21. In 1975 expenditure on labour market programmes increased by about one-third.

[36] Review of the Commonwealth Employment Service, above n 22.

[37] Committee of Inquiry into Labour Market Programs, *Report* (Canberra, AGPS, 1985) 91.

[38] See, eg, Commonwealth of Australia, Social Security Review, 'Income Support for the Unemployed in Australia: Towards a More Active System', Issues Paper No 4 (Canberra, DSS, 1988), which recommended that recipients of unemployment benefits become eligible for referral to labour market programmes after six months, and that more intensive contact between the CES and benefit recipients would aid the identification of especially disadvantaged jobseekers.

[39] Stretton and Chapman, above n 32, 27. By 1990, for example, there was only a single wage subsidy programme and a single community-based programme rather than several programmes of each type.

only reintroduced the problem in a slightly different form: it increasingly became identified as a welfare agency rather than a generalist employment exchange.

The End of the Public Employment Service in Australia: The First Phase

With the passage of the Social Security Act 1991 (Cth), spending on labour market programmes for the unemployed was increased by $150 million over three years. The Act introduced a new income support scheme – 'Newstart Allowance' (NSA) – for the long-term unemployed. The scheme involved the 'case management' of beneficiaries. A form of individualised assistance, case management involves a local official taking responsibility for linking relevant services together in a single strategy to meet the needs of a particular client. The case manager used new forms of authority to broker deals with separate agencies to procure those services thought most useful for the client.[40] In the employment services area, case management was first trialled in Victoria in the latter half of the 1980s after research found many long-term unemployed were unaware of the existence of, and their eligibility for, Commonwealth labour market programmes.[41]

CES case managers were given the flexibility to refer clients to specialist programmes that best suited their needs and the state of the local labour market without concern for expenditure limits on each programme.[42] Beneficiaries were interviewed by an employment adviser at the CES and discussed and completed a Newstart Activity Agreement (NSA Activity Agreement). The terms that could be included in such Agreements were defined, and had to be directed at securing employment.[43] In turn, those unemployed for more than 12 months were under increased obligation to accept referrals by the CES to training programmes, with failure to do so considered a breach of the 'work test', now renamed an 'activity test' to indicate its wider scope. As we saw in chapter seven, failure to enter into an Activity Agreement with the CES when required, or to abide by its terms, also amounted to a breach of the activity test, whether or not the claimant was actively seeking work according to the old work test criteria.[44] From March 1994 all new recipients of Newstart Allowance were referred to case management.

With its 1994 White Paper, *Working Nation*, the government signalled a further dramatic increase in expenditure on labour market programmes for the unemployed. An increase of $3 billion over four years was proposed, funding

---

[40] M Considine, 'Markets, Networks and the New Welfare State: Employment Assistance Reforms in Australia' (1999) 28 *Journal of Social Policy* 183, 186–87.

[41] Webster and Harding, above n 28, 19.

[42] ibid 29.

[43] See Social Security Act 1991 (Cth) s 606.

[44] ibid s 593.

650,000 places per year by 1995–96.[45] Programmes were targeted at the very long-term unemployed (those out of work for over 18 months) and early identification of those deemed likely to become so. Early identification was based on assessing CES registrants to determine their level of labour market disadvantage, taking into account factors such as English language ability, skill and age. Those assessed as at high risk of becoming long-term unemployed were offered a case manager and access to programmes such as remedial courses for literacy, numeracy, and English as a second language, vocational training, community-based work experience and subsidised employment. Case management assistance was also extended to all jobseekers who reached 12 months' unemployment, with the full range of labour market programmes available.[46] Individual Case Management Activity Agreements under these Working Nation initiatives had to include terms broadly similar to those in NSA Activity Agreements.[47]

Importantly, unemployed people entering intensive case management were given the choice of either public sector or independent case management providers. Competition between public and private providers of case management services was meant to lead to service improvement.[48] The Employment Services Act 1994 (Cth) established the Employment Services Regulatory Authority to encourage and regulate competition in the area of case management provision and to accredit and contract with private providers. Payments to providers were partly based on required outcomes, such as placing a 'client' in 13 weeks of unsubsidised employment, a labour market programme, full-time education or training. From 1994 to 1995 the CES had provided case management assistance to 376,900 jobseekers. The external network of contracted independent case management providers began to take referrals in March 1995, and by the beginning of 1996 there were over 400 community and private providers delivering case management.[49] By this stage the CES had withdrawn from offering case management services altogether. Instead a new Department of Employment, Education and Training organisation, Employment Assistance Australia (comprising staff mainly transferred from the CES, and operating out of the same premises as the CES) competed with contracted private and community-sector providers for a share in the new case management market.

Case management services – and the delivery of labour market programmes – had already reflected a mix of public and private provision prior to this period. The CES would, for example, sometimes buy places for jobseekers in existing

[45] Commonwealth of Australia, *Working Nation: Policies and Programs* (Canberra, AGPS, 1994) ch 5.
[46] ibid.
[47] Employment Services Act 1994 (Cth) s 39.
[48] Commonwealth of Australia, *Working Nation*, above n 45, 127.
[49] D Finn, *Working Nation: Welfare Reform and the Australian Job Compact for the Long Term Unemployed* (London, Unemployment Unit, 1997) 36. Some of these providers supplied a general service, while others provided specialist assistance to particular groups of jobseekers. The increase in independent providers represented a growth in market share from 6 per cent in May 1995 to 19 per cent in January 1996.

courses offered by the state-run technical and further education sector or by community or private sector providers. The process was largely regulated by the government making money available for programmes through its appropriation Acts and then contracting, under its executive power,[50] with private providers. The Employment Services Act 1994 (Cth) placed the case management services offered to recipients of Commonwealth unemployment assistance within a separate regulatory framework, and established a contestable market for such services. That is, rather than having an extended and more intensive system of case management operating through the existing structures of public provision of employment services, the government saw the increased emphasis of case management as justifying more radical institutional reform. As a 1994 Department of Social Security document put it,

> [i]t is essential that the paradigm ... shifts from one of client management to one of servicing a market. Only by taking a market perspective and a customer focus can the necessary specialisation and incentives be established to maximise the impact of Commonwealth expenditure on employment services.[51]

In making its case, the Department was drawing on the growing consensus that the public sector should no longer be insulated from the imperatives of competition. This in turn reflected a more general trend in bureaucratic practice to separate the government's policy function from its service delivery function.[52] The latter function can be devolved, through the use of contractors and quasi-markets, with greater scope for discretion and 'entrepreneurial' behaviour on the part of private providers of services.[53] The OECD had also raised the issue of contestability in the operation of public employment services, and endorsed the Australian reforms with the observation that '[f]urther experimentation along the Australian approach would be highly desirable'.[54]

The End of the Public Employment Service in Australia: The Second Phase

By subjecting the case management functions of the CES to competition, the 1994 reforms paved the way for a radical privatisation of CES functions

---

[50] Australian Constitution s 61.

[51] Department of Social Security, *From Client to Customer: An Approach to Re-engineering of Employment Services*, cited in M Wearing and P Smyth, '*Working Nation* and Beyond as Market Bureaucracy' in P Smyth and B Cass (eds), *Contesting the Australian Way: States, Markets and Civil Society* (Melbourne, Cambridge University Press, 1998) 235.

[52] See, eg, D Osborne and T Gaebler, Reinventing Government: How The Entrepreneurial Spirit is Transforming the Public Sector (Reading, Addison-Wesley, 1992).

[53] Considine, 'Markets, Networks and the New Welfare State', above n 40, 185–86.

[54] OECD, The OECD Jobs Strategy: Enhancing the Effectiveness of Active Labour Market Policies (Paris, Organisation for Economic Co-operation and Development, 1996) 27.

more generally. Emboldened by endorsements such as those of the OECD, the Howard Coalition government, elected in March 1996, extended the contestable market to job brokerage and forms of employment assistance other than case management. In effect, many of the traditional functions undertaken by the CES since 1946 were now to be undertaken by a mix of private, community and government organisations, members of the 'Job Network'. By the beginning of 1998, 148 Job Network members were from the private sector, 143 from the community sector and 19 government owned.[55]

Job brokerage and employer servicing, including public access vacancy boards, as well as jobseeker registration, remained with the CES until 1997. Then, responsibility for these tasks was transferred to a new entity, a Commonwealth services delivery agency called Centrelink, established pursuant to the Commonwealth Services Delivery Agency Act 1997 (Cth) and which administered the full range of Commonwealth social security payments. The task of registering and referring jobseekers to case managers was also transferred from the CES to Centrelink in the middle of 1997. After November 1997 the CES ceased to manage any labour market programmes. Between December 1997 and April 1998, management of the winding down of labour market programmes was transferred to Transition Services Units created in each State. As of 1 May 1998, most labour market programmes were disbanded and the operations of the CES ceased. The winding down of labour market programmes meant savings of $1.7 billion which were used to finance the operations of the new Job Network.

Centrelink became the initial point of contact for people seeking access to unemployment benefit. As well as maintaining a National Vacancy Database accessible through touch screens, Centrelink registered and classified those claiming unemployment benefit and referred claimants to Job Network members for employment services. Classification proceeded by jobseekers completing a Job Seeker Classification Instrument (JSCI) which sought to identify the type of employment assistance a client might require. Questions covered age, education, recent work experience, geographical location, language and literacy – those factors which were reckoned to correlate with long-term unemployment – and each was assigned a numerical weighting. On this basis, the jobseeker was referred to one of three levels of assistance: basic job matching and brokerage services; improved job searching skills (preparation of CVs and job applications, interview techniques and so on); or intensive, individualised employment assistance. This last level of assistance itself contained three sub-levels of assistance, depending on a client's degree of labour market disadvantage. The first sub-level was for claimants newly unemployed but who, for various factors, faced a strong risk of becoming long-term unemployed; the second for those long-term unemployed; and the third for people with disabilities and Aboriginal and Torres Strait Islander clients.

---

[55] United Kingdom, House of Commons Select Committee on Education and Employment, *First Report*, 1999, para 15.

There were no specific programmes which provider agencies were obliged to provide; they could use their government funds in any way they saw fit, although intensive assistance needed to be specified in an Activity Agreement pursuant to the Social Security Act 1991 (Cth). The streaming of claimants into the different levels of assistance also determined the payments that providers received. Agencies providing basic job matching and brokerage services received fees when they placed clients into jobs that lasted for at least 15 hours within a period of five consecutive days. Those providing the next level of services received the same fee, with a bonus if the jobseeker remained in the job for 13 consecutive weeks. Payments for the provision of intensive services were paid partly on referral of the jobseeker to the provider and the preparation of an Activity Agreement, with further payment once the client was placed in employment for 13 weeks, and the remainder after 26 weeks in placement.[56]

The Department of Social Security embraced the new market framework even more enthusiastically than it had in 1994:

> The movement in Australia to institute a competitive employment-placement market [rather than merely a case management market], with its payment for employment results, should increase greatly the emphasis on meeting the needs of individual customers. The market mechanism, too, will create strong financial incentives for employment service providers to help their unemployed customers with the most cost-effective forms of labour market assistance to improve their employability.[57]

Initially the government sought to implement its reform of employment services through amendments to the Employment Services Act 1994 (Cth).[58] When the amendments stalled in the Senate, the government proceeded without any enabling legislation, achieving substantially the result it wanted through a series of administrative arrangements. The government went ahead and contracted with private providers to provide a range of employment services;[59] the contracted providers then offered to unemployment benefit recipients the range of activities and services that they contracted with the government to provide. The terms under which the services were offered to benefit recipients and the extent to which continuation of receipt of benefit was dependent on performance of certain activities by the recipient remained governed, as they were prior to 1996, by the provisions of the Social Security Act 1991 (Cth). The only major change that the government had to make to its scheme in order to bypass the legislative route

---

[56] ibid para 17.

[57] Department of Social Security, 'Voice, Choice and Contract: Customer Focus in Programs for Unemployed People', Policy Discussion Paper No 9 (Canberra, DSS, 1997) 25.

[58] See Reform of Employment Services Bill 1996; Reform of Employment Services (Consequential Amendments) Bill 1996.

[59] The executive's capacity to enter into contracts is well established; it is not necessary for there to have been an appropriation of monies at the time of the contract, there being an implied condition in any contract that the government will not pay out any monies under the contract except with proper parliamentary appropriation. See Australian Constitution s 61; *NSW v Bardolf* (1934) 52 CLR 455.

was to ensure that providers tendered for, and were contracted to provide, a wider range of employment services than merely case management: that is, services such as job brokerage or 'intensive assistance' more broadly defined. By taking contracts beyond the scope of case management, the Commonwealth could avoid operation of the still extant Employment Services Act 1994 (Cth), which limited the executive power of the Commonwealth to entering contracts dealing with the provision of 'case management services' as statutorily defined.[60] The relationship between the Commonwealth (the then Department of Employment, Workplace Relations and Small Business) and the provider was governed by a contract, arising out of a tender process, while the relationship between the provider and the jobseeker was substantially governed by the existing terms of the Social Security Act 1991 (Cth) – in particular, those terms concerning the making of Activity Agreements. The Employment Services Act 1994 (Cth), which contained the legislative mandate of the CES, was not repealed, but became a dead letter. As long as there was no appropriation of government monies solely for case management services, there was nothing upon which the Act could operate.

A final feature of the initial iteration of the Job Network was the role of Employment National. This was a public employment placement enterprise, comprising mainly of staff from the old CES and Employment Assistance Australia. As well as competing with other providers for Job Network contracts, Employment National supplied services on a fee-for-service basis for the government in those areas where Job Network coverage was not otherwise achieved through the competitive tendering process. In compensating for market failure, Employment National took on elements of the community service obligations of the old CES. But Employment National had no statutory mandate, merely being established as a company wholly owned by the Commonwealth under corporations law. In the second-round tendering process concluded in December 1999, Employment National lost the bulk of its business to private providers (including church-based, not-for-profit providers), its share of the market for intensive assistance dropping from 40 per cent to 1 per cent. Employment National would not survive subsequent iterations of the Network.

The Evolution of the Job Network

That second tender round for employment services, like the first, was based on price and quality, but it saw the number of providers drop from 360 to just over 200, half of whom were not-for-profit agencies. Bids in the third round, in 2003, were judged on quality alone, by way of a 'star rating' system that was based on

---

[60] See Commonwealth of Australia, Senate Estimates Committee, Employment, Education and Training Legislation, Hearings, 19 August 1997.

both the number of clients placed in employment and the average time taken for such placements, with the rating weighted according to client mix and local labour market conditions. Sixty per cent of second round providers were 'rolled over' into the third round; 40 per cent of the providers were new tenderers, with the overall number of providers further reduced to just over 100 providers.

The third round put in place an 'Active Participation Model' that strongly prescribed the progress of claimants through the system. Clients coming into the system continued to have their level of assistance determined by their JSCI score, which in turn determined the payment to an employment assistance provider for a successful outcome for that jobseeker. The JSCI 'cut off' score used to determine whether a client was highly disadvantaged, and therefore required intensive assistance, was raised to reflect improved labour market conditions in much of the country.[61] The incoming jobseeker then signed an agreement and notionally chose a service provider. That choice had long been a chimera. Despite the hope that a quasi-market in job services would increase competition, as early as 2001 around two-thirds of jobseekers made no choice and were automatically referred to a provider.[62] Once clients entered the system, their progress through it was now largely determined by the requirements imposed by the government on all providers of employment services. The base level of assistance was Job Search Support; after three months this shifted to Intensive Assistance; and after a further three months this became Mutual Obligation, as outlined in chapter seven, with the default obligation being the Work for the Dole programme. After a further six months, the claimant proceeded to Intensive Support with customised assistance

The early Job Network was based on a hybrid model of regulation – goals and outcomes carefully prescribed by contract, but methods kept open and flexible – which led one commentator to characterise private providers as 'a new class of franchisees'.[63] Both Mark Freedland and Thorsten Stromback have also used the term 'franchise' to capture the effect of the privatisation of employment services.[64] Each of them is, I think, using the concept in a distinct way, but it is a distinction that might prove useful to our analysis. The distinction corresponds, roughly, to that between retail franchising and what is called business format franchising. The first involves applicants tendering to obtain exclusive rights to sell the franchisor's product for a defined period in a defined area. This has been a common understanding of privatisation projects since the mid-1980s, especially where the

---

[61] M Thomas, 'A Review of Developments in the Job Network', Parliamentary Library Research Paper No 15, 2007–2008 (Canberra, Parliament of Australia, 2007) 22.

[62] OECD, Activating Jobseekers: How Australia Does It (Paris, OECD, 2012) 70.

[63] M Considine, *Enterprising States: The Public Management of Welfare-to-Work* (Cambridge, Cambridge University Press, 2001) 172.

[64] M Freedland, 'The Marketization of Public Services' in C Crouch, K Eder and D Tambini (eds), *Citizenship, Markets, and the State* (Oxford, Oxford University Press, 2001) 95; T Stromback, 'The Job Network and Underemployment' (2008) 27 *Economic Papers* 286, 296.

service in question involves a natural monopoly. It more or less captures what has happened with the privatisation of government utilities, or with the public transport system in my home town of Melbourne. It's why we describe the resultant service provision as involving a '*quasi*-market'. For example, once Job Network tenders were accepted the Network was closed to other potential providers, the Commonwealth was the sole purchaser, and members of the Network had no collective exposure to competition for the life of the tender period. In Stephen Littlechild's succinct phrasing, the process involves 'competition *for* the market' rather than 'competition *in* the market'.[65]

Business format franchising, by contrast, involves a much greater degree of control and monitoring by the franchisor. The franchisee often signs up to the franchisor's production processes, quality control and accounting systems, group advertising and promotions. Fast food is the paradigm example, and the intention is to deliver a uniform experience to the customer of any franchisee.

Freedland seems to be invoking the notion of retail franchising as a useful way to think about the broad sweep of privatisation of government services generally. Stromback uses the model of business format franchising as a touchstone to make a much more specific point about the evolution of the Job Network. On his reading of the 2003–06 round of Job Network contracts, the Network had come to rely 'on a prescriptive specification of the service that providers should deliver, rather than allowing individual providers to develop the most effective forms of assistance in the community in which they operate'. The fine-grained specification of each stage of the process of assisting jobseekers set out in the 2003 contracts with providers, he notes, sat uneasily with the original conception of the Network, which was to free up employment assistance from the bureaucratic procedural strictures associated with centralised government provision.[66]

Stromback's observations are borne out by the fieldwork undertaken by Considine, Lewis and O'Sullivan. Front-line service providers in employment agencies reported that between 1998 and 2008 their activities had become more controlled and scripted.[67] Again, this shows a shift from the aspiration that accompanied the original roll out of the Network: that it would deliver a proliferation of innovative, entrepreneurial, individualised and discretionary approaches to client assistance. Like Stromback, Considine et al lay part of the blame on the increasingly prescriptive contract conditions. They come to the somewhat damning assessment that the standardisation of experience for both jobseekers and

---

[65] Cited in C Vejnayovska, *Selling the State* (London, Weidenfeld & Nicolson, 1987). The process regarding privatisation of government services differs, though, from that involved in commercial franchising (in, say, the petrol station sector). In stylised terms, the latter involves applicants *bidding* to pay the *highest* price for an exclusive licence; the former involves applicants *tendering* to provide the service at the *lowest* cost to government.

[66] Stromback, above n 64, 294–96.

[67] M Considine, J Lewis and S O'Sullivan, 'Quasi Markets and Service Delivery Flexibility Following a Decade of Employment Assistance Reform in Australia' (2011) 40 *Journal of Social Policy* 811, 822.

staff suggested that, rather than a profusion of innovation, there had resulted 'a "herd" of profit maximisers who are highly responsive to threats to their viability and who embrace standardisation of services as a way to minimise risks'.[68]

But it's worth remembering that business format franchising in general is not necessarily a bad thing, even if – or especially if – it results in an increasingly uniform experience for customers (although Stromback notes that franchising is best suited to roll out a market-proven product, which wasn't necessarily the case with the privatisation of employment services). The ongoing changes to the Job Network tender contracts represented very real attempts to partially standardise service delivery in response to perceived problems arising from the incentive structure put in place in the initial Job Network system.

One of these problems was 'creaming', which involved providers focusing their energies on easy-to-place jobseekers and pocketing the outcome fee. Another was 'parking', whereby providers took on difficult-to-place jobseekers and received the attached upfront fee, but then did little to assist them into work, or rotated them through artificial short-term jobs that maximised placement payments. Early analysis of the initial fee structure by some economists suggested that the most profitable option for providers would indeed be to take on referred disadvantaged clients without providing any meaningful assistance, with the service provision remaining viable on the basis of the steady stream of upfront payments that accompanied intensive assistance referrals together with outcome payments for more easy-to-place clients.[69] And the initial departmental evaluation of the Job Network presented evidence that some providers did organise their activities on precisely this basis. In effect, the fee structure provided an incentive for providers to *not* offer assistance to all eligible jobseekers.[70]

So rather than foster innovation, the 'black box' at the centre of the original tender contracts simply handed providers the discretion to ignore the most disadvantaged jobseekers in pursuit of profits. Standardising certain minimum requirements for all jobseekers was a logical response. So perhaps this is the inevitable outcome of such an experiment: in trying to marry innovation and discretion with equality of treatment and standardised service provision, the privatised network is doomed to career between under-regulation and what some would call 'aggressive over-regulation'.[71]

---

[68] ibid 826.

[69] See, eg, D Harding, 'What Incentives Does Job Network Create?' (1998) 4 *Mercer-Melbourne Institute Quarterly Bulletin of Economic Trends* 40.

[70] Commonwealth of Australia, Department of Employment, Workplace Relations and Small Business, *Job Network Evaluation Stage One: Implementation and Market Development*, Evaluation and Program Performance Branch Report 1/2000 (Canberra, Department of Employment, Workplace Relations and Small Business, 2000) 87–89.

[71] Considine, Lewis and O'Sullivan, above n 67, 830. On the negotiation of this problem in Britain, see M Considine, S O'Sullivan and P Nguyen, 'The Policymaker's Dilemma: The Risks and Benefits of a "Black Box" Approach to Commissioning Active Labour Market Programmes' (2018) 52 *Social Policy & Administration* 229.

The tension between discretion and proceduralisation played out in other ways. Case management techniques were grounded in risk management. Mid-century social insurance responses to unemployment necessarily incorporated notions of risk, but here I am drawing on the distinction between what Mitchell Dean calls different 'epistemes' of risk, distinguishing between actuarial or 'insurance risk' and 'case management risk'. The latter is assessed through the interpersonal practices of human service professionals.[72] Case management approaches in the employment services network are triggered by the JSCI, which proceeds on the assumption that the unemployed population can be abstractly classified according to a fine grid of sub-populations in order to assess probabilities of long-term unemployment.[73] It was designed to delve beneath the broad eligibility conditions to identify which individuals needed what levels of actual assistance in finding work. Importantly, despite the privatisation of employment services and the significant delegation of powers to Job Network agencies, the JSCI is applied by Centrelink staff and so the government, rather than the unemployed person or the Job Network agency, determined the level of assistance offered to the unemployed person. Administration of the JSCI is heavily proceduralised and automated, and so theoretically minimises the discretionary capacity of Centrelink employees (which, in turn, is expected to minimise costs associated with mis-classifying clients and delivering inappropriate or unnecessary assistance).[74] Centrelink staff used a standardised screen-based application, with questions asked verbatim, and 'best-practice' time protocols established how long the assessment should take.[75] This strict standardisation represented an attempt to limit the discretion inherent in what Michael Lipsky famously termed the 'street level bureaucracy' often associated with delivery of human services.[76] Yet subjective or 'soft' assessments, and the risk of misclassification, cannot be entirely eliminated. First, the JSCI relies on self-disclosure, from clients who might not want to disclose certain personal characteristics to a stranger (such as drug or gambling addiction) quite obviously increases the risk of a 'classification error' and who might not have appreciated that disclosure would determine the appropriate level of assistance.[77] Secondly, while many of the 'risk factors' identified by the JSCI derive from statistical profiling regarding who succeeds

---

[72] M Dean, Governmentality: Power and Rule in Modern Society (London, Sage, 1999).

[73] P Henman, 'Targeted! Population Segmentation, Electronic Surveillance and Governing the Unemployed in Australia' (2004) 19 *International Sociology* 173, 181.

[74] C McDonald, G Marston and A Buckley, 'Risk Technology in Australia: The Role of the Job Seeker Classification Instrument in Employment Services' (2003) 23 *Critical Social Policy* 498, 508.

[75] ibid 506.

[76] M Lipsky, *Street-level Bureaucracy: Dilemmas of the Individual in Public Services* (New York, Russell Sage, 1980); M Bouvens and S Zouridis, 'From Street-level to System-level Bureaucracies: How Information and Communications Technology is Transforming Administrative Discretion and Constitutional Control' (2002) 62 *Public Administration Review* 174.

[77] Productivity Commission, *Independent Review of the Job Network*, Report No 21 (Canberra, Ausinfo, 2002) para 9.2.

and who fails in the current labour market, for some unemployed the JSCI is supplemented by a secondary classification process through 'special needs assessment'. This is usually undertaken by occupational psychologists and dependent on much more discretionary judgements of Centrelink customer service staff, guided by a list of observable behaviours such as inappropriate eye contact, poor hygiene, inappropriate make-up application, appearance not in keeping with peers, inability to communicate effectively and so on.[78]

The psychological or therapeutic discourse that came to dominate the regulation of the unemployed, along with the focus on agreements and risk identification, produced a sense that case managers were working *with* rather than *over* the unemployed.[79] There is some evidence that interactions were increasingly marked by 'empathetic authority' and 'pedagogical authority' derived from the techniques used by human service professionals and social workers. These interventions were directed at getting the unemployed to regulate themselves in the form of embodying and desiring certain practices, identities, traits.[80] Assessment tools such as the JSCI produced a particular psychologised and individualised understanding of the unemployment problem, an understanding that potentially replicated a nineteenth-century focus on the character of the unemployed. Therapy and empowerment complemented and sometimes displaced coercion and discipline – or, perhaps, simply masked the coercive and disciplinary nature of the regulatory regime.

Contracts All the Way Down?

In Australia, as elsewhere, reforms to the delivery of employment assistance overlapped with wide-ranging changes to the nature of unemployment benefits. Rik van Berkel usefully separates 'program reforms', focused on eligibility for unemployment benefits (outlined in chapter seven), from 'operational reforms' directed at how the provision of employment assistance is organised (outlined in this chapter).[81] There's a natural tendency to suspect that the two are in some way linked, and that one could not proceed without the other. That suspicion is reinforced by the recurrent trope of 'contract'. And there does seem to be a neat symmetry about the reforms: at around the same time as claimants' relation with the state was being reconfigured through the contractual prism of 'Activity Agreements' and mutual obligation, the framework in which the adjudicating

---

[78] McDonald, Marston and Buckley, above n 74, 506, 509–11.

[79] G Marston and C McDonald, 'The Psychology, Ethics and Social Relations of Unemployment' (2003) 6 *Australian Journal of Labour Economics* 293, 311.

[80] ibid 302, 308, 311.

[81] R van Berkel, 'The Provision of Income Protection and Activation Services for the Unemployed in Active Welfare States: An International Comparision' (2010) 39 *Journal of Social Policy* 17.

agency operated was itself being contractualised. What emerged was a complex three-way relationship between the Job Network provider, the jobseeker 'client' and the government.

There is that old story about the sage who was asked on what the world stood, and who replied 'On a tortoise'. But on what does the tortoise stand? 'On another tortoise' was the reply. And that tortoise? 'On another tortoise'. You mean? 'Yes, it's tortoises all the way down' was the answer. The proliferation of contractual or contract-like arrangements makes it tempting to link late-twentieth-century programme reforms with operational reforms and to characterise the new world of welfare as contracts 'all the way down'. Freedland, for example, suggests that the new contractual relationships cohere to produce a mutually reinforcing 'marketization' of citizenship itself.[82] Thomas Bredgaard and Fleming Larsen also argue that there was a common agenda behind operational reforms and the desire to instil a 'work first' approach in programme delivery.[83] And Considine et al refer to 'double activation': the idea that stronger measures to activate claimants to find work were linked with financial incentives to better 'activate' providers to achieve outcomes.[84] More explicitly, Kanishka Jayasuriya highlights what he calls the 'chains of contracts' that now characterise welfare provision.[85]

But perhaps we should be cautious about concluding that the contractualisation of a jobseeker's situation is *necessarily* dependent on the contractual governance of an intermediate service provider.

First, the descriptor 'contractual' is being used in a loose way in these discussions. Peter Vincent-Jones distinguishes between administrative contracts, economic contracts and social control contracts. The first refers to those arrangements put in place within government bureaucracies whereby agencies are reconstituted as stand-alone 'business units' or 'cost centres' and are asked to meet certain performance and financial targets, but the agency remains a government agency, staffed by government employees. Economic contracts, by contrast, accompany the process of full-scale privatisation, whereby the government ceases to provide a service directly and instead purchases the provision of the service – employment assistance, for example – from an outside provider and the purchase and terms of delivery of the service is governed by a commercial contract between the government and the provider. Finally, the government might ask that individuals seeking access to state services sign up to 'agreements' that set

---

[82] Freedland, above n 64, 99–105. See also M Freedland and D King, 'Contractual Governance and Illiberal Contracts: Some Problems of Contractualism as an Instrument of Behaviour Management by Agencies of Government' (2003) 27 *Cambridge Journal of Economics* 465, 471.

[83] T Bredgaard and F Larsen, 'Quasi-Markets in Employment Policy: Do They Deliver on Promises?' (2008) 7 *Social Policy and Society* 341, 343.

[84] M Considine, J Lewis, S O'Sullivan and E Sol, *Getting Welfare to Work: Street-Level Governance in Australia, the UK, and the Netherlands* (Oxford, Oxford University Press, 2015) 32.

[85] K Jayasuri, 'The New Contractualism: Neo-Liberal or Democratic?' (2003) 73 *The Political Quarterly* 309, 309.

out what claimants must do in return for the service or assistance: these are social control contracts. The 'Activity Agreements', 'Preparing for Work Agreements' and 'Employment Pathway Plans' outlined in chapter seven are paradigm examples of social control contracts, but with the word 'contract' being used symbolically because these arrangements don't meet the legal criterion of a genuinely contractual relationship. The relationship between the government and employment service providers on the other hand is governed by an economic contract and, here, 'contract' does accurately describe the commercial reality of the relationship. So Jayasuriya's 'chain of contracts' might more accurately be thought of as a chain comprising both 'real' contracts and administrative instruments that simply try to mimic contracts.

Further, the 'chain of contracts' theory seems to be predicated on the understanding that programme reforms and operational reforms are of a piece. For Bredgaard and Larsen, there's a common neo-liberal rationality, so that when you combine the two reforms the effect of each is more profound. So for instance, if the terms of the contracts between governments and employment assistance providers impose strong performance incentives to move claimants off benefit, providers are more likely to negotiate tough contracts with claimants that pressure them to return to work or which carry an increased threat of sanction that will otherwise see them removed from benefit.[86] But what I've labelled 'programme reforms' – increasingly onerous requirements placed on jobseekers, imposed by way of Activity Agreements – in Australia preceded the operational reforms associated with the privatisation of employment services.

And not only did the programme reforms exist independently of any major operational reforms for over half a decade, once the Job Network was established there was reason to doubt whether the private provision of services did in fact bolster the government's policies regarding activation of claimants or undermine them. Deborah Mabbett suggests two possible factors that cast doubt on any mutually reinforcing connection between programme and operational reforms.

One involves the extent to which private providers were actually involved in negotiating the 'contract' with claimants and adjudicating subsequent compliance. The second concerns the incentives put in place by the providers' own contracts with government and which may have discouraged the reporting of breaches by claimants.[87]

While the relationship between the Commonwealth government and the provider was governed by a contract, arising out of a tender process, the relationship between the provider and the jobseeker remained substantially governed by the existing terms of the Social Security Act 1991 (Cth) – in particular, for those accessing intensive employment assistance, those terms concerning the making

---

[86] D Mabbett, 'Telling Tales from Abroad: Australia, the Netherlands and the Welfare-to-Work Proposals in the UK' (2009) 17 *Benefits* 137, 139–40; Freedland and King, above n 82, 471.
[87] Mabbett, ibid, 140.

of Activity Agreements.[88] The terms of the contracts between the Commonwealth and providers indicated that any Activity Agreement was not actually concluded with the provider. The role of the provider was limited to the negotiation of draft terms of an Agreement that then needed to be approved by a nominated Commonwealth officer. For the purposes of the Social Security Act, any Agreement was then between the nominated officer and the jobseeker, and the provider was contractually bound to the Commonwealth to deliver the services specified in the Agreement.[89]

So although Job Network members were required to monitor unemployed jobseekers' compliance with agreements and other aspects of the Social Security Act, it was Centrelink, the government agency, that remained responsible for determining whether non-compliance had actually occurred and for imposing sanctions on recommendation from Job Network members. So, for example, between July 1998 and August 1999, only 43 per cent of 'breach' recommendations made by Job Network members were applied by Centrelink. Both the overall rate of recommendation and the percentage of breach recommendations actually applied rose markedly near the end of this period, a fact a departmental evaluation attributed to an 'improved awareness of Job Network members of their role in applying the activity test, assisted by training delivered by Centrelink'.[90]

Evidence gathered under the contracted case management system in place from 1994 to 1996 had indicated that non-government providers recommended breaches at a lower rate than government providers, but, within the non-government group, not-for-profit community sector providers recommended breaches at a higher rate than private firms.[91] The Productivity Commission's 2002 study of the Job Network also highlighted a marked variation among private providers regarding notification of client breaches to Centrelink. Some researchers saw this variation as the consequence of how individual providers negotiated the inherent contradictions between their policing role, the profit motive, and their supportive role.[92] Many private providers saw the paperwork involved with 'breaching' a claimant as an administrative burden. Some saw breach notification as potentially damaging

---

[88] Social Security Act 1991 (Cth) ss 605–06. See T Brennan, 'Newstart Activity Agreements: Are They Contracts?' in R Creyke and M Sassella (eds), *Targeting, Accountability and Review: Current Issues in Income Support Law* (Canberra, The Centre for International and Public Law, Australian National University, 1998) 96.

[89] What mechanisms came into play should the Commonwealth officer *not* approve the draft Agreement remained unclear, but the first 'upfront' payment to providers for intensive assistance services was made once the provider and jobseeker agreed to complete a draft Agreement, whether or not the draft agreement was actually completed or whether or not the draft terms were approved by the Commonwealth: Brennan, ibid, 96.

[90] Commonwealth of Australia, Job Network Evaluation Stage One, above n 70, 116–20.

[91] Considine, *Enterprising States*, above n 63, 194–95.

[92] C Bigby and W Files, 'Street Level Leniency or Unjust Inconsistency? An Examination of Breach Recommendation Decision Making in a For Profit Job Network Agency' (2003) 6 *Australian Journal of Labour Economics* 277, 289.

the trust relationship they had with the jobseeker, and with the more vulnerable or disadvantaged jobseeker in particular.[93] So although employment assistance providers had technically 'signed up' to the task of monitoring clients' compliance, their interpretations of that contractual obligation seemed to differ. Rather than there being any simple correlation between privatisation and the policing of compliance, whether a jobseeker was reported for non-compliance by a private provider depended on what the Productivity Commission called, simply, 'the luck of the draw'.[94]

Providers' inclination or disinclination to set in train the sanctioning process by reporting breaches to Centrelink might also be related to Mabbett's second point. The decision to report might be a strategic one, related to the incentives put in place by the contracts between the government and the provider. The Productivity Commission acknowledged that rewarding providers by outcome could tempt them to 'vigorously' apply compliance measures in order to clear difficult-to-place clients from their books and make space for easier-to-place jobseekers. But the Commission thought that any strategic incentives which might exist to remove clients in this way were 'not that easy to exploit'.[95] Contracts rewarded providers for getting clients into employment. As we've seen, the initial structure of incentives may have led to certain opportunistic behaviour on the part of providers – the problems of 'parking' and 'creaming' of clients, discussed earlier – but they also created an incentive for providers to retain clients rather than have them disqualified for non-compliance.[96] The change in contract conditions in subsequent tender rounds, from a 'black box' to an increasingly prescriptive approach, was an attempt to deal with parking and creaming, but also arguably to address this issue of enforcing compliance.[97] Again, the need to constantly tinker with each round of tender provisions in an attempt to 'get it right' on this point suggests any correlation between privatisation and the better enforcement of activation measures – that goal of 'double activation' – can't be taken for granted.

But in a broader sense Freedland and others are probably right. Although neither 'contractualisation' of the unemployment–state relation nor the contractual provision of private employment services was the necessary precondition of the other, now that they do co-exist – and have done in Australia for two decades – we must be alert to how they operate as an ensemble.

* * *

The transformation of the public employment service in Australia, initially hailed as radical by international standards, has perhaps been more gradual than

---

[93] Productivity Commission, *Independent Review of the Job Network*, above n 77, paras 6.19–6.23.
[94] ibid para 14.22.
[95] ibid, para 9.20.
[96] Mabbett, above n 86, 140.
[97] ibid, 142.

is sometimes recognised An increasing emphasis on case management and the purchaser–provider model can be traced back to the second half of the 1980s. But questioning as to the CES's proper role began even earlier, in the mid-1970s – although the 1977 review of the Service noted, with apparent surprise, that the idea of 'disbanding the CES [and] allowing the market to expand its other existing mechanisms for filling jobs … was not put forward to the Review from any source'.[98]

Perhaps the CES's increasing responsibility for labour market programmes, which the Review endorsed, ensured the survival of the Service for another couple of decades. After all, the comparative advantage that a public employment service has over private commercial placement agencies is that rather than simply respond to existing patterns of supply and demand, its responsibility for government labour market programmes allows it to potentially alter patterns of both supply (through training programmes) and demand (through bestowing wage subsidies). Such advantage depends, of course, on the service maintaining a monopoly on such programmes. Once the CES had no monopoly in this area, along with no monopoly in placement services, its survival became increasingly precarious.[99] In Australia by the close of the twentieth century, the institution that Booth, Beveridge and a host of other reformers had seen as central to the 'invention' of unemployment – the government labour exchange – was no longer with us.

---

[98] Review of the Commonwealth Employment Service, above n 22.
[99] A Jordan, 'Employment, Unemployment and Social Policy: Response to Structural Change' (unpublished manuscript, 2000).

BIBLIOGRAPHY

Allport, C, 'Left off the Agenda: Women, Reconstruction, and the New Order Housing' (1984) 46 *Labour History* 1.

Anderson, G, *Fixation of Wages in Australia* (Melbourne, Macmillan, 1929).

Archer, V, 'Dole Bludgers, Tax Payers and the New Right: Constructing Discourses of Welfare in 1970s Australia' (2009) 96 *Labour History* 177.

Arup, C, 'Job Security or Income Support?' (1976) 7 *Federal Law Review* 145.

—— 'The Power of the Employer to Stand Down: Latitude and Constraints' (1978) 20 *Journal of Industrial Relations* 463.

Atalay, K, Kim, W and Whelan, S 'The Decline of the Self-Employment Rate in Australia' (2014) 47 *Australian Economic Review* 472.

Australian Bureau of Statistics, *Australian Social Trends 2000*, Cat No 4102.0.

—— 'Census of New South Wales 1891: Statistician's Report' (Sydney, 1891).

—— *Forms of Employment, Australia*, Cat No 6359.0.

—— *Informing A Nation: The Evolution of the Australian Bureau of Statistics*, Cat No 1382.0.

—— *Labour Force Status and Other Characteristics of Families*, Cat No 6224.0.

—— Labour Statistics: Concepts, Sources and Methods, Cat No 6102.0.55.001, February 2018.

Australian Interdepartmental Mission to Study Overseas Manpower and Industry Policies and Programmes, *Report* (Canberra, AGPS, 1974).

Bancroft, G, *The American Labor Force: Its Growth and Changing Composition* (New York, John Wiley and Sons, 1958).

Baxandall, P, 'Explaining Differences in the Political Meaning of Unemployment' (2002) 31 *Journal of Socio-Economics* 469.

—— *Constructing Unemployment: The Politics of Joblessness in East and West* (Aldershot, Ashgate, 2004).

Beveridge, WH, 'Labour Exchanges and the Unemployed' (1907) 17 *Economic Journal* 66.

—— 'Public Labour Exchanges in Germany' (1908) 18 *Economic Journal* 1.

—— *Unemployment: A Problem of Industry* (London, Longmans, Green and Co, 1931 [1909]).

—— *Full Employment in a Free Society* (London, Allen & Unwin, 1944).

Biernacki, R, *The Fabrication of Labour: Germany and Britain 1640–1914* (Berkeley, CA, University of California Press, 1995).

Bigby, C and Files, W, 'Street Level Leniency or Unjust Inconsistency? An Examination of Breach Recommendation Decision Making in a For Profit Job Network Agency' (2003) 6 *Australian Journal of Labour Economics* 277.

Black, C, 'The Origins of Unemployment Insurance in Queensland 1919–1922' (1991) 60 *Labour History* 34.

Boreham, P, Roan, A and Whitehouse, G, 'The Regulation of Employment Services: Private Employment Agencies and Labour Market Policy' (1994) 29 *Australian Journal of Political Science* 541.

Borland, J and Tseng, Y, 'Does "Work for the Dole" Work?' (unpublished paper, Department of Family and Community Services, 2003).

Bosch, G, 'Towards a New Standard Employment Relationship in Western Europe' (2004) 42 *British Journal of Industrial Relations* 617.

Bouvens, M and Zouridis, S, 'From Street-level to System-level Bureaucracies: How Information and Communications Technology is Transforming Administrative Discretion and Constitutional Control' (2002) 62 *Public Administration Review* 174.

Bray, M and Rimmer, M, 'Voluntarism or Compulsion? Public Inquiries Into Industrial Relations in New South Wales and Great Britain, 1890–4' in S Macintyre and R Mitchell (eds), *Foundations of Arbitration: The Origins and Effects of State Compulsory Arbitration, 1890–1914* (Melbourne, Oxford University Press, 1989).

Bredgaard, T and Larsen, F, 'Quasi-Markets in Employment Policy: Do They Deliver on Promises?' (2008) 7 *Social Policy and Society* 341.

Brennan, T, 'Newstart Activity Agreements: Are They Contracts?' in R Creyke and M Sassella (eds), *Targeting, Accountability and Review: Current Issues in Income Support Law* (Canberra, The Centre for International and Public Law, Australian National University, 1998).

Brewer, G, *Rough Justice: A Study of the Causes and Effects of the Termination of Unemployment Benefit* (Fitzroy, Brotherhood of St Laurence, 1978).

Brodkin, E and Marston, G (eds), *Work and the Welfare State: Street-Level Organizations and Workfare Politics* (Washington DC, Georgetown University Press, 2013).

Broomhill, R, 'Underemployment in Adelaide During the Depression' (1974) 27 *Labour History* 31.

Buchanan, J, 'Paradoxes of Significance: Australian Casualisation and Labour Productivity', paper presented to ACTU, RMIT, and *Age* Conference, Work Interrupted: Casual and Insecure Employment in Australia (Melbourne, 2 August 2004).

Burnett, J, *Idle Hands: The Experience of Unemployment, 1790–1990* (London, Routledge, 1994).

Butler, WP, 'Recruitment and Selection Procedures in Australian Industry' (1954) 10 *Personnel Practice Bulletin* 34.

Butlin, N, 'An Index of Engineering Unemployment, 1852–1943' (1946) 22 *Economic Record* 241.

Butlin, SJ, *War Economy 1939–1942* (Canberra, Australian War Memorial, 1955).

Butlin, SJ and Schedvin, CB, *War Economy 1942–1945* (Canberra, Australian War Memorial, 1977).

Campbell, I, 'A Historical Perspective on Insecure Work' (2013) 16 *Queensland Journal of Labour History* 6.

Campbell, I and Burgess, J, 'A New Estimate of Casual Employment?' (2001) 27 *Australian Bulletin of Labour* 85.

Card, D, 'Origins of the Unemployment Rate: The Lasting Legacy of Measurement Without Theory' (paper prepared for the 2011 meetings of the American Economic Association).

Carney, T, *Social Security Law and Policy* (Sydney, The Federation Press, 2006).

Carney, T and Hanks, P, *Australian Social Security Law, Policy and Administration* (Melbourne, Oxford University Press, 1986).

—— *Social Security in Australia* (Melbourne, Oxford University Press, 1994).

Carney, T and Ramia, G, *From Rights to Management: Contract, New Public Management and Employment Services* (The Hague, Kluwer Law International, 2002).

Chapman, B, 'Continuity and Change: Labour Market Programs and Education Expenditure' (1985) 18 *Australian Economic Review* 99.

Chesterman, J, 'Defending Australia's Reputation: How Indigenous Australians Won Civil Rights, Part One' (2001) 32 *Australian Historical Studies* 20.

—— 'Defending Australia's Reputation: How Indigenous Australians Won Civil Rights, Part Two' (2001) 32 *Australian Historical Studies* 201.

Clarke, VS, *The Labour Movement in Australasia: A Study in Social Democracy* (New York, Burt Franklin, 1970 [1906]).

Coase, RH, 'The Nature of the Firm' (1937) 4 *Economica* 386.

Cochrane, P, 'Anatomy of a Steel Works: The Australian Iron and Steel Company Port Kembla, 1935–1939' (1989) 57 *Labour History* 61.

Coghlan, TA, *Labour and Industry in Australia: From the First Settlement in 1788 to the Establishment of the Commonwealth in 1901* (Melbourne, Macmillan, 1969).

Cohen, M and Hanagan, M, 'Politics, Industrialization and Citizenship: Unemployment Policy in England, France and the United States, 1890–1950' (1995) 40(S3) *International Review of Social History* 91.

Colley, AG, 'New South Wales Unemployment Statistics' (1939) 11 *Australian Quarterly* 96.

Collins, H, *Regulating Contracts* (Oxford, Oxford University Press, 1999).

Committee of Inquiry into Labour Market Programs, *Report* (Canberra, AGPS, 1985).

Committee of Inquiry into Labour Market Training, *Labour Market Training in Australia* (Canberra, AGPS, 1974).

Commonwealth Bureau of Census and Statistics, *Labour Report 1925, No 16* (Melbourne, Government Printer, 1926).

—— *Labour Report 1936, No 27* (Melbourne, Government Printer, 1937).

—— *Labour Report 1939, No 30* (Melbourne, Commonwealth Government Printer, 1941).

—— *Labour Report 1946, No 36* (Melbourne, Government Printer, 1946).

—— *Labour Report No 35, 1945–46* (Melbourne, Commonwealth Government Printer, 1947).

—— *Census of the Commonwealth of Australia 30 June 1947, vol III: Statistician's Report* (Canberra, Commonwealth Government Printer, 1952).

—— *Census of the Commonwealth of Australia 30 June 1954, vol VIII: Statistician's Report* (Canberra, Commonwealth Government Printer, 1962).

—— *Census of the Commonwealth of Australia 30 June 1961, vol VIII: Statistician's Report* (Canberra, Commonwealth Government Printer, 1967).

—— *Census of Population and Housing, 30 June 1966*, Volume 1, Part 8 (Canberra, Commonwealth Bureau of Census and Statistics, 1969–73).

Commonwealth of Australia, *Commonwealth Record*, 4 July 1979.

—— *Commonwealth Record*, 1 May 1981.

—— Development and Migration Commission, *Report on Unemployment and Business Instability in Australia*, Parl Paper No 252 (1926–28).

—— *Full Employment in Australia*, Parl Paper No 11 (1945).

—— Joint Committee on Social Security, *Interim Report*, Parl Paper No 48 (1940–43).

—— Joint Committee on Social Security, *Second Interim Report*, Parl Paper No 71 (1940–43).

—— Joint Committee on Social Security, *Third Interim Report*, Parl Paper No 72 (1940–43).

—— 'Meeting the Challenge: Labour Market Trends and the Income Support System', Policy Discussion Paper No 3 (Canberra, Department of Social Security, 1993).

—— Parliamentary Committee on Social Security, *Minutes of Evidence* (Canberra, Commonwealth Government Printer, 1943).

—— Review of the Commonwealth Employment Service, *Report by Mr JD Norgard for the Minister for Employment and Industrial Relations*, Parl Paper No 177 (1978).

—— Royal Commission on National Insurance, *Minutes of Evidence: Unemployment, Destitution Allowances*, Parl Paper No 79 (1926–28).

—— Royal Commission on National Insurance, *Second Progress Report: Unemployment*, Parl Paper No 79 (1926–28).

—— Senate Estimates Committee, Employment, Education and Training Legislation, Hearings, 19 August 1997.

—— Social Security Review, 'The Case for Review of Aspects of the Australian Social Security System', Background/Discussion Paper No 1 (Canberra, Department of Social Security, 1986).

—— Social Security Review, 'Income Support for the Unemployed in Australia: Towards a More Active System', Issues Paper No 4 (Canberra, Department of Social Security, 1988).

—— *Unemployment Benefit Policy and Administration: Report of Inquiry*, Parl Paper No 243 (1977).

—— *Working Nation: Policies and Programs* (Canberra, AGPS, 1994).

—— Department of Employment, Workplace Relations and Small Business, *Job Network Evaluation Stage One: Implementation and Market Development*, Evaluation and Program Performance Branch Report 1/2000 (Canberra, Department of Employment, Workplace Relations and Small Business, 2000).

Connell, RW and Irving, TH, *Class Structure in Australian History: Documents, Narrative and Argument* (Melbourne, Longman Cheshire, 1980).

Considine, M, 'Markets, Networks and the New Welfare State: Employment Assistance Reforms in Australia' (1999) 28 *Journal of Social Policy* 183.

——— *Enterprising States: The Public Management of Welfare-to-Work* (Cambridge, Cambridge University Press, 2001).

Considine, M, Lewis, J and O'Sullivan, S, 'Quasi Markets and Service Delivery Flexibility Following a Decade of Employment Assistance Reform in Australia' (2011) 40 *Journal of Social Policy* 811.

Considine, M, Lewis, J, O'Sullivan, S and Sol, E, *Getting Welfare to Work: Street-Level Governance in Australia, the UK, and the Netherlands* (Oxford, Oxford University Press, 2015).

Considine, M, O'Sullivan, S and Nguyen, P, 'The Policymaker's Dilemma: The Risks and Benefits of a "Black Box" Approach to Commissioning Active Labour Market Programmes' (2018) 52 *Social Policy & Administration* 229.

Coombs, HC, *Trial Balance: Issues of My Working Life* (Melbourne, Sun Books, 1981).

Corden, J, 'Contracts in Social Work Practice' (1980) 10 *British Journal of Social Work* 143.

Cowling, S, 'Understanding Behavioural Responses to Tax and Transfer Changes: A Survey of Low-Income Households' (1998) Melbourne Institute of Applied and Economic Research, University of Melbourne Working Paper No 15/98.

Creighton, WB, Ford, WJ and Mitchell, RJ, *Labour Law: Text and Materials* (Sydney, Law Book Company, 1993).

Curtis, B, *The Politics of Population: State Formation, Statistics and the Census of Canada, 1840–1875* (Toronto, University of Toronto Press, 2001).

Daunton, MJ, *Poverty and Progress: An Economic and Social History of Britain 1700–1850* (Oxford, Oxford University Press, 1995).

Davidson, P and Whiteford, P, *An Overview of Australia's System of Income and Employment Assistance for the Unemployed* (Paris, Organisation for Economic Co-operation and Development, 2012).

Davies, P and Freedland, M, *Towards a Flexible Labour Market: Labour Legislation and Regulation Since the 1990s* (Oxford, Oxford University Press, 2007).

De Maria, W, 'New Society Blueprint or Political Ploy: The Work and Impact of the Joint Committee on Social Security' (1989) 35 *Australian Journal of History & Politics* 164.

Deacon, D, 'Political Arithmetic: The Nineteenth-Century Australian Census and the Construction of the Dependent Woman' (1985) 11 *Signs: Journal of Women in Culture and Society* 27.

Deakin, S, 'The Contract of Employment: A Study in Legal Evolution' (2001) ESRC Centre for Business Research, University of Cambridge Working Paper No 203.

Deakin, S and Wilkinson, F, *The Law of the Labour Market: Industrialization, Employment, and Legal Evolution* (Oxford, Oxford University Press, 2005).

Dean, M, *Governmentality: Power and Rule in Modern Society* (London, Sage, 1999).

Department of Labour and National Service, *An Analysis of Full Employment in Australia*, Labour Market Studies No 2, Melbourne, 1970.

Department of Social Security, 'Voice, Choice and Contract: Customer Focus in Programs for Unemployed People', Policy Discussion Paper No 9 (Canberra, DSS, 1997).

Derthick, M, *Policymaking For Social Security*, cited in P Pierson, 'The Study of Policy Development' (2005) 17 *The Journal of Policy History* 34.

Desrosieres, A, *The Politics of Large Numbers: A History of Statistical Reasoning* (Cambridge, MA, Harvard University Press, 1998).

Di Giorgio, F and Endres, A, 'The Changing Fortunes of CES Unemployment Statistics' (1983) 55 *The Australian Quarterly* 307.

Douglas, H and Chesterman, J, 'Creating a Legal Identity: Aboriginal People and the Assimilation Census' (2008) 32 *Journal of Australian Studies* 375.

Duncan, S and Edwards, R, *Lone Mothers, Paid Work and Gendered Moral Rationalities* (Basingstoke, Macmillan, 1999).

Dunlop, Y, 'Labour Market Outcomes of Low Paid Adult Workers', ABS Occasional Paper Cat No 6293.0.00.005 (Canberra, Australian Bureau of Statistics, 2000).

Eardley, T, Abello, D and Macdonald, H, 'Is the Job Network Benefitting Disadvantaged Jobseekers? Preliminary Evidence from a Study of Non-Profit Employment Services' (2001) Social Policy Research Centre, University of New South Wales Discussion Paper No 111.

Ebbels, N (ed), *The Australian Labour Movement, 1850–1907: Extracts From Contemporary Documents*, 2nd edn (Sydney, Australasian Book Society, 1976).

Endres, T, 'Designing Unemployment Statistics in New Zealand: A History Study in Political Arithmetic c1860–1960' (1982) 22 *Australian Economic History Review* 151.

Endres, T and Cook, M, 'Concepts in Australian Unemployment Statistics to 1940' (1983) 22 *Australian Economic Papers* 68.

—— 'Administering "The Unemployed Difficulty": The NSW Government Labour Bureau 1892–1912' (1986) 26 *Australian Economic History Review* 56.

Englander, E, 'The Inside Contract System of Production and Organization: A Neglected Aspect of the History of the Firm' (1987) 28 *Labor History* 429.

Ewing, KD, *The Right to Strike* (Oxford, Clarendon Press, 1991).

Fahey, C, 'Unskilled Labour and the Beginnings of Labour Market Regulation, Victoria 1901–1914' (2002) 33 *Australian Historical Studies* 143.

Fahey, C and Lack, J, 'Working at Sunshine: A Case Study of the Recruitment and Management of Labour in a Melbourne Manufacturing Enterprise, 1946–63' (2006) 90 *Labour History* 95.

—— 'The Great Strike of 1917 in Victoria: Looking Fore and Aft, and From Below' (2014) 106 *Labour History* 69.

Fahey, C and Sammartino, A, 'Work and Wages at a Melbourne Factory, the Guest Biscuit Works 1870–1921' (2013) 53 *Australian Economic History Review* 22.

Fenwick, C, 'Shooting for Trouble? Contract Labour Hire in the Victorian Building Industry' (1992) 5 *Australian Journal of Labour Law* 237.

Finn, D, *Working Nation: Welfare Reform and the Australian Job Compact for the Long Term Unemployed* (London, Unemployment Unit, 1997).

Fisher, SH, 'An Accumulation of Misery' (1981) 40 *Labour History* 16.

Fitzgerald, RT, *The Printers of Melbourne: The History of a Union* (Melbourne, Pitman, 1967).

Flanagan, R, '*Parish Fed Bastards': A History of the Politics of the Unemployed in Britain, 1884–1939* (New York, Greenwood Press, 1991).

Flatau, P and Dockery, M, 'How Do Income Support Recipients Engage with the Labour Market?', Policy Research Paper No 12 (Canberra, Department of Family and Community Services, 2001).

Foenander, O, *Wartime Labour Developments in Australia: With Suggestions for Reform in the Post-war Regulation of Industrial Relations* (Melbourne, Melbourne University Press, 1943).

—— *Industrial Regulation in Australia: A Study of Awards, Method of Remuneration Fixation, and the Status of Trade Unions Under the Australian Regulative System* (Melbourne, Melbourne University Press, 1947).

Forster, C, 'Australian Unemployment, 1900–1940' (1965) 41 *Economic Record* 426.

—— 'Unemployment and the Australian Economic Recovery of the 1930s' (1985) Department of Economic History, Australian National University Working Paper No 45.

Forsyth, A, 'The European Framework Agreement on Fixed-Term Work: An Australian Perspective' (1999) 15 *The International Journal of Comparative Labour Law and Industrial Relations* 161.

Fort, C, 'Developing a National Employment Policy, Australia 1939–45' (PhD thesis, University of Adelaide, 2000).

—— 'Regulating the Labour Market in Australia's Wartime Democracy' (2003) 34 *Australian Historical Studies* 213.

Frances, R, *The Politics of Work: Gender and Labour in Victoria, 1880–1939* (Melbourne, Cambridge University Press, 1993).

Freedland, M, 'The Marketization of Public Services' in C Crouch, K Eder and D Tambini (eds), *Citizenship, Markets, and the State* (Oxford, Oxford University Press, 2001).

—— 'The Segmentation of Workers' Rights and the Legal Analysis of Personal Work Relations' (2015) 36 *Comparative Labor Law & Policy Journal* 241.

Freedland, M and King, D, 'Contractual Governance and Illiberal Contracts: Some Problems of Contractualism as an Instrument of Behaviour Management by Agencies of Government' (2003) 27 *Cambridge Journal of Economics* 465.

Freedland, M et al, *Public Employment Services and European Law* (Oxford, Oxford University Press, 2007).

Galenson, W and Zellner, A, 'International Comparison of Unemployment Rates' in National Bureau of Economic Research (ed), *The Measurement and Behavior of Unemployment* (Princeton, NJ, Princeton University Press, 1957).

Garland, JM, 'Some Aspects of Full Employment, Part II' (1945) 21 *Economic Record* 23.

Gifford, JLK, *Economic Statistics for Australian Arbitration Courts: Explanation of the Uses Criticism of Existing Statistics and Suggestions for their Improvement* (Melbourne, Macmillan, 1928).

Gomez Garrido, M, 'From the Industrial Reserve Army to the Invention of Unemployment: Between Social History and Historical Ontology' (2004) European University Institute Working Paper SPS No 2004/18.

Gospel, HF, *Markets, Firms and the Management of Labour in Modern Britain* (Cambridge, Cambridge University Press, 1992).

Gray, M et al, 'Changes in the Labour Force Status of Lone and Couple Mothers, 1983–2002', Research Paper No 33 (Melbourne, Australian Institute of Family Studies, 2003).

Gray, S, 'The Elephant in the Drawing Room: Slavery and the Stolen Wages Debate' (2007) 11 *Australian Indigenous Law Review* 30.

Green, DG and Cromwell, L, *Mutual Aid or Welfare State: Australia's Friendly Societies* (Sydney, Allen & Unwin, 1984).

Gregory, RG, Klug, E and Thapa, PJ, 'Lone Mothers Work and Welfare: An Assessment of the Impact of Taper Rate Reduction and Related Reforms', paper prepared for the Social Policy Evaluation and Analysis Centre, Research School of Social Sciences, Australian National University, mimeo, 2005.

Gregory, RG, et al, 'The Australian and US Labour Markets in the 1930s' in B Eichengreen and TJ Hatton (eds), *Interwar Unemployment in International Perspective* (Dordrecht, Springer, 1988).

Grundy, J, *Bureaucratic Manoeuvres: The Contested Administration of the Unemployed* (Toronto, University of Toronto Press, 2019).

Hacking I, 'Making Up People' in TC Heller, M Sosna and DE Wellbery (eds), *Reconstructing Individualism: Autonomy, Individualism and the Self in Western Thought* (Stanford, CA, Stanford University Press, 1986).

—— *The Social Construction of What?* (Cambridge, MA, Harvard University Press, 1999).

Hagan, J, *Printers and Politics: A History of the Australian Printing Unions 1850–1950* (Canberra, Australian National University Press, 1966).

Hall, R, 'Labour Hire in Australia: Motivation, Dynamics and Prospects' (2002) Australian Centre for Industrial Relations Research and Training, University of Sydney Working Paper No 76.

Hancock K, et al, *Report of the Advisory Committee on Commonwealth Employment Service Statistics* (Melbourne, Australian Government Publishing Service 1973).

Harding, D, 'What Incentives Does Job Network Create?' (1998) 4 *Mercer-Melbourne Institute Quarterly Bulletin of Economic Trends* 40.

Harris, J, *Unemployment and Politics: A Study in English Social Policy, 1886–1914* (Oxford, Oxford University Press, 1972).

—— *William Beveridge: A Biography* (Oxford, Clarendon Press, 1977).

—— 'From Sunspots to Social Welfare: The Unemployment Problem 1870–1914' in B Corry (ed), *Unemployment and the Economists* (Cheltenham, Edward Elgar, 1996).

Hasluck, P, *The Government and the People, 1942–1945* (Canberra, Australian War Memorial, 1970).

Hauser, P, 'The Labour Force and Gainful Workers: Concept, Measurement and Comparability' (1949) 54 *American Journal of Sociology* 341.

Henman, P, 'Targeted! Population Segmentation, Electronic Surveillance and Governing the Unemployed in Australia' (2004) 19 *International Sociology* 173.

Hennock, EP, 'Poverty and Social Theory in England: The Experience of the 1880s' (1976) 1 *Social History* 67.

Higman, B, *Domestic Service in Australia* (Melbourne, Melbourne University Press, 2002).

Hobsbawm, EJ, 'The Tramping Artisan' in EJ Hobsbawm (ed) *Labouring Men: Studies in the History of Labour* (London, Weidenfeld and Nicolson, 1964).

Howard, C, 'The Promise and Performance of Mutual Obligation' in C Aspalter (ed), *Neoliberalism and the Australian Welfare State* (Taichung, Casa Verde, 2003).

Howe, J and Mitchell, R, 'The Evolution of the Contract of Employment in Australia: A Discussion' (1999) 12 *Australian Journal of Labour Law* 113.

Hunter, R, 'Women Workers and Federal Industrial Law: From *Harvester* to Comparable Worth' (1988) 1 *Australian Journal of Labour Law* 147.

ILO, *Man-power Mobilisation for Peace* (Montreal, International Labour Office, 1943).

—— *Employment, Unemployment and Labour Force Statistics: A Study of Methods* Studies and Reports, New Series, No 7, Part 1 (Geneva, International Labour Office, 1948).

—— *The Sixth International Conference of Labour Statisticians, Montreal, 4–12 August 1947*, Studies and Reports, New Series, No 7, Part 4 (Geneva, International Labour Office, 1948).

Innes, J, *Knowledge and Public Policy: The Search for Meaningful Indicators*, 2nd edn (New Brunswick, Transaction Publishers, 1990).

Isaac, JE, 'Manpower Planning in Australia' (1960) 82 *International Labour Review* 403.

Jayasuri, K, 'The New Contractualism: Neo-Liberal or Democratic?' (2003) 73 *The Political Quarterly* 309.

Jordan, A, *Long Term Unemployed People under Conditions of Full Employment*, Research Report, Commission of Inquiry into Poverty (Canberra, AGPS, 1975).

—— *Work-Test Failure: A Sample Survey of Terminations of Unemployment Benefit* (Canberra, Department of Social Security, 1981).

—— 'Labour Market Programs and Social Security Payments' (1994) (December) *Social Security Journal* 60.

—— 'A Generation of Growth in Female Employment, But How Much Change?' (1995) (December) *Social Security Journal* 78.

—— 'Employment, Unemployment and Social Policy: Response to Structural Change' (unpublished manuscript, 2000).

Kewley, TH, *Social Security in Australia 1900–72* (Sydney, Sydney University Press, 1973).

Keyssar, A, *Out of Work: The First Century of Unemployment in Massachusetts* (Cambridge, MA, Cambridge University Press, 1986).

King, D, *Actively Seeking Work? The Politics of Unemployment and Welfare Policy in the United States and Great Britain* (Chicago, IL, University of Chicago Press, 1995).

Kirby, PEF, 'An Overview of Australian Experience with Manpower Policies' in CE Baird et al (eds), *Youth Employment, Education and Training: Conference Papers* (Canberra, Centre for Economic Policy Research, ANU, 1982).

Knibbs, GH, *Social Insurance: Report of the Commonwealth Statistician*, Vol 2, Parl Paper No 72 (1910).

Kumar, K, 'From Work to Employment and Unemployment: The English Experience' in RE Pahl (ed), *On Work: Historical, Comparative and Theoretical Approaches* (Oxford, Blackwell, 1988).

Laplagne, P et al, 'The Growth of Labour Hire Employment in Australia' (2005) Productivity Commission Staff Working Paper (Melbourne, Productivity Commission).

Law, A, 'Idlers, Loafers and Layabouts: An Historical Sociological Study of Welfare Discipline and Unemployment in Australia' (PhD thesis, University of Alberta, 1993).

—— 'Surfing the Safety Net: "Dole Bludging", "Surfies" and Governmentality in Australia' (2001) 36 *International Review for the Sociology of Sport* 24.

Le, A and Miller, P, 'Job Quality and Churning of the Pool of the Unemployed', ABS Occasional Paper Cat No 6293.0.00.003 (Canberra, Australian Bureau of Statistics, 1999).

Lee, J and Fahey, C, 'A Boom for Whom? Some Developments in the Australian Labour Market, 1870–1891' (1986) 50 *Labour History* 1.

Lesser, L, 'Labor Disputes and Unemployment Compensation' (1945) 55 *Yale Law Journal* 167.

Lever-Tracy, C and Quinlan, M, *A Divided Working Class: Ethnic Segmentation and Industrial Conflict in Australia* (London, Routledge & Kegan Paul, 1988).

Linge GJR, *Industrial Awakening: A Geography of Australian Manufacturing 1788–1890* (Canberra, Australian National University Press, 1979).

Lipsky, M, *Street-level Bureaucracy: Dilemmas of the Individual in Public Services* (New York, Russell Sage, 1980).

Long, C, 'The Concept of Unemployment' (1942) 57 *Quarterly Journal of Economics* 1.

Louis, LJ, *Trade Unions and the Depression: A Study of Victoria, 1930–1932* (Canberra, Australian National University Press, 1968).

Mabbett, D, 'Telling Tales from Abroad: Australia, the Netherlands and the Welfare-to-Work Proposals in the UK' (2009) 17 *Benefits* 137.

Macgregor, DH, 'Labour Exchanges and Unemployment' (1907) 17 *Economic Journal* 585.

Macintyre, S, *Australia's Boldest Experiment: War and Reconstruction in the 1940s* (Sydney, NewSouth Press, 2015).

Mansfield, M, 'The Why Work? Syndrome' (1988) 22 *Social Policy & Administration* 235.

—— 'Labour Exchanges and the Labour Reserve in Turn of the Century Social Reform' (1992) 21 *Journal of Social Policy* 435.

—— 'Flying to the Moon: Reconsidering the British Labour Exchange System in the Early Twentieth Century' (2001) 66 *Labour History Review* 24.

—— 'Blind Spots and Awkward Corners: "Precarisation" through the Perspective of Unemployment Construction' (paper prepared for the 11th biennial French Sociology of Work Conference, London Metropolitan University, 20–22 June 2007).

Marsden, D, *A Theory of Employment Systems: Micro-Foundations of Societal Diversity* (Oxford, Oxford University Press, 1999).

Marston, G and McDonald, C, 'The Psychology, Ethics and Social Relations of Unemployment' (2003) 6 *Australian Journal of Labour Economics* 293.

McDonald, C, Marston, G and Buckley, A, 'Risk Technology in Australia: The Role of the Job Seeker Classification Instrument in Employment Services' (2003) 23 *Critical Social Policy* 498.

McGregor, R, *Indifferent Inclusion: Aboriginal People and the Australian Nation* (Acton, Aboriginal Studies Press, 2011).

McLaughlin, E, 'Work and Welfare Benefits: Social Security, Employment and Unemployment in the 1990s' (1991) 20 *Journal of Social Policy* 485.

McLean, I and Richardson, S, 'More or Less Equal? Australian Income Distribution Since 1933' (1986) 62 *Economic Record* 67.

McQueen, R, 'Company Law as Imperialism' (1995) 5 *Australian Journal of Corporate Law* 187.

—— 'Master and Servant Legislation in the 19th Century Australian Colonies' in D Kirkby (ed), *Law and History*, vol 4, (Bundoora, School of Legal Studies, La Trobe University, 1987).

Meagher, G, *Friend or Flunkey? Paid Domestic Workers in the New Economy* (Sydney, UNSW Press, 2003).

Merrett, D and Seltzer, A, 'Personnel Practices at the Union Bank of Australia: Panel Evidence from the 1887–1900 Entry Cohorts' (2000) 18 *Journal of Labor Economics* 573.

Merrilees, B, 'Hidden Unemployment of Women in Australia' (1977) 19 *Journal of Industrial Relations* 50.

Merritt, A, 'The Historical Role of Law in the Regulation of Employment – Abstentionist or Interventionist?' (1982) 1 *Australian Journal of Law & Society* 56.

Merritt, J, 'The Federated Ironworkers' Association in the Depression' (1971) 21 *Labour History* 48.

Mitchell, R, 'Union Security and the "Hiring Hall": A note on the Sanctioning of Union Labour Supply Arrangements in Australian Labour Law' (2003) 16 *Australian Journal of Labour Law* 343.

Mitchell, R and O'Donnell, A, 'Participation, Exchange, and Rights and Obligations in Labour Markets and Work Relationships' in C Arup et al (eds), *Labour Law and Labour Market Regulation* (Sydney, The Federation Press, 2006).

Morris, R, 'The Employer's Free Selection of Labour and the Waterfront Closed Shop' (1981) 23 *Journal of Industrial Relations* 49.

Moses, S, 'Labour Supply Concepts: The Political Economy of Conceptual Change' (1975) 418 *Annals of the American Academy of Political and Social Sciences* 26.

Murphy, J, 'Path Dependence and the Stagnation of Australian Social Policy Between the Wars' (2010) 22 *The Journal of Policy History* 450.

—— *A Decent Provision: Australia Welfare Policy, 1870 to 1949* (Farnham, Ashgate, 2011).

—— 'Conditional Inclusion: Aborigines and Welfare Rights in Australia, 1900–1947' (2013) 44 *Australian Historical Studies* 206.

Murray, B, 'Full Employment and the Employment Service: with Special Reference to Australia and the Commonwealth Employment Service' (PhD Thesis, University of Melbourne, 1952).

Murtough, G and Waite, M, 'The Diversity of Casual Contract Employment', Productivity Commission Staff Research Paper (Canberra, AusInfo, 2000).

National Committee to Promote the Breakup of the Poor Law, Royal Commission on The Poor Laws and Relief of Distress, *The Minority Report of the Poor Law Commission Vol 2* (London, 1909).

New South Wales, *Official Year Book of New South Wales 1934–35* (Sydney, Government Printer, 1937).

—— Labour Hire Task Force, *Final Report* (Sydney, NSW Department of Industrial Relations, 2003).

O'Donnell, A, 'Non-Standard Workers in Australia: Counts and Controversies' (2004) 17 *Australian Journal of Labour Law* 89.

—— 'Fixed Term Work in Australia' in H Nakakubo and T Araki (eds), *The Regulation of Fixed-Term Employment Contracts: A Comparative Overview* (The Hague, Kluwer Law International, 2010).

O'Donnell, A and Mitchell, R, 'The Regulation of Public and Private Employment Agencies in Australia: A Historical Perspective' (2001) 23 *Comparative Labor Law and Policy Journal* 7.

O'Malley, P, *Risk, Uncertainty and Government* (London, Glasshouse Press, 2004).

OECD, 'Activity for All in Tomorrow's Society', *OECD Employment Outlook* (Paris, Organisation for Economic Co-operation and Development, 1987).

—— 'The Path to Full Employment: Structural Adjustment for an Active Society', *OECD Employment Outlook* (Paris, Organisation for Economic Co-operation and Development, 1989).

—— *The OECD Jobs Strategy: Enhancing the Effectiveness of Active Labour Market Policies* (Paris, Organisation for Economic Co-operation and Development, 1996).

—— *Activating Jobseekers: How Australia Does It* (Paris, Organisation for Economic Co-operation and Development, 2012).

Osborne, D and Gaebler, T, *Reinventing Government: How The Entrepreneurial Spirit is Transforming the Public Sector* (Reading, Addison-Wesley, 1992).

Oswald Barnett, F, *The Poverty of the People in Australia* (Melbourne, Good Companions Christian Social Order Group, 1944).

Owens, R, 'The "Long term or Permanent Casual": An Oxymoron or a "Well Enough Understood Australianism" in the Law?' (2001) 15 *Australian Bulletin of Labour* 118.

Palmer, G, *A Guide to Australian Economic Statistics* (Melbourne, Macmillan, 1963).

Patmore, G, 'Systematic Management and Bureaucracy: The New South Wales Railways Prior to 1932' (1988) 1 *Labour & Industry* 306.

Pech J and Innes, H, 'Women in the Australian Labour Market 1966–96: The Impact of Change on the Social Security System' (1998) (December) *Social Security Journal* 3.

Peck, J and Theodore, N, '"Workfirst": Workfare and the Regulation of Contingent Labour Markets' (2000) 24 *Cambridge Journal of Economics* 119.

Pigou, AC, *Unemployment* (London, Williams and Norgate, 1924).

—— *The Theory of Unemployment* (London, Macmillan, 1933).

Pincus, J, 'Aspects of Australian Public Finances and Public Enterprises, 1920 to 1939' (1985) Department of Economic History, Australian National University Working Paper No 53.

Porter, A, *Gendered States: Women, Unemployment Insurance, and the Political Economy of the Welfare State in Canada, 1945–1997* (Toronto, University of Toronto Press, 2003).

Powlay, J and Rodgers, K, 'What's Happened to the Work Test?' (1995) (December) *Social Security Journal* 67.

Productivity Commission, *Independent Review of the Job Network*, Report No 21 (Canberra, Ausinfo, 2002).

Puniard, A and Harrington, C, 'Working Through the Poverty Traps: Results of a Survey of Sole Parent Pensioners and Unemployment Beneficiaries' (1993) (December) *Social Security Journal* 1.

Quinlan, M, 'Pre-Arbitral Labour Legislation in Australia and Its Implications for the Introduction of Compulsory Arbitration' in S Macintyre and R Mitchell (eds), *Foundations of Arbitration: The Origins and Effects of State Compulsory Arbitration, 1890–1914* (Melbourne, Oxford University Press, 1989).

—— 'Australia, 1788–1902: A Workingman's Paradise?' in D Hay and P Craven (eds), *Masters, Servants and Magistrates in Britain and the Empire, 1562–1955* (Chapel Hill, NC, University of North Carolina Press, 2004).

Raper, M, 'Examining the Assumptions Behind the Welfare Review' in P Saunders (ed), *Reforming the Australian Welfare State* (Melbourne, Australian Institute of Family Studies, 2000).

Reeves, WP, *State Experiments in Australia and New Zealand Vol 2* (Melbourne, Macmillan, 1969).

Reference Group on Welfare Reform, *Participation Support for a More Equitable Society: Final Report* (Department of Family and Community Services, Canberra, 2000).

Roe, J, 'Perspectives on the Present Day: A Postscript' in J Roe (ed) *Social Policy in Australia: Some Perspectives 1901–1975* (Sydney, Cassell Australia, 1976).

Romeyn, J, *Flexible Working-Time Arrangements: Fixed-Term and Temporary Employment*, Industrial Relations Research Series, No 13, Department of Industrial Relations, 1994.

Ronald Walker, E, 'The Unemployment Problem in Australia' (1932) 40 *Journal of Political Economy* 210.

—— *Unemployment Policy: With Special Reference to Australia* (Sydney, Angus and Robertson, 1936).

—— *The Australian Economy in War and Reconstruction: Issued under the Auspices of the Royal Institute of International Affairs* (New York, Oxford University Press, 1947).

Rowley, C, *The Remote Aborigines* (Canberra, ANU Press, 1971).

Rowse, T, 'The People and Their Experts: A War-Inspired Civics for HC Coombs' (1998) 74 *Labour History* 70.

—— *White Flour, White Power: From Rations to Citizenship in Central Australia* (Melbourne, Cambridge University Press, 1998).

—— 'Curtin and Labor's Full Employment Promise', paper presented at 'From Curtin to Coombs: War and Peace in Australia' seminar (Curtin University of Technology, 25 March 2003).

—— *Indigenous and Other Australians Since 1901* (Sydney, NewSouth, 2017).

Russell, FAA, *Australian Industrial Problems: Some of the Problems and Results of the Law of Industrial Arbitration Under Statutes of New South Wales and the Commonwealth of Australia Before and During the War, 1914–1918* (Sydney, Butterworths & Co, 1918).

Ryan, P and Rowse, T, 'Women, Arbitration and the Family' (1975) 29 *Labour History* 15.

Salais, R, 'Labour Conventions, Economic Fluctuations and Flexibility' in M Storper and A Scott (eds), *Pathways to Industrialization and Regional Development* (London, Routledge, 1992).

Salais, R, Baverez, N and Reynaud, B, *L'Invention du Chômage: Histoire et Transformations d'une Catégorie en France des années 1890 aux annés 1980* (Paris, Presses Universitaires de France, 1986).

Sanders, W, 'The Politics of Unemployment Benefit for Aborigines: Some Consequences of Economic Marginalisation' in D Wade-Marshall and P Loveday (eds), *Employment and Unemployment: A Collection of Papers* (Darwin, ANU North Australian Research Unit, 1985).

Saunders, P, 'Improving Work Incentives in a Means-Tested Welfare System: The 1994 Australian Social Security Reforms', Discussion Paper No 56 (Sydney, Social Policy Research Centre UNSW, 1995).

Schweber, L, 'Progressive Reformers, Unemployment, and the Transformation of Social Inquiry in Britain and the United States, 1880s–1920s' in D Rueschemeyer and T Skocpol (eds), *States, Social Knowledge, and the Origins of Modern Social Policies* (Princeton, NJ, Princeton University Press, 1996).

Seltzer, A, 'Labour, Skills and Migration' in S Ville and G Withers (eds), *The Cambridge Economic History of Australia* (Melbourne, Cambridge University Press, 2015).

Seltzer, A and Sammartino, A, 'Internal Labour Markets: Evidence From Two Large Australian Employers' (2009) 49 *Australian Economic History Review* 107.

Shaver, S, 'Design for a Welfare State: The Joint Parliamentary Committee on Social Security' (1987) 22 *Historical Studies* 411.

Sheehan, P and Stricker, P, 'The Collapse of Full Employment 1974 to 1978' in R Scotton and H Ferber (eds), *Public Expenditure and Social Policy in Australia Volume II: The First Fraser Years 1976–78* (Melbourne, Longman Cheshire, 1980).

Sheridan, T, *Mindful Militants: The Amalgamated Engineering Union in Australia 1920–1972* (Cambridge, Cambridge University Press, 1975).

—— 'Planners and the Australian Labour Market 1945–1949' (1987) 53 *Labour History* 99.

—— *Division of Labour: Industrial Relations in the Chifley Years, 1945–1949* (Melbourne, Oxford University Press, 1989).

—— 'Australian Wharfies 1943–1967: Casual Attitudes, Militant Leadership and Workplace Change' (1994) 36 *Journal of Industrial Relations* 258.

Skidelsky, R, *John Maynard Keynes, Volume Two: The Economist as Saviour 1920–1937* (London, Macmillan, 1992).

Smee, R, '"Some Problems in the Measurement of Unemployment" – A Comment' (1969) 11 *Journal of Industrial Relations* 253.

Smith, L, 'Economic Security and Unemployment Insurance' (1910) 20 *Economic Journal* 513.

Snooks, GD, 'Robbing Peter to Pay Paul: Australian Unemployment Relief in the Thirties' (1985) Flinders University Working Paper in Economic History No 41.

—— *Portrait of the Family Within the Total Economy: A Study in Longrun Dynamics, Australia 1788–1990* (Cambridge, Cambridge University Press, 1994).

Southall, H, 'Neither State nor Market: Early Welfare Benefits in Britain' in B Palier (ed), *Comparing Social Welfare Systems in Europe: Volume 1* (Paris, MIRE, 1994).

Spicker, P, *What's Wrong With Social Security Benefits?* (Bristol, Policy Press, 2017).

Spierings, J, 'Magic and Science, Aspects of Australian Business Management, Advertising and Retailing, 1918–1940' (PhD Thesis, University of Melbourne, 1990).

Steinfeld, RJ, *The Invention of Free Labor: The Employment Relation in English and American Law and Culture, 1350–1870* (Chapel Hill, NC, University of North Carolina Press, 1991).

Steinke, J, 'Some Problems in the Measurement of Unemployment' (1969) 11 *Journal of Industrial Relations* 39.

Stern, E, '"Industrial Disputes" and the Jurisdiction of the Federal Industrial Tribunal' (LLM Thesis, University of Melbourne, 1993).

Stevens, S, 'Problems in the Interpretation of Australian Statistics of Unemployment' (1963) 39 *Economic Record* 142.

Stretton, A and Chapman, B, 'An Analysis of Australian Labour Market Programs' (1990) Centre for Economic Policy Research, Australian National University Discussion Paper No 247.

Stricker, P and Sheehan, P, *Hidden Unemployment: The Australian Experience* (Parkville, Institute of Applied Economic and Social Research, University of Melbourne, 1981).

Stromback, T, 'The Job Network and Underemployment' (2008) 27 *Economic Papers* 286.

Studer, B, 'Social Policy as Gender Technology: The Social Construction of 'the Unemployed' in Switzerland in the First Half of the Twentieth Century' (paper prepared for the 5th European Social Science History Conference, Berlin, 24–27 March 2004).

Sutherland, P with Anforth, A, *Social Security and Family Assistance Law* (Sydney, Federation Press and Welfare Rights Centre, 2001).

Tham, JC, 'Industrial Action and Unemployment Income Support' (2002) 15 *Australian Journal of Labour Law* 40.

—— 'Towards an Understanding of Standard Employment Relationships Under Australian Labour Law' (2007) 20 *Australian Journal of Labour Law* 123.

Thomas, M, 'A Review of Developments in the Job Network', Parliamentary Library Research Paper No 15, 2007–08 (Canberra, Parliament of Australia, 2007).

Thompson, EP, 'Time, Work Discipline and Industrial Capitalism' (1967) 38 *Past & Present* 56.

Threlfall, M, 'A Critique of the Statistics that Support European Employment Policy' (2005) 88 *Radical Statistics* 22.

Tierney, R, 'The Pursuit of Serviceable Labour in Australian Capitalism: The Economic and Political Contexts of Immigration Policy in the Early Fifties, with Particular Reference to Southern Italians' (1998) 71 *Labour History* 137.

Topalov, C, 'The Invention of Unemployment: Language, Classification and Social Reform 1880–1910' in B Palier (ed), *Comparing Social Welfare Systems in Europe: Volume 1* (Paris, MIRE, 1994).

Turner, I and Sandercock, L, *In Union is Strength: A History of Trade Unions in Australia 1788–1983*, 3rd edn (Melbourne, Nelson, 1983).

United Kingdom, House of Commons Select Committee on Education and Employment, *First Report*, 1999.

van Berkel, R, 'The Provision of Income Protection and Activation Services for the Unemployed in Active Welfare States: An International Comparision' (2010) 39 *Journal of Social Policy* 17.

VandenHeuvel, A and Wooden, M, *Casualisation and Outsourcing: Trends and Implications for Work-Related Training* (Adelaide, National Centre for Vocational Education Research, 1999).

Vejnayovska, C, *Selling the State* (London, Weidenfeld & Nicolson, 1987).

Victoria, *New Zealand: Report on the System of Dealing with the Unemployed*, Parl Paper No 32 (1899–1900).

—— *Unemployment: Report of the Board of Inquiry*, Parl Paper No 5 (1900).

Victorian Council of Social Service, *Workers' Rights and Unemployment* (Collingwood, VCOSS, 1976).

Victorian Department of Labour, Sustenance Branch, *The Administration of Social Services (Unemployment Relief)* (Melbourne, Government Printer, 1933).

Ville, S and Merrett, D, 'The Development of Large Scale Enterprise in Australia, 1910–64' (2000) 42 *Business History* 13.

Vincent-Jones, P, *The New Public Contracting: Regulation, Responsiveness, Rationality* (Oxford, Oxford University Press, 2006).

Vosko, L, 'Gender Differentiation and the Standard/Non-Standard Employment Distinction: A Genealogy of Policy Interventions in Canada' in D Juteau (ed), *Social Differentiation: Patterns and Process* (Toronto, University of Toronto Press, 2003).

Waite, M and Will, L, 'Fixed-Term Employees in Australia: Incidence and Characteristics', Productivity Commission Staff Research Paper (Canberra, AusInfo, 2002).

Walters, W, 'The Demise of Unemployment?' (1996) 24 *Politics & Society* 197.

—— *Unemployment and Government: Genealogies of the Social* (Cambridge, Cambridge University Press, 2000).

Ward, E, 'A Sample of Unemployment in Victoria' (1938) 14 *Economic Record* 23.

Watts, R, *The Foundations of the National Welfare State* (Sydney, Allen & Unwin, 1987).

Wearing, M and Smyth, P, '*Working Nation* and Beyond as Market Bureaucracy' in P Smyth and B Cass (eds), *Contesting the Australian Way: States, Markets and Civil Society* (Melbourne, Cambridge University Press, 1998).

Webster, E and Harding, G, 'Outsourcing Public Employment Services: The Australian Experience' (2000) Melbourne Institute, University of Melbourne Working Paper No 4/00.

Weeks, P, *Trade Union Security Law: A Study of Preference and Compulsory Unionism* (Sydney, Federation Press, 1995).

Whiteside, N, *Bad Times: Unemployment in British Social and Political History* (London, Faber, 1991).

Whiteside, N and Gillespie, J, 'Deconstructing Unemployment: Developments in Britain in the Interwar Years' (1991) 44 *Economic History Review* 665.

Williams, JL and Williams, K (eds), *A Beveridge Reader* (London, Allen & Unwin, 1987).

Williams, R, *Keywords: A Vocabulary of Culture and Society* (London, Fontana, 1988).

Windschuttle, K, *Unemployment: A Social and Political Analysis of the Economic Crisis in Australia* (Ringwood, Penguin Books, 1979).

Wooden, M and Harding, D, 'Recruitment Practices in the Private Sector: Results from a National Survey of Employers' (1998) 36 *Asia Pacific Journal of Human Resources* 73.

Wright, C, *The Management of Labour: A History of Australian Employers* (Melbourne, Oxford University Press, 1995).

Wurth, W, *Control of Manpower in Australia: A General Review of the Administration of the Manpower Directorate, February 1942–September 1944* (Sydney, Government Printer, 1944).

Yeatman, A, 'Mutual Obligation: What Kind of Contract Is This?' in P Saunders (ed), *Reforming the Australian Welfare State* (Melbourne, Australian Institute of Family Studies, 2000).

INDEX

Aboriginal peoples
  child endowment and pensions   98–9
  employment on government settlements,
      missions and pastoral stations   101
  equal pay   103
  exclusion from the census   98
  integration into a regulated, wage-based
      labour market   102, 103
  State-based classifications   99
  unemployment benefit
      entitlement to   99, 100, 103
  Wards' Employment Ordinance
      102–3
  Welfare Ordinance   102
ABS   97, 114
'Active Participation Model'   157
'active society'
  flexible labour markets, and   140
  move towards   119–22, 137–8, 139, 140
Activity Agreements   126–9, 130, 131,
      163, 164
'activity test'   122, 123–6
  'actively seeking'   124
  additional 'requirements   124–5
  part-time employment, and   136–7
  'suitable work'   123
  'unsuitable work'   123–4
  'Work for the Dole' programme   125
ACTU   65, 72
administrative contracts   162
agency workers   115
Anderson, G.   72
arbitration
  regularisation of conditions of
      employment   27
Australian Bureau of Statistics (ABS)
      97, 114
**Australian Council of Trade Unions
      (ACTU)**   65, 72
awards regulation   20
  seasonal and casual workers   25

Bailey, K.   144
Bancroft, G.   75

Beeby J   26–7
Beveridge, W.   7, 13, 14, 37, 38, 45, 46,
      47, 48, 49, 70, 80, 86, 95
Black, C.   41
'black ban'   89
Bland, H.   144
Booth, C.   7, 11, 12, 13, 46
breach notifications   164–5
'breadwinners' and 'dependants'
      97, 98
  censuses   28, 29, 30, 32
Bredgaard, T.   162, 163
Brewer, G.   109, 110
Britain
  'casual labour problem'   10, 11, 12,
      13, 14
  poor law   8–9, 11
  seasonal and cyclical fluctuations and
      irregularities   9, 10
  street-level demonstrations   10
  unemployment as a political issue
      10, 11
  waged labour   9
Broomhill, R.   18
Brotherhood of St Laurence   109, 110
business format franchising   158, 159

Calwell, A.   98
Campbell, I.   117
Carney, T.   90, 132
case management services   152–3
Cass, B.   121
'casual' employees   112–13, 114
  annual leave   113, 114
  designation as 'casual'   114
'casual labour problem'   8, 14–15, 16, 18,
      26, 27
  Britain   10, 11, 12, 13, 14
censuses
  'breadwinners' and 'dependants'   28, 29,
      30, 32
  defining unemployment   43
  occupational groups
      'usual gainful occupation'   29, 30, 32

occupational status   30
    'unemployed', meaning of   30, 31
    part-time employment   32
    see also **population surveys and post-war
        censuses**
Centrelink   154, 160, 161, 164, 165
CES *see* **Commonwealth Employment
        Service**
Chifley, B.   62, 64
Churchill, W.   37, 47, 48
classes of labourers   12
Coghlan, T.   28, 29, 31
collective bargaining   21
Collins, H.   129
**Commonwealth Bureau of Census and
        Statistics**   28, 32, 66
**Commonwealth Court of Conciliation
        and Arbitration**   5, 17, 73
**Commonwealth Employment Service
        (CES)**   1, 7, 64, 69, 70, 71, 72,
        89–90, 141
    assistance for the long-term
        unemployed   148
    case management assistance   152, 153
    decline of   154, 166
    establishment of   143
    immigrants   146–7
    initial problems faced   144–5
    labour market programmes   148–50, 151,
        152, 154, 166
    objectives of   143, 144
    privatisation of CES functions   153–4
    role of   141–2, 143
    unemployment benefit scheme, and
        147–8
'compulsorily unemployed'   31
Considine, M.   158, 162
contractualisation   161–2, 163, 164, 165
    administrative contracts   162
    economic contracts   162, 163
    social control contracts   162–3
'control test'   23, 24
Cook, M.   43
Coombs, H. C.   64, 65, 67, 68, 81, 143, 144
Curtin, J.   58, 62, 63, 64, 65
Curtis, B.   92

Davies, P.   129
Deakin, A.   37
Deakin, S.   24, 27, 42, 84
Dean, M.   160
decasualisation   27, 46, 48, 49

**Department of Labour and National Service
        (LNS)**   55, 61
'dependents' and 'breadwinners'
    censuses   28, 29, 30, 32
    married women   97, 98
Depression, the   18, 19, 27, 52, 80
Derthick, M.   90–91
**'deserving and undeserving
        unemployed'**   12, 13
Directorate of Manpower   55–6, 57, 63, 67,
        89, 90, 143
'discouraged jobseekers'   96, 97
'dole bludger'   104, 107
'double activation'   162, 165

economic contracts   162, 163
Egham Free Registry   45
employment
    interactive relationship between employment
        and unemployment   6
Employment Assistance Australia   152
Employment National   156
**Employment Services Regulatory
        Authority**   152
Endres, T.   43
Evatt, B.   64, 84

family-owned and managed firms   17
'family wage'   93, 95, 119
Firth, G.   65
Fisher, S.   15
fixed-term employees   114–15
Foenander, O.   27
**formalised, 'standard' employment
        relationship**
    emergence of   20
Forster, C.   18
Fort, C.   94
Fraser, J.   87
Freedland, M.   129, 157, 158, 162
'frictional' unemployment   104
friendly societies   33–4
full employment
    Employment Service   67, 68, 69
    international policy   64–5
    promoting the mobility of labour   66
    White Paper   65, 66–9
Funnell, W.   63, 67, 68, 81, 83, 89, 143

Garland, J. M.   53–4
Gifford, J.   36
Gillespie, J.   19, 39

'go-slow' 89
Green, K. 108
Gregory, B. 18, 19

Hacking, I. 2, 3, 4
Hanks, P. 132
'hard-core unemployed' 104
Harris, J. 40, 44, 48, 141
Hasluck, P. 102
Hayden, B. 105, 106, 132–3
Heydon J 23
'hidden unemployment' 96, 97
Higgins J 26
Holloway, J. 63, 82, 83, 88
Holt, H. 55, 84
Howe, B. 121
Howe, J. 24

ILO *see* International Labour Office
immigrants
    CES, and 146–7
industrial disputes
    unemployment benefits scheme, and 85,
        86, 87–9
Innes, J. 96
internalisation of market transactions 5–6
International Labour Office (ILO) 76, 97, 144
    role of national labour exchanges 142

Jayasuriya, K. 162, 163
job brokerage services 154, 155
job creation schemes 78
Job Network 154, 156, 157, 158, 159, 164
Job Search allowance (JSA) 122, 123
    Activity Agreements 126
Job Seeker Classification Instrument
        (JSCI) 154, 157
    'case management risk' 160, 161
jobless households 119
joblessness
    forms of 1
Johnston, R. M. 28
Joint Committee on Social Security
        58, 59, 60
Jordan, A. 80, 104, 106, 107, 110, 118, 135–6
JSA *see* Job Search allowance
JSCI *see* Job Seeker Classification Instrument

Keane, R. 82, 83, 87
Kewley, T. 90
'key man' strikes 87, 88
Keynes, J. M. 70

Kirby, P. 150
Knibbs, G. H. 28, 37, 38, 39, 51

labour exchanges 6–7
    Australia 49–54
        casual employment, and 51
        history of 49–51
        proposals for national scheme 51–2, 57,
            61, 65
        sustenance and relief work 52–3
        unemployment insurance, and 52
    Britain 45–9
        decasualisation 48–9
        history of 45, 46
        proposal for a national scheme 46–7, 48
        social surveillance 49
        unemployment insurance, and 48, 49
    purpose of 45
'labour farms' 41
labour force framework 75, 76, 77, 78, 79,
        81, 96, 97
    appropriateness of 118
'labour market disorganisation' 8, 13, 14,
        26, 27, 46
labour market programmes 148–50, 151,
        152, 154, 166
labour mobility
    importance of 120
    promoting the mobility of labour 66
Larsen, F. 162, 163
length of employment contracts 22
limited liability 16–17
Lipsky, M. 160
Littlechild, S. 158
Llewellyn Smith, H. 37, 38, 48
LNS *see* Department of Labour and National
        Service
lone parents
    means test 136
long-term secure employment 16
long-term unemployed 121
Lowry, A. 47

Mabbett, D. 163
'malingerers' 7, 49, 61, 71, 80
Mansfield, M. 49
married women 93
    debarred from claiming unemployment
        benefit 97–8
    dependents, as 97, 98
    'discouraged jobseekers' 96–7
    'family wage' 93, 95

immediate post-war period
  discouraged from employment   95
  not classed as unemployed   95–6, 97
  preference for part-time work   97
  wartime work   93–5, 98
master and servant legislation   20–21, 23
  conflation of 'master/servant' and
    'employer/employee'
    relationships   23–4
McGregor, R.   102
means test   133, 134
  encouraging claimants to access part-time
    and casual work   134, 135,
    136, 137
  lone parents   136
Mendelsohn, R.   60
Menzies, R.   58
Ministry of Post-War Reconstruction
  64
Mitchell, R.   24
Murphy, J.   40, 99
'mutual obligation'   130–31
Myers, D.   110

**National Development and Migration
    Commission**   8
**National Employment and Training
    (NEAT) scheme**   149, 150
National Service Offices   55, 56, 57
national statisticians
  upsurge of interest in official statistics   28
  see also **censuses**
National Welfare Fund   62
NEAT scheme   149, 150
Newstart Allowance (NSA)   123, 151
  Activity Agreements   126, 151
Nimmo, J.   60, 61, 63, 65
non-employment rates
  men   118
**'non-standard' employment
    relationships**   111–12
  life-cycle stages   116, 118
  restrictions on   116, 117, 118, 120
NSA *see* **Newstart Allowance**

occupational groups
  censuses
    'usual gainful occupation'   29, 30, 32
occupational status
  censuses   30
    'unemployed', meaning of   30, 31
OECD   119, 120, 121, 153

open-ended employment contracts   5, 73,
  74, 112
O'Sullivan, T.   40
'out-of-work' benefits schemes
  trade unions   34, 35, 38, 85

'parking' and 'creaming' of clients
  159, 165
part-time employment   112
  'activity test', and   136–7
  censuses   32
  married women
    preference for part-time work   97
Peck, J.   139
Pigou, A.   43
poor law   8–9, 11
population surveys and post-war censuses
  defining and counting unemployment
    74–9
  labour force framework   75, 76, 77, 78, 79
Porter, A.   95
post-war labour market   73–4
poverty
  causes of poverty   12, 13
**private provision of employment
    services**   155, 156, 157, 158, 159
  licensing of employment agencies   145
  opposition to private employment
    agencies   144
**profile of employment opportunities
    available to social security
    claimants**   139
protective labour legislation
  scope of   22–3, 24
public works   41

reciprocal obligation   129, 130, 131, 140
**Regional Employment Development Scheme
    (REDS)**   149
'responsibilisation'   131
retail franchising   157–8
returned servicemen
  preference in employment   65, 68, 95
Roe, J.   90
Ronald Walker, E.   18
Rowe, F. H.   81
Rowse, T.   101, 102
Ryan, R.   59

Salvation Army   141
sanctions   131–3
school leavers   108

self-employment   112
social assistance
　'active programmes'   120–21, 122
social construction of unemployment   2, 3
social control contracts   162–3
Social Security Review   121, 122, 123,
　　129, 130
social surveillance
　labour exchanges   49
social surveyors   11
　causes of poverty   12, 13
　classes of labourers   12
　surveys of the London working class
　　11–12
Southall, H.   35
Spicker, P.   135
'stand down clauses'   25–6
'standard employment relationship'   111
Steinke, J.   96
Stewart, F.   59
Stromback, T.   157, 158
structural unemployment   104
subcontracting   15, 17, 20, 24

Theodore, N.   139
Threlfall, M.   118
Topalov, C.   14
trade unions
　ACTU   65, 72
　control over employment conditions   21
　'out-of-work' benefits schemes   34, 35, 38
　　industrial disputes   85
　'placement agencies', as   145–6
　unemployment statistics   32–3, 35–6

unemployment
　concept of   1
　political issue, as a   10, 11
unemployment benefits scheme
　　1, 58–64, 72
　abolition of   123
　Aboriginal peoples
　　entitlement to   99, 100, 103
　'activity test'   122
　administration of the scheme   62–4
　CES, and   147–8
　'dole bludger'   104, 107
　eligibility   62, 79
　industrial disputes, and   85, 86, 87–9
　Joint Committee on Social Security   58,
　　59, 60
　low take-up   90

　married women   97–8
　non-contributory system   59, 60, 61, 84
　rate of payment   60
　school leavers   108
　work test   60–61, 79, 80, 81, 82, 83, 84, 85,
　　105, 106, 107, 108, 109, 110
　　discretion   81, 84, 110
　　formula   82, 83, 84
　　'involuntary' unemployment   83, 84
　　liberalising of the test   106
　　reciprocal obligation   129, 130
unemployment insurance schemes   36–41,
　　42–3
　defining unemployment   38, 42, 43, 44
　see also labour exchanges
unemployment rate   90, 118
'usual gainful occupation'   29, 30, 32

van Berkel, R.   161
Victorian Council of Social Service
　　(VCOSS)   109, 110
Vincent-Jones, P.   131, 162

wage bargaining   117
wage policy   17–18
Walters, W.   6, 8, 20, 43, 70–71, 137, 138
Ward, E.   36
Ward, Eddie   55, 64, 83
Wards' Employment Ordinance
　　(WEO)   102–3
wartime labour administration   54–5
　Department of Labour and National
　　Service   55
　directions to accept employment
　　56, 57
　Directorate of Manpower   55–6, 57
　National Service Offices   55, 56, 57
Webb, B.   7, 46, 47
Webb, S.   7, 46, 47
weekly hiring   25, 26, 27
Welfare Ordinance   102
Whiteside, N.   10–11, 19, 39, 92
Wilkinson, F.   42, 84
Wilson, R.   55, 64
women
　labour force participation   116
　see also married women
'Work for the Dole' programme
　　125, 130
work rationing   18, 19
work test
　Britain   80

unemployment benefits scheme   60–61, 79,
    80, 81, 82, 83, 84, 85, 105, 106, 107,
    108, 109, 110
  discretion   81, 84, 110
  formula   82, 83, 84
  'involuntary' unemployment   83, 84

  liberalising of the test   106
  reciprocal obligation   129, 130
Wurth, W.   53, 55, 56, 94

**'young people without apparent
    disability'**   105

www.ingramcontent.com/pod-product-compliance
Lightning Source LLC
Chambersburg PA
CBHW062029270326
41929CB00014B/2371